MEANING AND TEXTUALITY

Historically there has been a wide gulf between European and Anglo-American thought on the philosophy of language, in part because it is often difficult to find important European works in English translation. *Meaning and Textuality* represents key elements of the ground-breaking new theory on signs and discourse that has come out of Europe in the past few decades.

Meaning and Textuality is an investigation into methods useful to the analysis of language and literature. Rastier seeks ways to better understand signs, with emphasis on their relation to action and culture. He proposes a theoretical framework for the semantic description and typology of texts. Towards this end he establishes a critical debate among various streams of research before arriving at a synthesis of literary semiotics, thematics, and linguistic semantics. The author sees this synthesis as a means by which to reconcile the rigour of linguistic analysis with the complexity of literary interpretation. In the later portion of the book he tests his propositions in a series of detailed investigations of French literary texts by Zola, Maupassant, Mallarmé, Apollinaire, and Jodelle. Each study examines a new problem such as narrative ambiguity or referential impression.

This book will be welcomed by scholars in any discipline concerned with discourse analysis and the close reading of texts.

(Toronto Studies in Semiotics)

FRANÇOIS RASTIER is Professor of Semantics and Director of Research at the Centre National de la Recherche Scientifique, Paris.

FRANK COLLINS is a professor in the Department of French, University of Toronto.

PAUL PERRON is a professor in the Department of French and Principal of University College at the University of Toronto.

FRANÇOIS RASTIER

Meaning and Textuality

Translated by Frank Collins and Paul Perron

UNIVERSITY OF TORONTO PRESS
Toronto Buffalo London

Toronto Buffalo London
Printed in Canada

ISBN 0-8020-4167-1 (cloth)
ISBN 0-8020-8029-4 (paper)

This book is a translation of *Sens et textualité* (Paris: Hachette) 1989.

Toronto Studies in Semiotics
Editors: Marcel Danesi, Umberto Eco, Paul Perron, and Thomas A. Sebeok

Printed on acid-free paper

Canadian Cataloguing in Publication Data

Rastier, François
Meaning and textuality

(Toronto studies in semiotics)
Translation of: Sens et textualité.
Includes bibliographical references and index.
ISBN 0-8020-4167-1 (bound)   ISBN 0-8020-8029-4 (pbk.)

1. Semantics. I. Collins, Frank. II. Perron, Paul.
III. Title. IV. Series.

P325.R3713 1997   401′.43   C97-930765-1

University of Toronto Press acknowledges the financial assistance to its publishing program of the Canada Council for the Arts and the Ontario Arts Council.

Contents

Foreword

This English edition sees the light a few years after the original, and the author cannot decently be moved by his past rashness, nor can he call upon the reader to note how much progress he has made since. I shall simply say that I have modified this work very little, not that I did not wish to but because the translators worked more quickly than anticipated. I did not have time to profit from Quintillian's wise maxim that the pen accomplishes as much when it excises as when it adds. I have thus added a few paragraphs. Some of these additions attempt to take into account comments made by various colleagues in their letters as well as in their reviews.

I should also like to thank the translators, whose talents benefit this work. I am pleased to acknowledge a debt to Paul Perron, without whom this English edition would not have seen the light of day.

At every stage of its edition and translation, the original title of this work has given rise to recurring Freudian slips that insist heavily on sensuality, or even sexuality. I had to rectify this on numerous occasions, and the disappointed expression on the face of the person I was addressing informed me all too well of the kind of book I would have to write in order to meet the public's expectations.

Introduction

Words, sentences, and texts remain the objects of distinct disciplines separated by academic rather than by scientific boundaries. Lexicology and syntax still fall within the realm of linguistics, but the study of texts is generally turned over to other disciplines, such as poetics, semiotics, hermeneutics. Though a restricted form of linguistics, centred on morphosyntax, still dominates, I wish to demonstrate, on the one hand, that a text cannot be reduced to a series of sentences, and on the other, that it constitutes not only the empirical object, but also the real object of linguistics.

A. Without underestimating their contribution I shall explain why various textual linguistics and rational theories of text that have been worked out over the past twenty years or so have not attained a satisfactory level of development.

Discourse analysis inspired by Harris's work has produced only minor results, the inevitable price it had to pay for its anti-semantic bent. At the very least, however, it has shown that textual linguistics cannot be founded on the distribution of signifiers. Textual linguistics inspired by Chomsky, which developed especially in West Germany, did not meet with a happier fate: such work first attempted, unsuccessfully, to represent the text as a tree that in turn links syntactic trees. For want of an adequate semantic theory, it sought in various ways to reconcile vericonditional and pragmatic semantics. For a long time its formalist ambitions kept it at a programmatic stage.[1]

Other theories of text, arising from within disciplines other than linguistics, have attempted to meet these needs. Discursive semiotics, and particularly Greimassian semiotics in France, has amassed a fairly rich experience. But its universalism and its speculative involution have led to the formulation of theories too powerful for our use, in so far as they are disconnected from natural languages. Pragmatics, another branch of the philosophy of signification,[2] has also investigated textual structures through research on argumentation and conversational analysis. However, its links to linguistics remain imprecise.[3] In fact, as I have shown elsewhere, pragmatics has, in part, replaced rhetoric after the fall of the trivium. This is why it examines interlocution rather than the text proper. In Artificial Intelligence and in cognitive psychology, several partial theories of text have been created that make it possible to undertake the automatic analysis of narrative (understood in the very loose sense as the report of events). Here, I can cite work done by Rumelhart, Abelson, Schank, Lehnert, Dyer; and refer the reader back to the debate on narrative grammars (see Rumelhart, 1980). Nevertheless, I should like to underscore that these theories remain ad hoc, unsystematic; they ignore other theories of text; and most important, they are not involved with linguistics at all. From the outset, and with a certain presumption, they assimilate the semantic with the conceptual[4] in proclaiming their universality. In short, I refuse to choose between, on the one hand, theories of text that claim to originate in linguistics but are condemned to failure by a formalist thrust that makes them neglect semantics; and on the other, semiotic and cognitive theories that have no direct link with linguistics, and reduce textual semantics to a combination of concepts or of universal primitives that do not take into account the specificity of the languages in which the texts are articulated.

Of course, to assert itself, textual linguistics must give semantics its due. Even then, it still must prove itself. It certainly is not sufficient for it to cloak itself in self-proclaimed scientificity in order to attain the status of other disciplines such as law, poetics, literary criticism, hermeneutics – all of which describe texts without claiming to be scientific. Textual linguistics operates short of these, but can learn a great deal from them.

B. The textual semantics I implement originates in general linguistics and not in universal linguistics. In order to correspond to their designation, universal grammars (Chomsky, Montague, Shaumyan) inevitably neglect the connection between languages, cultures, and history.[5] They develop 'intrinsic' semantics, weak imitations of syntax not linked to any 'field of application.' Their formalist ambitions lead them to consider meanings as simple variables.

Moreover, textual semantics obviously cannot be satisfied with the dozens or even several hundred well-calibrated sentences, artificially isolated from any context, that are the rule of universal grammars. In order to describe the richness of contextual relationships, linguistics cannot remain in the comfortable but confining space of the sentence. In reaffirming its status as a non-formalist social science it opens up onto texts, and, by this, onto cultures and onto history. It progresses through contact with related disciplines – that is to say, all the other social sciences – and can even exercise a claim to their territory.

Let us take a simple example. In the sixth line of his octet *Farewell to Wei Wan*, Li Qi writes: 'In the evening, you hear the beetle of the washerwomen in the park.' In order to make the inference 'noise of the beetle' → |'Autumn'|, one must know that in ancient China in autumn (in this case, in the eighth century) all quilted clothes were brought out of their chests, to be washed for winter. Without this knowledge, the relationship of semantic equivalence, an elementary form of isotopy, could not be established between the line and its counterpart in the first stanza ('Last night, for the first time, there was ice on the river'). All knowledge that comes from another discipline is not only licit, but requisite, in so far as it allows for the actualization of a semantic relationship that conforms to the cohesion of the text and to the norms of its genre.

Furthermore, textual semantics stems from general linguistics by its method. Working out a comparative method also was essential for establishing a general linguistics. When applied to texts, the comparative method was necessary for setting up the first scientific theories of textuality: in folklore studies with Bédier, Propp, Mélétinski; in comparative mythology with Dumézil; in anthropology with Lévi-Strauss. In these disciplines it brought about scientific revolutions whose impact has not always been clearly noted.[6] What I am proposing here is a conceptual frame unified by the comparative method for the semantic typology of texts. Defined concepts are simply universals of the method, and we do not have to formulate a realist hypothesis for them, establishing them as cognitive archetypes, or other primitives – as is often the case today. This theory can be called unified, as it operates both short of the word and beyond the sentence. Who can say that it does not express the vow to reassemble the *logos*, which, according to Aristotle, can consist of a single word or the entire *Iliad*? Its foundations have been worked out in detail elsewhere (Rastier, 1987a) and it would be unseemly, indeed discourteous to return to this.[7] Let me simply mention three characteristics:

(i) It is *componential*, even though it impugns the principal postulates of 'classical' componential semantics.
(ii) It is *differential*, because meaning stems from value (in the Saussurian sense of the term). Pertinent linguistic differences determine the phenomena of reference – or, more precisely, the referential impression – and secondarily the truth effects (in the weak sense).
(iii) It is *dynamic*, as its objective is to describe interpretative paths in the contextual transformations of all levels of units as well as in the continuous reorganizations of representations throughout the text.

C. This book accepts three major limitations, which have made it possible for me to complete it.

a) It describes only literary texts, although the theory it calls on claims to have a wider domain of validity.[8] Aside from the fact that these texts are most agreeable to study, it can be said that their complexity puts the descriptive instruments to the test. However, on the contrary, would choosing literary texts not provide us with a simple way out? Their cohesion is a guide to the scholiast. Hence, from this perspective it would be more worthwhile to study a sonnet by Mallarmé than a non-directive interview about the social import of the local organizers of a social district. We must also remember that in the domain of rhetoric, poetics, and even hermeneutics,[9] the essential aspects of our tradition related to textual studies were formed through the study of literary texts.

However, this restriction also provides us with several openings.

(i) Language arts exploit and bring to the fore principles related to how the cognitive apparatus functions; notably, language arts allow one to pose the problem of semantic perception that has mainly gone unnoticed.

Note: *Perception* and *semantic* apparently clash in being placed side by side, when a long tradition, taken up by Fodorian modularism, makes meaning the exclusive property of the central nervous system. However, besides the fact that perception is not simply an ascendant process, only a 'positivistic' conception of language could dismiss from the outset the hypothesis that sound and meaning are treated in a manner that is at least in part analogous. Comprehending a linguistic string is essentially an activity of recognizing semantic forms,[10] whether they happen to be already learned or constructed during processing.

Just as the graphic arts reveal the laws of visual perception when they make use of optical illusions,[11] language arts exploit semantic illusions (in the first place, the mental images that determine the referential impression). In this, they reveal the laws of perception of meaning.[12] That is why aesthetics could open up cognitive research to areas of unrealized richness.

(ii) I have opted for a linguistics open to norms. Literary norms, such as norms, defining genres, are part of this domain (without going over to literary studies in their instituted academic form).

(iii) Linguistics must not break its natural connections to philology; rather, it should reinforce them. Its very status as a social science depends on it, and it is notably philology that allows one to conceive linking language and text to culture and history. Now, literary texts are best studied from a philological point of view.

Finally, if textual linguistics must still prove itself, it can also be through renewing the conditions of reading texts that have already been widely commented upon.

b) I make no claim to exhaustiveness,[13] which is largely illusory, even in the study of a short text. Fortunately, there will always be someone who, fully within his or her rights, will go one better.

I do not intend to collect monographs on the works of various authors, but rather to illustrate remarkable forms of textuality by means of punctual descriptions. In short, I claim neither to 'renovate,' for our ends, text commentary – the paltry heir of the *lectio* – nor to use 'linguistic methods' to counterbalance for all that, the indestructible discourse of 'belles lettres.' On the contrary, the studies that follow are governed by the concerns of semantics, even though they share with criticism[14] the same empirical object.

c) A last limitation is related to the almost exclusive privilege given to the semantic level. Before one undertakes a stylistic analysis (understood as a study of the correlations between levels), it is necessary to gain more knowledge about the semantic level. Now, semantics still remains largely conjectural, all the more so since logic, pragmatics, and cognitive psychology today are vying to supplant it. And the validity of an *autonomous* linguistic semantics (autonomous, but not independent) is still only very rarely recognized.

In part 1 of this work, I define a problematics and then propose some descriptive concepts that are brought into play in part 2. This succession of two parts should not be misleading: the theory presented is seen as rational, but it does not claim to be deductive.[15] It does not precede practice. It was worked out through descriptive practice and to satisfy the needs of that practice.

As much as possible, I have tried to simplify my conceptual apparatus and terminology. If it is adequate, a small network of concepts can prove more operative than a complex theory that only reproduces itself in the present state of research.

For the most part, this work has been hitherto unpublished. However, chapter 10 was published in *Langue française* (61: 1984); chapter 12 was the object of a partial preliminary study (1972); and finally, a brief outline of chapter 13 appeared in *Fabula* (2: 1983).

It is my pleasure to thank all my listeners, correspondents, friends, and colleagues, whose advice has kept me from self-contradiction and allowed me to temper as well as to tolerate the rashness of this book. Most of all, I thank Josselyne Santer and Yves-Marie Visetti.

Symbols and Abbreviations

a : b :: c : d	a is to b what c is to d
vs	opposition
→	afference; rewriting
⇒	indexation
↔	relation of identity; relation comparing/compared

'sign'
signifier
/seme/
'sememe'
//semantic class//
| 'content made up by rewriting' |
ATT: attribute
ERG: ergative
ACC: accusative
DAT: dative
BEN: benefactive
INS: instrumental
LOC: locative
RES: resultative
FIN: final

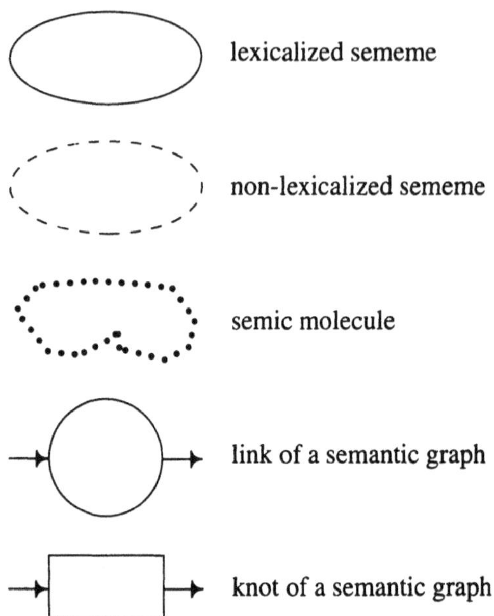
lexicalized sememe
non-lexicalized sememe
semic molecule
link of a semantic graph
knot of a semantic graph

PART ONE

INTERPRETATIVE SEMANTICS AND FORMS OF TEXTUALITY

1

On the 'Objectivity' of Meaning

Only say what is open to several interpretations.

Cioran

The way of treating textual meaning naturally depends upon the type of objectivity that one assumes it has. It conditions the very possibility of the existence of a scientific semantics, if one admits that in order for a discipline to be considered a discipline, it must have not only a problematics and methods, but also an object.

A. Even though anyone can have the impression of gaining access to the meaning of a text, we know that the linguistic content is not an immediate given.[1] It is only because of recent cognitive research linked to the automatic treatment of language that we have been able to appreciate the hitherto unsuspected complexity of the processes of interpretation. Once it was agreed that semantic facts, like other facts, are constructed, a false dilemma arose – a dilemma that for the past twenty years, at least in France, has dominated research on the interpretation of textual meaning: either receivers discover the immanent meaning of a text by appropriate procedures; or they construct it, and this meaning explodes into an indefinite plurality, the plurality of readers.

The first thesis was defended by a structuralist current: by applying the universal principles of decoding to the 'text alone'[2] (as isolated from its linguistic and 'pragmatic' surroundings), any reader, armed with the right method, could elicit its meaning. In fact, the proposed method remained so general, or so unexplicit, that it could lead to very diverse descriptions of the same text.[3] Discussions on this matter by those espousing various schools of thought will remain sterile for as long as the theory in question has not proposed criteria for evaluating descriptions stemming from it. Immanentism here is rooted in a long tradition that antedates any project for the scientific description of meaning, that of religious exegesis, founded on revelation. Meaning is immanent to the text, as it has been deposited there – by God or by a man, it does not matter whom. From this arise strategies of unveiling, of drawing out, etc.[4] Another way of misconceiving the type of objectivity of meaning (just as unilateral as the preceding one, but for opposite reasons) consists in postulating the indefinite plurality of meaning, which is then situated in the subject, whose unconscious, structured like a language, speaks instead of the text. Thus, meaning becomes transcendent to the text, whose readings amount to rewritings that are, in psychoanalytic terms, as drive oriented as possible.

One could have hoped that this 'desiring' theory of meaning, even though it did not succeed in describing texts, would at least produce an agreeable variety of readings. This certainly is not the case, as these 'drive oriented' readings of texts have uncovered only the most Oedipal of dramas,[5] the most heavily sexualized symbols.[6] Thus, postulating an immanent fundamental meaning no more limits the diversity of 'structural' readings than postulating a plural meaning, which is in fact transcendent, avoids the drudgery of an ageing psychoanalysis.

B. To avoid oversimplification, it is advisable to re-examine the concept of objectivity. The long dominant philosophical tradition of Western idealism has conditioned us to separate the intelligible from the sensible, thought from matter, subject from object. Affirming the absolute objectivity of meaning, or its absolute subjectivity, does not resolve anything, and it is not sufficient to be twice unilateral in order to be complete. The rigid positioning of subject and object has already been questioned by the sciences.[7] Semantics itself can also contribute to its relativization. On the one hand, there is an objectivity of meaning, to the degree that the text constrains – albeit without completely determining – plausible readings.[8] First of all, the semantic fields appearing in the text are constituents of the referential impression it induces (for example, one cannot evade the fact that 'Salut' – see chapter 12 below – is also, as the Groupe Mu would say, a 'story of sailors'). Moreover, the text, be it only because of its genre, contains interpretative instructions, which, whether they happen to be explicit or otherwise, cannot be neglected without interpretation being reduced to deficient rewriting. All this serves to constrain the possible interpretative paths, and even the reader's mental imagery. In short, if in the Spanish inns of old, pilgrims dined on their own provisions, this occurred nevertheless in the often precarious shelter of a few walls and a roof.

Yet we can admit that meaning has no existence of its own beyond its utterance and its interpretation. Certainly, philosophical tradition has conditioned us to an instrumental conception of language, whereby it is considered to be the simple vehicle of thought that is autonomous, indeed independent, with regard to it.[9] However, one suspects that there are 'things to say' that happen to be independent of putting them into words.[10] Even admitting this, one still suspects that they fall within the domain of semantics. In short, meaning is not immanent to the text as a message, but as a situation of communication including, moreover, a transmitter and a receiver (see chapter 3) as well as a set of conditions (norms, including the textual genre and determined social practice). These conditions can be called pragmatic, but in the sense of an encompassing pragmatics.

Note: The question discussed here was raised in the context of the sentence, where one distinguished its signification, an inherent content defined independently of the communicative situation and of the linguistic context, as distinct from the meaning of the utterance, which itself is relative to these factors.[11] However, meaning is not added to a signification that is already there. On the contrary, signification results from an abstraction carried out by the linguist starting from meaning. As proof of this: the identification of sememes depends upon the communicative situation; if one does not take this into account, one creates a polysemy or, more precisely, an artificial indetermination. Thus, according to Fauconnier, *she has great legs* would be 'ambiguous' because these legs could be great to eat. Certainly, and in Bradbury, a *difficult book* could be difficult to burn. Herein lies the fodder for never-ending colloquiums.

Let us keep in mind that signification that is immanent to the sentence is an artefact created by linguists and that it remains inevitably equivocal. Even though inversely, its meaning, reputed to be oblique and difficult to define, remains generally univocal in a given context[12] and a given situation. In an interpretative (and no longer generative) perspective the distinction between a semantic component that would deal with signification, and an (integrated) pragmatic component that would reinterpret it to give an account of meaning, seems then to lose all usefulness. In short, semantics is bound to deal with meaning, without delegating its study to pragmatics, even if it happens to be integrated with it.

Therefore, we distance ourselves from a purely 'positivistic' conception of objectivity. Meaning as object does not have the pure exteriority an object has for the positive sciences: it is an interaction between a text, subjects, and a situation (or set of communicative conditions). Meaning's immanence to the text alone becomes blurred. Not only must we admit that the meaning of an utterance varies according to context, but we must also give ourselves the theoretical means to describe this variation.[13] The semantics of the utterance, and that of the sentence, cannot have real autonomy. Neither can that of the text, although for other reasons. First, a text is never isolated and derives its meaning from mediate relations with other texts, since it is an instance of a genre (see chapter 3). And especially, to actualize the slightest components of its meaning, one must often have recourse to encyclopaedic knowledge stemming not only from the social sciences but also from the natural sciences. It is admittedly difficult to arrange these factors into a hierarchy, but linguistics must take into account the effective use of languages, without leaving it up to related disciplines, although it may demand indefinitely retracing its boundaries.

C. Let me explain finally why, in spite of its name, interpretative semantics cannot be taken for a philosophical hermeneutic. Of the three hermeneutic processes – comprehension, interpretation, and application (in Gadamer's, and then Szondi's, account of them) – we should retain only the second if, deprived of the first process determining it, it could subsist without losing the plenitude that philosophers say it has. However, are these three points, distinguished by contemporary philosophical hermeneutics, not new avatars of the *subtilitates* of the pietistic hermeneutics of the Enlightenment – *intelligendi*, *explicandi*, *applicandi*? Do these three moments not redeploy in the act of reading, since Luther denied that the Scriptures have any polysemy and most especially rejected allegoresis, the multiplicity of the two, three, or even four meanings that the Catholic church recognized in them?

What is the relationship between comprehension and explanation? In Jauss's literary hermeneutics, the former corresponds to the moment of the reader's aesthetic emotion, which appears to me to be analogous to the act of faith in religious hermeneutics. This immediate comprehension is primary only for a phenomenology that assigns primacy to an originating intuition. In the circle that unites comprehension and interpretation, the former always dominates, as it originates in a faith – or, in less compromising terms, a questioning, an expectation. It is understandable, then, why a hermeneutic always knows which meaning it must find. This is why Ricoeur was able to define hermeneutics as an unveiling of the meaning that is hidden under an apparent meaning: this hidden meaning is not discovered but found in the interpretation, as it appears, immediately, as epiphanic, in the moment just prior to comprehension. This is why Ricoeur finally described psychoanalytic hermeneutics so well: because it also proceeds from a faith that is, moreover, secularized and has deteriorated into belief, if not into superstition.

Textual semantics remains far short of all philosophical hermeneutics. It defines the linguistic conditions of interpretation. It can describe some interpretations and evaluate them with respect to these conditions, but it does not, strictly speaking, produce an interpretation.[14] In short, it does not look for one of several hidden meanings; in the case of a plurality of meaning, it describes their relative accessibility, and evaluates their degree of plausibility. And above all, it does not know which kind(s) of meaning it must find. These restrictions measure the necessary distance that linguistics as a science takes with respect to philosophical hermeneutics – no matter how indebted to the latter it happens to be.

Once the moment of comprehension as a global intuition has been eluded, the reader ceases to master textual meaning straightaway: comprehension being only one of the elements that make it up. Rather than being the depository of a more or less profound meaning,[15] the text appears as a series of constraints that draw out the interpretative paths. Individual readers are free to follow a personal route, to deform or to neglect at will the paths indicated by the text, according to their objectives and their historical situation. Paradoxically, this confirms the intersubjective objectivity of meaning. If, for example, a group of readers are asked to pick out recurrences of a semantic feature, each reader will have different scores that indicate individual competencies. However, the objectivity of the isotopy revealed will be much less debatable.

Seen in this light interpretative semantics can do perfectly well without an interpreter, whether it happens to be Riffaterre's 'superreader,' or Jauss's 'cultured professor.' Such abstractions are not rare in universal linguistics (cf. the 'ideal speaker' for Chomsky). However, empirical rationalism from which we claim to stem, dismisses such speculative types. Instead of turning towards philosophical hermeneutics, we therefore turn our attention towards psycholinguistics, to clarify experimentally the performances of real readers. The author of these lines is certainly only one reader among many; he travels through the same labyrinths, but he counts his steps, so as to preserve the hope of drawing up the plan of his journey.

Just as it has no supreme reader, neither does a text necessarily have one true meaning. Although this postulation distinguishes interpretative semantics from the philologic tradition as well as from the self-assured interrogations of philosophical hermeneutics, nevertheless, it does not disqualify it. There is some meaning, and this partitive is not evocative of a subtle matter, ether, or phlogistic,[16] from which 'positivistic' and formalist linguists would save us at any cost. It suggests that a text must be thought of as a set of constraints placed on the production of meaning (by its author, as much as by its readers). It is up to semantics to study and develop a hierarchy of descriptive readings[17] that conforms to its principles as well as to philological deontology; as productive readings stemming from other objectives.

Finally, the author is not the ultimate guarantor of interpretation. The intentionality of the transmitter on which pragmatics would found linguistic description is at the very most conjecture. Authors can be mistaken, or fool us, and they are not necessarily the best placed either to listen to themselves or to read their own works. At the very most, one could invoke a principle of charity that credits their texts with the most interesting interpretation.

If, therefore, the meaning of a text is constructed rather than given, its objectivization is not a unique process that is fixed once and for all. It is admittedly founded upon the material objectivity of the text but not founded or guaranteed by it. The objectivization of textual meaning can recur indefinitely in new situations. It does not, for all of this, escape from a rational, indeed scientific, description, as Interpretative Semantics can claim to describe how the constraints imposed by a text upon its successive readers are reconciled or opposed to the constraints imposed by the situations in which these readings are produced. In a given historical situation, the guarantee – simply fiduciary – of objectivization resides in a shared plausibility: the same holds, to varying degrees, for social consensus that institutes the relative truth of meaning for all units, from word to text. As for the foundation of objectivization, this rests in the laws of semantic perception,[18] which allow for the representation of the textual world. These laws do not differ fundamentally from the laws of sensorial perception, which determine representations of the real world, so that one can sometimes pair up the representations of these two mutually inclusive worlds.

2

Difficulties of Avant-Garde Hermeneutics

In the deformation of a text, something similar occurs to what happens in the case of a crime: the difficulty lies not in carrying out the misdemeanour but in covering it up.

S. Freud

Up to the end of the eighteenth century, the hermeneutic problem was set out within the context of exegesis. As P. Szondi has shown, literary hermeneutics grew out of religious hermeneutics.[1] Freudian psychoanalysis[2] was another profane (or at least secularized) hermeneutics that developed. These two hermeneutics have converged into a neo-Freudian, Lacanian current that over the past decades has overshadowed most debates on the interpretation of literary texts.

Let us here start with the hermeneutics that calls itself post-structuralist,[3] since it developed theses that are still very much alive and that have steered research on textuality away from a rational problematics. These theses are not articulated systematically, but this does not in any way detract from their popularity. As a matter of fact, the contrary is true. It is possible to find them demonstrated in *Le plaisir du texte*, Barthes' little book, which continues to have immense repercussions, as it announces the foundations of avant-gardist hermeneutics; here is how (I shall underscore the main themes):

(i) 'The text has a human form, it is a figure, an anagram of the body? Yes, but of our erotic body' (30).

(ii) 'This is surely the *inter-text*: the impossibility of living outside of the infinite text – whether the text happens to be Proust, the daily newspaper or the television screen: the book makes meaning, meaning makes life' (59).

(iii) 'Although the theory of text has especially designated significance (in the

> meaning that Julia Kristeva assigns to the word), as a space of *jouissance*, although she affirmed the erotic and critical value of textual practice, these proposals are often forgotten, suppressed, smothered' (101).

Uttered in the tone of an oracle, this clearly anti-scientific theory of text concluded that textual genres were finished (see chapter 3, part 4). Let us take up successively the three themes that I have just introduced.

I. The Textual Content Is Libidinal and/or Scriptural

This essentialist thesis first and foremost is applied to texts worthy of the name of 'break,' 'revolutionary' texts, written by authors such as Mallarmé, Lautréamont, Artaud, Joyce, Bataille, and let us not forget Sade, the only one who is invariably invoked. When it comes to interpreting a reputedly obscure text, one is tempted to choose as one's guiding principle a certainty about what the text *must* be saying. Making the text say it then becomes basically a subsidiary element of the method. The strength of patristic exegesis resides precisely in the firmness of its principles. Thus, Saint Augustine justifies any interpretation that conforms to faith, no matter the author's intention.[4] Now, the interpretation's conformity can cause an isotopic change. For example, according to Saint Augustine, if a candidate for conversion 'hears even in the Scriptures a word of a carnal strain, he must still believe, even though he does not understand it, that it signifies a spiritual truth, relative to saintly behaviour and to afterlife' (*De catechizandis rudibus*, XXVI, 50).

The same holds for avant-gardist hermeneutics, only inversely: in any text worthy of the name of text one must detect the signification 'of a carnal strain.' Thus, in *les chevelures pouilleuses de l'espace* (Lautréamont), Kristeva reads the word *phallus*. Using the same method, it is possible to read *valise* or *falaise*; but apparently their libidinal charge would seem to have been insufficient.[5] In this way, the dogmatic magisterium of the Freudian school has caricaturally replaced that of the Church. Moreover, avant-gardist hermeneutics does not for all this manage to avoid the reductionism it reviles elsewhere. What is more, the text, which is literary and therefore auto-referential, is supposed to designate only writing; and its ultimate meaning would constitute a scriptural isotopy. This thesis, linked to the Romantic aesthetic, undoubtedly originates in Schelling's affirmation of the *tautegorical nature* of myth; and develops in the mystique of art for art's sake illustrated by fin-de-siècle poetry. It can direct the reading of those authors, such as Mallarmé, who clearly articulated it, but scarcely of authors such as La Fontaine, for example.[6] Libidinal and scriptural meanings are not mutually exclusive. The contrary is true for those who espouse the libidinal theory of writing (see Barthes, *Le Plaisir*) and 'the ... jubilant unity of (sexual) pleasure and writing.'[7] Clearly, these 'meanings' belong to some texts, but to postulate them everywhere, and to value them no matter what, is to make a useless act of faith.

I shall now take up the problems of method.

II. Interpretation Can Operate Short of the Morpheme

In other words, analysts can and indeed must combine the letters of the phonemes of the text according to the postulates that guide them. This very powerful technique of rewriting was systematized by the Jewish mystics,[8] and the Fathers of the Church did not disregard it. Its use in literary analysis is not really new. In the last century, for example, Benjumea turned it to good account in his commentary of *Don Quichotte*.[9] Precedents aside, avant-gardist hermeneutics restores respect to this technique by finding inspiration in two well-known authors.

(i) Freud, who, for example, analysed in this manner *glejsan*, the invocation of the 'man among the rats' (I follow Gandon's presentation, *Sémiotique et négativité*, Paris, Didier, 1986, 24): *gl* = *glücklich* (makes happy); *l* = also: everyone; *e*: forgotten; *j* = *jetzt und immer* (now and forever); *s*: forgotten. Often associated with this construction are the beloved, a certain *Gisella*, and the semen (*Samen*) of her lover.[10]
(ii) Saussure, by the anagrammatic theory of saturnine verse, which remained unpublished right up to the sixties.[11]

These two 'founding' examples were exploited in philosophy by Derrida in his *dissemination* theory;[12] in psychoanalysis by Lacan in his theory of the *signifier*. In literary analyses, research on the dissemination of the signifier for the most part aims to give an account of textuality. They follow two main approaches:

(i) *Attributing a symbolic value to each phoneme*. I. Fonagy, in *Les bases pulsionnelles de la phonation*,[13] states, for example, that /m/ appertains to orality, /f/ to the phallic (the author sees here an ambiguity between 'aggressiveness' and 'relief'); /s/, in its own right ambiguous, is sometimes phallic, sometimes urethral. These 'semantic values' combine independently of the text's morphemes and their content, which therefore has become parasitic.[14] For example, here is the 'libidinal' significance of the third stanza of 'Prose pour des Esseintes':[15] 'There is released from the whole of the stanza, a signification that is mimetic, pluralized and fractured, and that can be called the constitution of a dual unity, a reminder of the identification with the maternal body; a return into the mother – a symbolic incest; an attempt to experience genitality – but one soon sees that this is exclusively in the signifying process – after having gone through the aggressiveness and the phallicism of the first two stanzas that have activated the signifying process of the text.'[16]

Admittedly research on phonetic or graphic symbolism opens up very interesting perspectives (cf. Guiraud's unjustly forgotten work on protosemantism), especially with respect to literary texts. However, symbolic codes are neither omnipresent nor built on a definitive 'libidinal base.' They are relative to languages, to textual genres, to authors. Bringing them to the fore requires (rather than excludes) a close, microsemantic analysis of the text, in order to establish plausible correlations. In a word, in this field, the neo-Freudian dogmatism of avant-gardist hermeneutics is somehow regressive.

(ii) *Composing one or several key words that stem from letters or phonemes found in the text.* This second way happens to be the one preferred.

Since Talmudic times, it has been widely used in religious hermeneutics to read the secret names of God in the Torah. The genius of the Phoenicians having drastically reduced the number of letters, everyone can easily find any words one wishes in any fairly extensive text. Here the fundamental problem of pertinence arises. It is less difficult to find anagrams than to succeed in reducing their number by formulating plausibility criteria. Saussure attempted to find the *rules* for the production of anagrams, which could possibly apply to a genre, but avant-gardist hermeneutics did not follow him on this point. It hardly looked for interpretants outside texts (acquaintance with literary theories, like that of the *Grands Rhétoriqueurs*, or that of *Oulipo*); nor for internal interpretants – for example, topographic indications, positions of metre that reveal acrostics, etc.).

Jakobson's research on anagrams[17] in poetry offers some telling examples. Being attentive to 'the fury of phonetic interplay as defined by Ferdinand de Saussure in his letter to Meillet,' he noticed, regarding the poems entitled 'Spleen' in Baudelaire's *Les Fleurs du Mal*: 'The last poem bearing this title makes some clear allusions to this theme-word and progressively anagramatises it, especially by repeating the diphones *sp*, *pl*, and, with an exchange of the liquids *spr* ... As for the last line, it sketches an anagram of the complete term: Line 4 *Sur mon crâ*N*e inc*LIN*é* PL*ante* S*on dra*P*eau* N*oir*.'[18]

However, if we accept *spleen* as a theme word, we shall have no trouble finding it elsewhere; for example in 'Le cygne,' line 4: *Ce* SIM*o*IS *menteur qu*I *par vos* PL*eurs grand*I*t* (with an exchange of nasals and not liquids); or in 'Les petites vieilles,' line 1: *Dans les* PLI*s* SIN*ueux des vielles ca*PI*ta*L*es*. Let us acknowledge that the position of *spleen* as title constitutes in itself an interpretant. Nothing is more likely: as a matter of fact, use would have it that the title resume, as it were, the content of the text; why not its expression, since in poetry, as Pope advises, *the sound must seem an echo of the sense*?[19] Yet this question is misleading and we should come up with another one. In literature, the phonic level of a text, including the title, generally has remarkable phonic recurrences that are often codified by the genre; must the origin of this be located in the 'theme words' (or 'key words'), and, if the answer is affirmative, under what conditions?

An answer can be found in the first quatrain of a sonnet by Dante: 'Se vedi li occhi miei di pianger vaghi / per novella pietà che'l cor mi strugge / per lei ti priego che da te non fugge, / Signor, che tu di dal piacere i svaghi' '(If you see that my teary eyes are thirsting / For a new anguish to destroy my heart / Lord! for the sake of one who does not desert you / For pity's sake, distract them from this pleasure.').

Jakobson feels that *pietà* is a key word, according to prosodic and morphologic considerations.[20] Then he asserts: 'The first key word *pietà* is surrounded by a string of words that echo ... its attack, that is its initial /p/, alone or accompanied by the semi-vowel /i/, sometimes with an expressive [?] /r/ that is either inserted between the two or added at the end of the word: 1 PI*anger* ~ 2 P*e*R ~ PI*età*[?] ~ 3 P*e*R ~ PRI*ego* ~ 3 PI*ace*R.'[21]

Yet many other words are anagrammatized: *occhi* in line 2, *cor* in line 1, etc. Therefore, everything depends on which key word is chosen, the one whose anagram is being sought. Moreover, the anagram is an *artefact* of the analyst, used to confirm the very risky choice of a key word. Just as by using the same type of criteria one can find other key words, one can find other anagrams, and not have the means for finding that they are implausible.[22]

We can observe certain tangible limits in the choice of the anagrammatized key words in Jakobson as well as in other authors. They correspond to minimal syntagms,[23] in the languages studied. In conformity with a tenacious prejudice that has existed in the philosophy of language since Plato, they are always (to our knowledge) chosen among (proper or 'common') nouns, although words from other morphological categories could just as well claim the honour of being key words. In fact, the criteria for choosing a key word are of little importance to us, as this is the very principle we are challenging. In linguistic analysis by rights all words are equal. Admittedly, the text or its environment can, explicitly or not, insist on certain words,[24] but it does not follow that phonic (or semic) recurrences must originate in these words, even if in some way they are condensed in them. Phonic (and semic) recurrences constitute one of the fundamental factors of textuality. Now, not only are they not *explained* through this search for and discovery of anagrams, but their complexity is also overlooked. On the one hand, the key word is instituted within paradigms of phonic or graphic symbols whose recurrences one tries to identify in the text; but, at the same time, their syntagmatic nature is overlooked: their contiguities, their relative positions,[25] their rhythms, their disposition within the whole of the text. Moreover, one is working on phonemes, which are already complex unities; and this analytical level lacks finesse, as it is the infra-phonemic (*phemic*) structures that account in the main for effects of phonic cohesion and discohesion and, hence, for textuality at the level of expression. In short, as I shall confirm later when dealing with thematics, the microsemantic and microphonemic bundles that in part found textuality cannot be summed up by words: they remain unnamed in any language.

Note: I am alluding here to the content plane, where an analogous problem arises. The content of a key word could be disseminated. In fact, several authors have extended the principle of anagrammism to textual content. For example, for Riffaterre, a (poetic) text is engendered by a *matrix*, which includes a 'core word.' This word can belong to the text, and constitute, for example, its title. The matrix develops into an utterance or an implicit text, called a *hypogram*. In short, 'the poem results from the transformation of a word or a phrase in a text or even from the transformation of texts into one, larger text.'[26] Naturally, this version of extended anagrammatism encounters the same objections I presented before.

III. The Meaning of a Text Is to Be Found in the Intertext

The notion of intertextuality, which undoubtedly owes much of its success to its own vagueness, has spawned an abundant literature. In its common use, it covers all the various kinds of relationships between texts.[27] For linguists, every text is quite obviously made up of pre-existing bits and pieces, not only morphemes but phraseologies, stereotyped, paremiologic formulas. All in all, every text is a cento. In what way does intertextuality affect textuality, and particularly at the semantic level? Avant-garde hermeneutics considers that the content of a text can reside wholly or in part in the intertext. This is where Arrivé situated 'the place of manifestation of the connotated isotopy': 'this place is not the text, but the intertext, the intertext being in turn defined as the set of texts between which the relations of intertextuality function ... In turn, according to J. Kristeva, intertextuality is defined "as the textual interaction within a single text."'[28]

How then can we identify the texts that are part of the intertext, and that therefore account for textual content? With the exception of quotations, parodies, or explicit allusions, the difficulty of choosing criteria comes to the fore here.[29] Thus Riffaterre suggests that the original 'matrix' of the text can reside in the intertext: then, for example, he includes 'l'azur sonneur,' in 'Fêtes de la faim' (Rimbaud), as a 'bitter allusion to the Mallarméan intertext (the only explanation for this strange syntagma)' (1983, 104–5). This intertext is supposedly the poem entitled 'L'Azur'; so be it, but even remaining within the confines of Mallarmé, one could just as well choose 'Le sonneur.' Neither is there anything that prevents the mention of Baudelaire, Hugo, Gautier, among others who turn out azures. How then does one avoid idle cross-referencing from text to text? The key to this problem lies in the cohesion of the text studied: this cohesion determines the allusion's textual function and, by this, its plausibility as well.

An 'allusion' is an instruction to refer to an external interpretant, any semiotic, but not necessarily linguistic, unit that allows for the actualization of semantic components (either inherent or afferent) of the text studied. If the instruction is explicit, the reference is plausible, but its effect on the interpretation of the text still remains to be shown. By explicit instruction, we mean also instructions to investigate further: for example, the title of Borges' poem 'On His Blindness' (1984) in itself constitutes such an instruction (because of the break in cohesion between the English of the title and the Spanish of the text): the conjunction of the features / Englishness / (language of the title), / poetry / (genre of the text), / blindness / (content of the title) allows one to arrive at Milton, whose sonnet XXIII (in the 1673 edition) is entitled 'To Mr Syriak Skinner upon His Blindness.' One then certainly still needs to describe semantically the interrelation between the two texts. If the instruction is not explicit, it can only be identified a posteriori, once the intrinsic interpretation of the text has allowed one to judge the plausibility of the allusion.[30]

Every textual sequence, even every sign, can function in two different ways: intratextually and intertextually (or more generally and more precisely speaking, inter-semiotically). It is the intratextual function that determines the extratextual function. This determination is of a general nature: in fact, the intratextual function is of the order of meaning (the set of relationships between elements of the contents of a text) and the intersemiotic function, of the order of *designation*: thus, meaning determines designation.[31] Hence, the intrinsic interpretation of 'Fêtes de la faim' and the intratextual function of 'l'azur sonneur' will allow us to judge the pertinence of a reference to Mallarmé.

Even if I were to show that a text consisted of a string of allusions, indeed, a collage of citations, I should still know nothing about its textuality, as such, which is exactly what makes it different from an inventory of words and phrases. In short, only the study of textuality makes it possible to found that of intertextuality and, for having neglected this, avant-garde hermeneutics has often limited the study of relationships between texts to uncontrolled comparisons between singular texts. If they do reveal forms of intertextuality, these forms are generally the most superficial ones. In fact – or this is at least my hypothesis – there exists a systematics of relationships between texts, within any given cultural domain. Making comparisons between texts is just one way of (re)constructing this systematics, but naturally, does not exhaust it. Finally, these comparisons must be elaborated with a view to such a reconstruction, otherwise they are quickly reduced to bouts of idle erudition.

Let us take, as an example, the first two lines of *Orlando furioso* (1532 edition):

> Le donne, i cavallier, l'arme, gli amori,
> le cortesie, l'audaci imprese io canto.

Here are some plausible connections:[32]

> Arma virumque cano (Virgil, *Aeneid*, I, 1)
>
> Le donne e'cavalier, li affani e li agi
> che ne 'nvogliava amore et cortesia (Dante, *Purgatorio*, XIV, 109–10)
> d'arme e d'amore (*Mambriano*, I, 5, 7)
> Armes, Amours, Dames, Chevaleries (Deschamps, *Balades de moralitez*, CXXIII, 1)
> Però diversamente il mio verziero
> de amore e de battaglie ho già piantato
> (Boiardo, *Orlando innamorato*, 1. III, V, 2, 1–2)

The following table shows this more precisely.

	I	II	III	IV	V
Virgil	arma			virumque	cano
Dante		amore cortesia	le donne	e'cavalier	
Mambriano	d'arme	d'amore			
Deschamps	Armes	Amours	Dames	Chevaleries	
Boiardo	de battaglie	de amore			ho già piantato
Ariosto	l'arme l'audaci imprese	gli amori le cortesie	le donne	i cavallier	io canto

I harbour no illusion concerning my table. It would be possible to come up with different ones by taking, as another parangon, cited excerpts different from the two lines of Ariosto. Choosing the line from Deschamps, for example, would have in all likelihood prevented one from establishing a link with the *Aeneid*.[33]

Granted this restriction, the table can be exploited only if one has recourse (i) to the context of the excerpts, (ii) to knowledge of the genres to which the cited texts belong. They line up under three headings:[34]

(i) *topical*:

- 'Singing' signals lyrical poetic genres.
- The oppositions 'ladies' vs 'knights' and 'loves' vs 'weapons'[35] are homologous in feudal topoi. Relations of afference therefore are established between components of these two taxemes.[36]

(ii) *tactic* (or syntagmatic disposition):

- 'I sing ...' appears in the exordium of the long poems (Virgil, Ariosto) or at the beginning of the canto (Boiardo) and then at its resolution ('ho già piantato').
- If 'ladies' and 'knights' are concurrent, they are arranged in that order, conforming to the courtly rules that are still valid. The order of the manifestation of 'loves' and 'weapons' is not fixed.[37]

(iii) *dialogical* (represented interlocution):

- The narrator of the epic poem represents himself in the first person in the exordium and/or at the beginning of the canto (Virgil, Dante,[38] Boiardo, Ariosto).
- The time of the great deeds that are being sung by far precedes that of the represented enunciation: this is obvious in Virgil; in Dante, Guido del Duca misses former times; Boiardo writes in the preceding book: 'Così nel tempo che virtù fioria / ne li antiqui segnori e cavallieri / con noi stava allegrezza e cortesia / e poi fuggirno per strani sentieri' (I.II, 1,2,1–4) ; and last, the 1516 edition of *Orlando furioso* gives us in the first line: 'Di donne e cavallier li antiqui amori.'[39]

In short, this minute example shows sufficiently well for our purposes that the connections from text to text, indeed from author to author, do not allow one to account actually for phenomena of intertextuality. Thus, in neglecting this fundamental factor of textuality, that every text belongs to a genre as well as, more particularly, to a historically dated use of a genre, avant-garde hermeneutics bypasses intertextuality, upon which it had, however, founded its method. Now that linguistics extends its object to include texts – to the point where it encounters the boundaries of neighbouring disciplines, at the forefront of which are ethnology and history – it is still the comparative method that can allow it to master the accumulation of data. In this way, the principles of comparativism found the scientific study of textuality and intertextuality.

None of the three theses that we have just examined is, for all this, without foundation. There certainly exist (i) texts with libidinal or scriptural isotopies, (ii) anagrammatic texts, (iii) texts whose intrinsic interpretation demands having recourse to other texts. However, none of these theses defines textuality, even when the study is restricted to literary texts; even more, their generalized application leads one to neglect the fundamental structures of textuality.[40] Let me now clarify what these structures are, before establishing an interpretative semantics that can account for hermeneutic procedures and yet avoid their limitations.

3

Situations of Interpretation and Typology of Texts

Since the meaning of a text is immanent to an interpretation situation, and types of texts are determined by typical situations, the interpretative paths that allow for the (re)construction of textual meaning are determined by the *type* of the text. Various hermeneutics do not allow one to consider this matter in its generality, as they focus on a determined type of text (especially literary, religious, legal). Linguistics, on the other hand, when it examines the text, considers it as a stage of language[1] and confines itself to generality, at the risk of delegating the study of textual types to neighbouring disciplines, like poetics.

I. Re-evaluating the Heritage of Rhetoric

In order to build a textual typology, one can hardly rely on the clouded tradition of rhetoric. Granted, linguistics and other disciplines that deal with the text have borrowed[2] a great deal from it (rhetoric) and, after it disappeared, divided up the scraps of its doctrinal body. However, rhetoric has never really been a scientific discipline – even if it is important at present to safeguard its rational kernel.[3] In fact, from its inception, it was conceived of as a technique, and its taxonomical categories as well as its descriptive concepts are linked to practical objectives.[4]

It also has some notable limitations:

(i) Since it helps to produce the texts of a given society, it deliberately remains ethnocentric, no matter what its claims to universality happen to be.
(ii) It is historically connected to certain types of discourses: judicial, deliberative, epideictic, epistolary (*ars dictaminis*), literary.
(iii) It is normative, rather than descriptive.
(iv) It is a technique of production and not of interpretation.

Finally, the theories of language upon which it rests have, if not expired, been forgotten, so much so that the concepts it produced can not be reused without epistemological precautions. All of these restrictions distance it from an interpretative semantics that is connected neither to a given society nor to a type of discourse.

II. The Question of Genre

In addition to rhetoric, which identified various types of eloquence, the question of genre has been addressed by poetics.[5] This question has been its central objective from Aristotle to Hegel. All the same, if it still continues, the debate in poetics over genres and their typology deals only with literature, indeed, even more restrictively, with poetry. Every period has attempted to make its genres fit into the tripartition (falsely attributed to Aristotle) established between the lyrical, the epic, and the dramatic, even if it had to declare them irregular to do so.[6] A profusion of typologies stem from this that we shall not dwell on here. As genres are not distinctive to literature, and even less to poetry, and since we wish to formulate linguistic criteria, let us take up this question from another direction.

A genre is a program of positive or negative prescriptions and authorizations that regulate the generation of a text as well as its interpretation; they do not arise from the functional system of language, but from other social norms. There is no text (or utterance) that can be produced solely by the functional system of language (in the restricted sense of being given linguistic form). In other words, language is never the only semiotic system at work in an utterance, as other social codifications, notably the genre, operate in every verbal communication. One will readily object that texts or utterances appear freed from competing codifications. Let us set aside those produced by computer programs, not only because they still activate only small fragments of the functional system, but also because they obey other limitations imposed by the domain of application (not to mention by state of the art). Let us rather look to linguistic examples, which are supposed to illustrate pure linguistic forms, or at least those generally examined in this light.

Strictly speaking, they are not utterances but sentences, that is to say, abstract theoretical objects, cut off from any concrete communicative situation, and therefore devoid of non-linguistic codifications that are distinctive to such a situation.[7] If the example chosen does not belong to the language object, it at least belongs to 'metalanguage': a very much codified subgenre made up of linguists' parlance.[8] And each occurrence takes on its signification within this context. Each school keeps reiterating its own examples, using them as rallying signs. They point out affiliations, and veneration for certain schools has filled European grammar texts with examples translated from American English, just as they were previously translated from Latin. In the same way that every time a genre is mentioned, they have their own topics,[9] their own heroes (Max, Pedro), their own stereotyped situations ('if you are thirsty, there is beer in the fridge'). Some are even given the status of a type (donkey-sentences, hamburger-sentences). In short, no text, not even any sentence, or *a fortiori* no utterance escapes the conventions of a genre.

Before trying to find the reason for this, we should dispel an apparent contradiction regarding genres, between the objective of linguistics (describing languages) and that of semiotics belonging to the post-Saussurian tradition. Too often, the object of linguistics is reduced only to 'form.' Linguistic 'substance,' judged not pertinent relative to the linguistic system, is in fact structured by systems that are not taken into account by restrictive linguistics. It is this 'semiotically formed substance' constituted by systems not described by linguistics (e.g., genres), but which function in every text, that, according to Hjelmslev, constitutes the 'point of contact between language and other social institutions.' Does this mean therefore that the study of textual genre should be the concern of semiotics and not linguistics? Let us agree rather that nothing that is part of language is beyond the realm of linguistics, and that textual semiotics has only served to compensate for the insufficiencies of a linguistics that is too restrictive. In short, the study of genres rightfully belongs to the domain of linguistics. The role then of semiotics is to consider the interaction of the various systems that produce a text, as well as its insertion into the communicative situation from which it derives its meaning.

III. Why Genres?

An act of communication is not the simple transmission of messages between two idealized interlocutors, like Saussure's Sender and Receiver, Jakobson's A and B, or Bloomfield's Jack and Jill.[10] The use of a language is first and foremost a social activity; so much so that every situation of communication is determined by a social practice that institutes and constrains it. It is on this evidence that I form my assertions concerning the omnipresence of genres. By exalting initiative and individual liberty, our society has certainly come to hide it from our view: it remains true that we cannot say no matter what to no matter whom no matter when. The linguists who have studied less talkative societies are well aware that for these traditional societies language is a serious thing, and that its use is clearly codified. By formulating a general but western deontology of linguistic use in his very famous conversational maxims, Grice quite simply forgot that sometimes it is necessary to be silent, and sometimes to be talkative.[11]

There is associated with each type of social practice a type of linguistic use that can be called *discourse*:[12] hence juridical, political, medical discourse, etc. Discourses seen in this light correspond to paradigmatic formations that are semantic domains.[13] As a general rule, at the heart of a semantic domain there is no polysemy. In other words, more precisely, the polysemy of signification and/or meanings of a lexicographical entry is explained for the most part by the multiplicity of domains in which that entry can receive an interpretation. The lexicographical indicators like *agric.* (agriculture) or *alch.* (alchemy), etc., constitute an empirical typology of domains and, indirectly, of discourses.

Every speaker participates in several social practices and must therefore possess several discursive competencies. Each one assumes the mastery of one or several genres. For example, in his or her professional life, a hospital doctor practices three written genres: summaries of observations, scientific articles, and letters to colleagues. These genres implement, respectively (and I exaggerate only slightly here) laconic, Attic, and Asianic styles. At the very least, some rhetorical decorations, absent in the first case, sometimes grace the third. All in all, a discourse is organized through various genres, which correspond to so many differentiated social practices within the same field – to such a degree that a genre is what attaches a text to a discourse. A typology of genres must take into account the incidence of social practices on linguistic codifications.[14] Even literary genres, which today we often think of as stemming from the same discourse, can correspond to differentiated social practices. For example, each of the lyrical genres of classical Greece (such as the hymn, the ode, the dithyramb, the threnody, or the epithalamium) was dedicated to a specific social function. The origin of genres is found then in the differentiation of social practices. It is not sufficient to say, along with Todorov, that our genres stem from the ones preceding them; we still must show how genres are formed, how they evolve, and how they tend to disappear along with the social practices they are associated with.[15]

IV. The Twilight of Genres?

Let me now explain why genre research runs into difficulties. Contemporary poeticians have produced remarkable work[16] that none the less comes up against two types of limitations: empirical limitations, since they deal only with genres that today are considered literary; theoretical limitations, as they challenge the models inherited from classical poetry, generally in the name of a typology of levels or textual functions that have no definable relations with linguistics.

These limitations reflect the ambiguity of the very status of poetics, which is a mixture of aesthetics and linguistics. When linguists dare to look beyond the sentence, they do so without a great deal of assurance. If they do mention the problem of genre, it is usually only to avoid it. Here are some references to this question. The useful work by Brown and Yule (*Discourse Analysis*, 1983) does not allude to genre. Coseriu courageously asserts that linguistics 'not only encounters, but includes' the theory of genres (1981, 152); however, he goes no further. Finally, in his monumental anthology on the analysis of discourse, Van Dijk specifies only: 'We disregard differences between types of discourse, in other words, between genres. Although the most general principles are valid for each type of discourse, there can be differences in the superficial traces of coherence, additional constraints on local or global coherence, or specific semantic properties, valid for some discourse-types (e.g. narratives vs poems vs prefaces)' (1985, II, 121). Even if genres are considered here as superficial phenomena, they still need to be described scientifically.

On the other hand, Greimas and Courtés reduce genres to ideological formations that need not be taken into account by means of a scientific topology of texts: 'Genre designates a class of discourse[17] and it is recognizable by sociolectal criteria. These can originate either in an implicit classification which is based, in oral traditional societies, on a particular categorization of the world, or in a "genre theory" which, for a number of societies, takes the form of an explicit taxonomy of non-scientific nature. Such a theory, clearly stemming from cultural relativism and based upon implicit ideological postulates, has nothing in common with the typology of discourses the establishment of which is being attempted, and which starts from a recognition of the specific formal properties of the discourses' (1979 [1982] 135).

If these theories of discourse neglect the study of genre, it is doubtless because their universalist pretensions cannot accommodate the cultural character of genres. For them, it all comes down to describing macrostructures by a textual (or narrative) syntax envisaged as being universal (in the same way as universal grammars).[18] This universalism of principle rests on a formalist conception of scientific knowledge that is not easily compatible with the status of the social sciences. By wishing to imitate the pure sciences, we are led to neglect the fundamentally cultural nature of languages and of other sign systems. At the very least, in a spirit of compromise, linguistics and semiotics should endeavour to consider the unity of language through the diversity of languages and, in the end, the unity of humanity through the diversity of cultures. In short, I see no contradiction between the general facts that every text stems from a genre, and that every genre stems from a particular culture.

Beyond scientific preoccupations, contemporary thought on genres appears to have been influenced by the modern literary aesthetic. This is not surprising, since genre theories traditionally focus on literature as their primordial object. Now, the modern aesthetic, which dilutes Romantic thought, considers that a literary text is above all the expression of a personal inner self or, for the avant-gardists, of a desiring subjectivity. The social factors that genres reflect are therefore neglected or denied. Many artists consider then that authentic creation comes about with the destruction of genres. A good text must be un-classable. Exemplary texts that are 'revolutionary,'[19] that 'break with the past,' refer to no genre, except to parody it.[20]

In *Le plaisir du texte*, Barthes wonderfully articulates this avant-gardist thesis: 'How can the text "extricate itself from" the war of fictions and sociolects? – By a progressive effort of depletion. First, the text liquidates all metalanguage, and it is because of this that it is a text: no voice (Science, Cause, Institution) *props up* what it says. Then to the very end, *to the point of contradiction*, the text destroys its own discursive category (its "genre") ... Through transmutation (and not only by transformation), it is a matter of bringing about a new philosophical state of language-matter' (50–1).

Outside these pythic but sibylline remarks,[21] and outside literary research (which in fact leads to the creation of unnamed new genres), genres are and always will remain healthy. Guides on the art of letter writing, on the art of writing theses, or résumés, or dissertations, all attest to this. In its development, the automatic analysis of languages encounters the problem of genre, in the analysis as well as the generation of texts.[22] Finally, the knowledge of genres remains indispensable in the interpretation of texts, even literary and avant-garde texts. It allows us to define the interpretants, to formulate criteria for the plausibility of readings, and to contribute to determining reference, whether it happens to be fictional or not.

V. Towards a Linguistic Foundation of Textual Typology

Beaugrande and Dressler consider that a typology of texts cannot be based on the 'traditional criteria' of linguistics (1984, 238). However, linguistics is evolving and for us what follows still remains within its domain. Since meaning is immanent to the communicative situation, the manner in which it is represented naturally is very important.

A. Linguistic Functions

The main contemporary representations of linguistic functions are based on the sign model presented by Karl Bühler (1934 [1965]). The sign functions as such through its relations with the sender, the receiver (*Empfänger*), and the referent (*Gegenständen und Sachverhalten*). Relative to each of these three poles, the sign pertains to a different semiotic type: it is a symptom in relation to the sender, a signal in relation to the receiver, and a symbol in relation to the referent.[23]

Let us assume that this functional theory of the sign holds for the text in as much as it is a combination of signs, indeed for the text as sign (did Peirce and Hjelmslev not maintain, each one in his own way, that the text is a sign?). However, this model does not take into account the situation of communication, that is to say, the relations between sender, receiver, and referent, that are mediated not only by the sign. Moreover, its a priori nature[24] leaves no place for the social conditions that determine the communicative situation, and does not, for this reason, make it possible to establish a typology of situations.

Jakobson reintroduced and popularized Bühler's functional concept and made it more sophisticated without however proposing anything to equal it. The function that Bühler called *Ausdruk*, and then *Kundgabe*, and that links the sender to the message, Jakobson calls the *emotive*; he calls *conative* that which links the message to the receiver (Bühler's *Auslösung* or *Appell* function); and he calls Bühler's *Darstellung* (the function linking the message to what it represents) the referential. He borrows from Malinowski the notion of a phatic function that is not really distinct from Bühler's *Appell*; he adds a metalinguistic function that seems no different from the referential function, as there is only one specific case of it (the reference to signs);[25] finally, he adds also a poetic function characterized by 'the intent (*Einstellung*) of the message as a message, putting the accent on the message for its own sake' (1963, 218). However, as Coseriu remarked, the archetypal example of poetic function given by Jakobson (*I like Ike*) is a political slogan mainly pertaining to the conative function. This very objection shows that the identification of functions and the determination of their hierarchy cannot occur without knowledge of the type of discourse that characterizes the text. If *I like Ike* had been taken from the personal notebooks of a Victorian naïve person, where *Ike* designated some conceited dandy or other, Coseriu could not have formulated his objection. Indeed, it is not the typology of functions that founds the typology of discourses, but the latter that makes it possible to suggest what function dominates in the text.[26]

Several difficulties inherent to a functional typology of texts come to the fore:

(i) The inventory of functions stems from a comprehensive pragmatics and not from linguistics as such. In fact, the theory of functions is part of general semiotics and is equally valid for non-linguistic signs.

(ii) As the hypothesis that a text proceeds from a single function is generally dismissed, textual types become defined rather by the dominance of one function over others. However, it must then be presumed that the same function is dominant throughout the text, otherwise every text would stem in part from all of the types. It also remains difficult to formulate criteria of dominance. As the quantitative criteria appear excluded, unless one can classify the signs themselves as 'specialized' in one or another function, it becomes necessary to identify in each text the structures that are judged to be typical of a function. Other than Jakobson with respect to the poetic function, no one to my knowledge has attempted to do this.

(iii) Finally, the functional types obtained in this way inevitably confuse texts stemming from diverse discourses. Take, for example, the typology that Beaugrande and Dressler see as defining certain texts (1984, 239 ff.). Descriptive texts 'serve to fill areas of knowledge in which the centres of control are objects or situations'; narrative texts are 'those that organize actions and events in a sequential order'; lastly, argumentative texts are 'those that ... underscore as true vs false or positive vs negative the recognition or the evaluation of determined ideas or convictions.' This kind of typology, as the authors acknowledge, will accept a 'blending of descriptive, narrative and argumentative functions' in the most diverse of texts. However, what could be the interest of a typology that could not manage to differentiate the present work, for example, from *Jerusalem Delivered*? The dominance of a function would certainly allow one to distinguish three types of texts, to classify Tasso's masterpiece in the second category (where narration dominates) and my laborious treatise in the third (where argumentation dominates). But, in fact, Beaugrande and Dressler are compelled to rely on encyclopaedic knowledge with respect to the situation of communication: for example, the technical file of a slide projector contains 'some elements of argumentative texts' but mainly stems from a descriptive function because it 'has as its goal the description of the use and handling of a given apparatus' (241). On the other hand, the American Declaration of Independence belongs, along with the book you are reading at present, to the third category (because it 'strives to convince one that America had the right to "choose" her "political ties" with England' [240]).[27]

To circumvent this type of difficulty, one could impugn the notion of dominance or at least only envisage each function separately, in order to produce typologies relative to the sender, the receiver, the referent, or any other functional pole. In fact, there has been no shortage of typologies founded on the presumed intention of the sender (to educate, please, instruct, etc.) or on the expected effect on the receiver (enthusiasm, boredom, etc.). Speech-act theory has taken up this problematic in its own manner. These typologies are not founded upon linguistic theories of the text, but on philosophic theories of intentionality (see Searle, 1985) from which praxeology is derived, or even an aesthetics. As for the classification of texts according to the type of referent, this ultimately relegates our problem to physics, indeed (according to phenomenologists) to metaphysics. Finally, nothing leads us to expect that these unilateral and extra-linguistic typologies be mutually compatible, since the interaction of the functional poles upon which they are founded will have been neglected from the very outset.

In short, if functional theories account for the relation between a text and its conditions, it is by defining communication as an archetype, independently of any situation.[28] In addition to shedding hardly any light on intra- and intertextual relations, they do not take into account all the relations of the text to its conditions of communication. Notably, arising as they do from a reflection on the sign (see Bühler), they rather neglect the systems at work in a text – one of which is language itself.[29] The necessary mediation between the text and its functional poles is, in my opinion, to be found first and foremost in these sociolectal formations: genres and discourses. They codify the relation between texts and their situations of communication, as well as the situations themselves.

B. The Conditions of Communication and Interpretation

The following diagram does not claim to present the archetypal situation of communication, but only to give an inventory of the necessary conditions for communication.

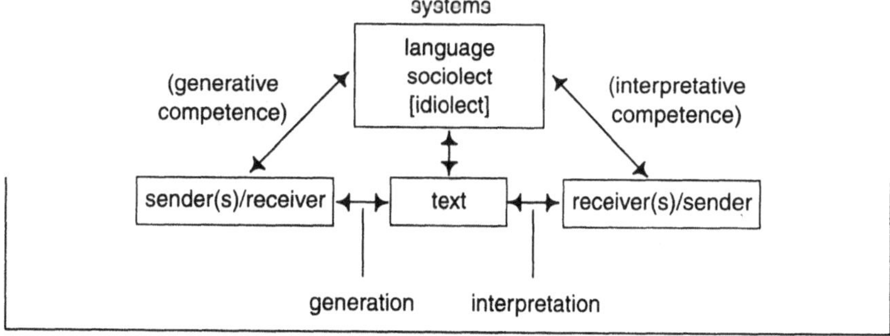

Let me clarify the status of the parts of this diagram:
1) The *sender* and the *receiver* are as a rule considered to be subjects.[30] Just the same, it is convenient to divide each of these two notions.

(i) For my purpose, the sender and the receiver are first and foremost *places* occupied by actors (and not by persons). Actors are defined as groups of roles linked by a semiotics of social relations (see chapter 5 on dialectics). These actors may be human or not (e.g., they could be computer systems), and may or may not be endowed with intentionality. They may be individuals or collectives (e.g., the text of a law of Parliament that concerns the national community), and may or may not correspond to persons endowed with a historical existence that may or may not have been attested to (Homer, the authors of *One Thousand and One Nights*). The actors of enunciation proper (which include the interpretation as well as the generation of a text)[31] maintain complex relations with the actors of represented enunciation (see chapter 6, 58–61, on dialogics). For example, the Author[32] of *A la recherche du temps perdu* corresponds to two actors of the represented enunciation: the Narrator and Marcel. Genres codify the type and the number of roles of the represented enunciation.

(ii) At another analytical level, which goes beyond our analysis, since it is psychological and sociological, the sender and the receiver are persons who temporarily assume the roles of actors of the enunciation proper.[33] They are different notably because they are persons endowed with generative and interpretative competencies. Their relation to the text is not unilateral (pure activity or pure passivity) but must be understood as an interaction: the text acts upon its author, who produces, but also interprets it (auto-correction, rereadings, etc.); and the reader acts on the text, in one respect, by (re)producing it (he anticipates it, completes it, catalyses it – in the Hjelmslevian sense – indeed, in the case of a productive reading, even rewrites it).

Enunciation thus supposes: (i) the choice by a person of a type of role, either sender or receiver; (ii) the production and interpretation of the text. The concepts of sender and receiver are used to introduce a mediation between the text and the persons participating in the situation of communication. The text, therefore, is not the simple and immediate expression of a subjectivity (in spite of modern and postmodern clichés on art as howl,[34] for example). On the contrary, the subject is not constituted only by the production and interpretation of texts, in spite of what Benveniste says: 'The foundation of subjectivity is in the exercise of language' (1966, 262). It is first of all by assuming the roles of sender and receiver as they are codified by society that an individual affirms her or his subjectivity, or, in other words, confirms her or his subjection.[35]

2) Several types of systems are at work in any given text.

(i) Functional language (as opposed to historical language; cf. Coseriu, 1976) remains too exclusively the object of linguistics. The rules of this system are considered to be imperatives; they consist of prescriptions and interdictions. We often forget licences, which make up the object of what Donatus called *permissive grammar*.

(ii) A *sociolect*,[36] which, within the framework of a functional language, consists of positive and negative prescriptions. A sociolect stems from a social practice rather than from a particular social group: we all possess several sociolectal competencies that are linked to these practices (sports, politics, teaching, etc.). Each has its lexicon structured in a semantic domain, and its own textual genres (sports column, oath of loyalty, lecture, etc.).

(iii) The *idiolect* is a system of textual norms that are characteristic of a sender. Although all speakers have their own habits and peculiarities, they do not all possess systematized idiolectical competencies. The norms of an idiolect can in fact contradict and transgress those of a genre (which stem from a sociolect), and even of a language.[37] It is in literary texts that one finds the most developed examples of idiolectical formations. Clearly, every text does not offer such formations; all the more so since certain genres exclude them (business letter, for example).

These three types of systems are in constant interaction. In synchrony, they interfere naturally in the texts. Is it then up to a more evolved linguistics or a restricted semiotics to describe these interactions? I shall leave this question open, in the hopes that the progress of systemics will provide the theoretical tools needed to better ask it. Furthermore, in diachrony, these systems evolve into temporalities of different orders. For the idiolect, the unit of measure could be the decade (thus, the Mallarmean idiolect extends over thirty years); for the sociolect, the century (for example, French 'classical literary language' has fallen into disuse in less than two centuries); in functional language, it comes down to permanencies or evolutions that stretch out to a millennium (one could say that in French the formation of the system of the article from Latin has not been achieved even yet). This distinction between systems – or rather, for an unrestrained linguistics, between *degrees* of systematization – remains necessary to explain the incidence of social history on language. For example, individual innovations can become stereotypes and end up being integrated into the lexicon.[38] Thus, it could be said that the lexicon is a kind of *frozen doxa*.

All in all, there correspond degrees of fixedness, whose ultimate outcome is morphological integration, to the different temporalities I have evoked.[39]

3) The *surrounding* (or the non-linguistic context, in the widest sense) includes the text, the sender and the receiver. It contains the interpretants necessary for the actualization of the text's contents. It is arranged in three zones of increasing scope:

(i) The semiotics associated with the text (mimics, gestural, graphic, typographic, diction, music, images, illustrations, etc.). One or several associated semiotics are always present; and it could be said that linguistic communication is of a plurisemiotic nature.[40]
(ii) The situation of communication and, most notably, the social practice within which the text is situated, and which takes into account its choice of genre, as well as other sociolectal formations.
(iii) The encyclopaedic knowledge *of* the society where the communication occurs; and, including the preceding, *on* this society. They most certainly include all available knowledge on the sender and the receiver.

Having recourse to all sorts of encyclopaedic knowledge from all sorts of origins, on the express condition that it be required by textual or generic directives, and/or that it reinforces the cohesion of reading, is not a tactic of dubious facility that would cause linguistics to dissolve into ethnology, history, or other disciplines. Any research that aids in the interpretation of a text is linguistically justified, even if the required knowledge is not part of linguistics. From this there arises a fundamental problem for interpretative semantics. If the surrounding changes, the content of the text also changes, since it is immanent to a situation of communication that is now modified. As a general rule, in the case of a change of era or culture, it degenerates, through loss of knowledge. Hence, schematically:

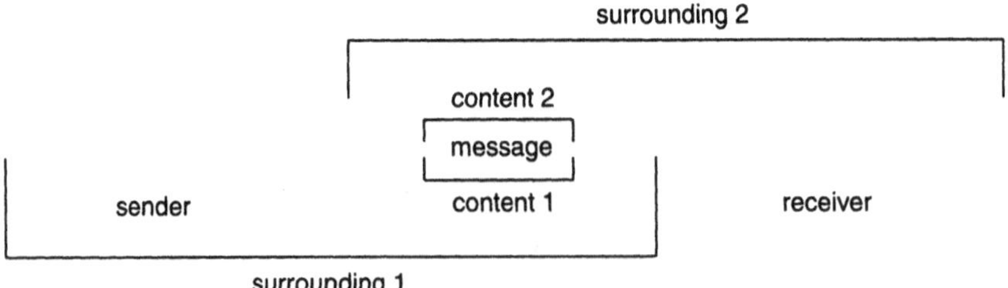

Two directions are then possible:

(i) *Productive* reading reinterprets the text according to the receiver's preference, and makes it correspond to new situations and referents, although it may even mean partially rewriting it.[41]
(ii) *Descriptive* reading responds to the modest but ambitious objective of restoring the text's content[42] by reconstructing the surroundings of the initial communication. As far as scientific discipline goes, only interpretative semantics can claim to do this. It necessarily builds on the results of philology; even more so, the developments of these two sectors of linguistics are mutually conditioned.

The project of the restoration of one or several initial meanings has been naturally criticized by religious hermeneutics (the revealed text surpasses worldly historicity: since it is sacred, it is not historical, but historial – Henry Corbin would say), as well as by literary hermeneutics (under the pretext that masterpieces are inexhaustible). For example, Riffaterre writes: 'Must one have recourse to historical method? Revive the fossilized conventions that emerge from it by reconstructing a bygone aesthetic?' In spite of modernist pejoratives (such as *fossilized*) I should respond in the affirmative: this method is *necessary* (although not sufficient), be it only to establish the text. Riffaterre continues: 'But first, the applications of this method to literature have serious limitations: supposing one could really reconstruct the milieu that had conditioned the genesis of the work and oriented the original readings of it towards a certain interpretation, it is inadmissible to limit a poem to its first avatar, since it contains within itself much more potential than was developed by its first readers' (1971, 189). Perhaps, but: (i) a first avatar is not *already* a 'reincarnation'; (ii) the text does not straightaway contain within itself its possible readings: the progressive modification of its surrounding creates new situations of communication, that allow for new interpretations; (iii) the history of the readings of a text must be retraced from its origin: the first are not in essence the best, but at least we must be aware of them in order to retrace this history, and relate it to modifications in the surrounding.

Finally, the surroundings must not be confused with the referent. In the communication situation, we have not left room for reference as such. Yet Jakobson distinguishes, among the six factors of communication, the 'context' or 'referent' that gives rise to the 'referential' function (also called 'denotative' or 'cognitive'; see 1963, 214). Not only does the problem of reference stem from the philosophy of language rather than from linguistics, but it is posed *after* the (re)construction of meaning and therefore depends not only on the text and the system, but on their interrelations with the surrounding and the interlocutors. The thesis of denotative, literal meaning that is immediately understandable, and upon which vericonditional semantics is founded, is unacceptable under these conditions.

4) As for the *text*, finally, chapters 4 to 7 describe each of the four systematic components organizing its semantic level: *thematics, dialectics, dialogics, tactics*. They define and organize the descriptive concepts useful in the analysis of texts and in the typology of genres.

4

Thematics

Thematics gives an account of invested contents and of their paradigmatic structures.

Before continuing, I must redefine the notion of *theme*, which supplanted that of topos after the dismemberment of rhetoric. This notion remains imprecise;[1] in general, a theme is a lexeme used as a generic denominator. For example, a thesis on the theme of *water* in the novelist Bosco's work[2] will exploit the occurrences of *river*, *sea*, *pond*, etc. Obviously, the results would be different if the theme of the *river* or even of *liquid* had been chosen. Each theme conceived of in this manner owes its existence solely to an arbitrary choice (even if it can be confirmed by the intuition of uncommon recurrences). Each one can give access to a semantic universe, but can also lead to impasses, by masking the systematic character of this universe. Narrative functions are also designated as *themes* (for example, submission in Racine), as well as more complex structures (for example, the bride sold).

The same imprecision remains beyond the realms of literary studies. In Artificial Intelligence, many authors consider the notion of theme to be an established concept, and use it[3] as a foundation for theories of textual cohesion. None the less, the nature of thematic continuity still needs to be described semantically.

I. Elements of Thematic Typology

How can multiplying ad hoc themes, which are potentially as numerous as the lexemes of a natural language, be avoided? We must also take into account progress made in fundamental semantics, and not remain 'at the surface of signs,' even if lexical or simply morphemic recurrences can make up very valuable interpretants. In the first place, I shall remain within it, in order to decompose the theme into semantic features (or *semes*), even at the risk of dissolving it. A theme may have no name in any language.

If, as is ordinarily done, one takes as a theme the content of a lexeme (a *sememe*), one can elucidate the structures of the semantic universe described by identifying the recurrences of its generic features (that constitute its *classeme*) and/or those of its specific features (that constitute its *semanteme*). For example, water in Bosco can be studied as an element (like earth, air, and fire, if one indulges in Bachelardian reveries) and/or as having specific 'qualities,' for example, movement, liquidity, transparency. A distinction between two types of themes stems from the fundamental distinction between generic and specific semes.

Generic themes reveal semantic classes in a text by the recurrence of their members and, in some cases, by their designation. Three types of generic themes correspond to the three types of semantic classes:[4]

(i) The *taxeme* is the minimal class where sememes are interdefined: for example, 'cigarette,' 'cigar,' 'pipe' are contrasted within the taxeme //tobacco//. Thus, the 'theme' of tobacco in *Madame Bovary* is noticeably articulated through the opposition between 'cigar' (of the Viscount, Rodolphe), 'pipe' (of Léon, Rodolphe), 'cigarette' (of Emma), which is correlated as one would expect with many narrative oppositions. This type of 'theme' can be called *microgeneric*.

(ii) The *domain* is a more general class, which includes several taxemes. It is 'linked to the experience of the group' (Pottier 1974), in so far as it structures the linguistic representation of a codified social practice. Most lexicographic indicators like *mar.* (marine) or *cuis.* (cuisine) are in fact designations of domains.[5] Studying a theme like food in Zola's *L'Assommoir* would amount to studying the domain of //food//. This type of theme could be called *mesogeneric*.

(iii) *Dimension* is the most general of classes. *Dimensions* are articulated together by major oppositions that cross semantic units, for example //animate// vs //inanimate//, //animal// vs //human//, //animal// vs //vegetable//. These oppositions can be lexicalized; for example, respectively, 'one' vs 'it,' 'snout' vs 'mouth,' 'venomous' vs 'poisonous.' A theme that corresponds to a dimension can be called *macrogeneric*: for example, animality in Maupassant constitutes such a theme.

Detecting the recurrence of a generic theme amounts, in the end, to formulating a generic isotopy. The three types of themes laid out above correspond to the three types of generic isotopies (see Rastier 1987a, chap. 5).

Now, let us turn to *specific themes*. Since the opposition between specific and generic semes is as relative as it is fundamental, let us simplify matters by saying that specific semes are not linked to any determined class. Therefore, a lexical content[6] like those ordinarily chosen as themes, by its generic components, is linked to at least one semantic class.

We shall look rather for noticeable recurrences of specific semes, independent from determined lexicalization. As a notable phenomenon, texts create *semic molecules* through the recurrence of groupings of relatively stable specific semes. For example, in *L'Assommoir*, the grouping of the semes /hot/, /viscous/, /yellow/, and /harmful/ is repeated throughout the text, diversely lexicalized, in whole or in part, by words such as *juice*, *pee*, *sauce*, *snot*, *butter*, *paunch*, *copper*, *oil*, *moon*, *drop*, etc. Thus, this molecule is not linked to any determined class, even though its lexicalizations belong to very diverse classes. This is precisely what allows it to recur throughout the whole text (see chapter 10).

If one really wanted to get back to a sign-linguistics and/or to a hermeneutics of dissemination, one could try to determine which of these lexicalizations have all the semes of the molecule and choose from among them a key word, *alcohol*, for example. However, the commonsense logic that would make the other lexicalizations metaphors of *alcohol* is rather arbitrary,[7] and especially restricts the interpretative paths. Let us represent by a related graph the *associative network* of the molecule studied, that is to say, the set of its lexicalizations and of their active context. Orienting the arcs of the graph in such a way that all paths lead to *alcohol* at the same time eliminates dozens of possible connections between the other lexicalizations, which equally impoverishes the interpretative path.

Let us keep in mind that by their occurrence, the semic molecules induct entire networks of specific isotopies. They are not linked to any determined lexicalization. A molecule has the status of a type. During the same interval of textual time, its occurrences can take on very diverse degrees of typicality to the point of displaying only one of its semes. Moreover, the composition of a molecule can vary, in the same semantic universe and in the same world, between two intervals of textual time.[8] Far from being static units, molecules constitute potent morphogenes.

In short, generic – and notably mesogeneric – isotopies and the *networks* inducted by semic molecules are thus the two primary factors of semantic cohesiveness. This cohesiveness doubtless plays an essential role in textuality. Because of this, the concept of *theme* can be explained in detail and become founded in microsemantics.

Let me review the preceding points and propose some inevitably imperfect equivalencies with the terminological oppositions used in other fields:

Semantics:	generic themes	specific themes
Gestalttheorie:	ground	figure
Artificial intelligence:	topic	focus
Literary criticism:	subject	theme
Ancient rhetoric:	style[9]	'topoi'

It seems that only textual semantics can propose a unified description of the two orders of phenomena. And such a description is based on a microsemantics. Indeed, the same occurrence of a morpheme can concurrently reveal a generic theme (by its classeme) and a specific theme (by its semanteme). In the case of a plurivocal reading, it presents at least two generic themes and at least two occurrences of a specific theme.

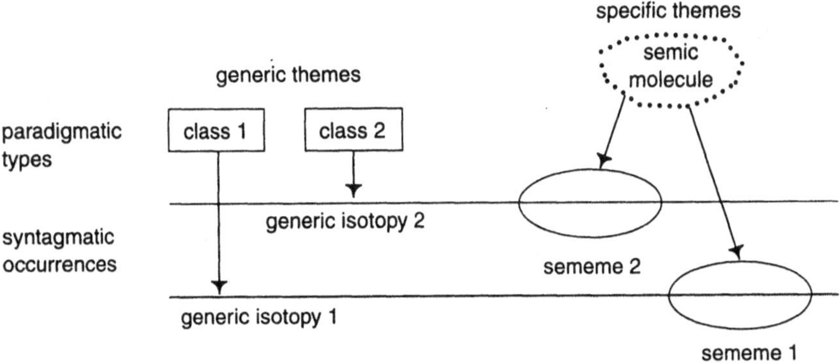

Thus, in *L'Assommoir*, 'sauc(e)', on the generic isotopy of //food// manifests the same semic molecule (/yellow/, /hot/, /viscous/, /harmful/) as 'sauc(ée)', on the generic isotopy of //weather// (see chapter 10, 122).

In short, the thematics that I propose is purely semantic, as it is founded on the identification of semic recurrences (of an order inferior to the sememe, which is already a complex content). The recurrences of complex signs (such as lexemes) and even simple signs (such as morphemes) can only serve, in the best of cases, as interpretants signalling the existence of an associative network.[10]

II. The Construction of Specific Themes[11]

It is generally taken as given that every text 'represents' a succession (that is rarely logical or chronological) of processes affecting entities. I shall not go on regarding the ontologies proposed by the philosophy of language to define their referential correlates or regarding the theories of mental objects that have been worked out in cognitive research. In addition to its being difficult and perhaps useless to distinguish between entities and processes, it is important first to elaborate on which semantic constraints allow for the construction of representations. This necessary prerequisite concerns interpretative semantics: classes of occurrences, whose groupings of invariable features are instituted as types (precisely, specific themes) are constituted. For this, paraphrastic relations are identified: the study of parasynonymies and of anaphores is not sufficient; syntactic parallelisms, parataxis, or isophones, which are interpretants of equivalence relations, must also be taken into account.[12]

For example, at the end of the first act of *El Burlador de Sevilla* (Tirso de Molina), Thisbé speaks to Dom Juan (I, 1006–7): 'A falso huesped, que dexas / una muger desonrada ...'[13] and later (I, 1017–20): 'Engañòme el cavallero / debaxo de fé, y palabra / de marido, y profanò / mi honestidad, y mi cama.'[14]

Taking anaphores into account (with or without co-reference), it could be acknowledged that 'falso huesped' and 'cavallero debaxo de fé' are semantically equivalent (although not identical): the guest was a cavalier; to be false is to be without honour. However, 'ladron' and even (by hypallage) 'fiero' could be added to this list, according to the lines 999–1002: 'Ay choza, vil instrumento / de mi deshonra, y mi infamia, / cueva de ladrones fiera, / que mis agravios ampara.'[15]

Dom Juan's act is characterized by a class of sememe-occurrences: desonrada, engaño, profanò, desonra, infamia, agravios.

In short, the class invariables so constituted by homologation are grouped in semic molecules. As types, they allow for the analysis of occurrences that reveal the same entities or the same processes (whatever their place in the text) because they are recognized as occurrences of the same molecule.[16]

Note: Those familiar with narrative analysis will have noted that the specific theme I have designated by 'Dom Juan' is none other than an *actor* (in the technical sense). Admittedly though, actors are themes just like any others: proper nouns, indeed the feature /human/, do not justify a priori that narrative analysis be focused on them, to the detriment of other contents. Moreover, thematics and narrative analysis are separated only on the basis of poor academic reasons. In this case, the contents of actors must be constructed by the same methods as other themes.

III. Variables and Thematized Graphs

What is the internal structure of specific themes (and notably of semic molecules), and how are they interlinked? I have chosen for this a graphic representation inspired by Sowa (*Conceptual Structures*, 1984). This formalism of graphs that I have used in a specifically semantic rather than conceptual manner has the merits of being potent, generalizable, elegant, easily implementable, and founded on mathematics.[17]

These closely related graphs can make up cycles (unlike the 'nice syntactic trees' popularized by Chomskyism). Their nodes are labelled by semantic units of every level (beginning with semes, semic molecules, and sememes). Their links are labelled by semantic primitives[18] (like cases, for example). Strictly speaking, in graphic representation, the designations of the nodes are included within rectangles, those of the links, within circles; 'propositional' representation, between brackets and parentheses respectively. As they have important properties in textual semantics, these graphs can be paired and transformed. They can represent the three layers of textual analysis. In the microsemantic layer, the nodes represent features and the links, primitives; in the mesosemantic layer, actants and cases, respectively; in the macrosemantic layer, actors and dialectical functions, respectively.[19]

For example, relations of case can articulate the features of a sememe just as well as the actants (in the sense ascribed them by Tesnière) of an utterance or the actors of a narrative. What is more, groupings of semes can be assembled in a sememe or dispersed throughout a text. This all serves to authorize the expansions and condensations by which one characterizes the functioning incorrectly called metalinguistic: thus, in determined genre conditions, a sememe can be the equivalent of an utterance (definition, paraphrase), or of a text (title). It is in the mesosemantic layer that specific themes are invested in the graphs (then said to be *thematized*). These are the primitives we use to label their links: the attributive, the dative, the benefactive, the ergative, the accusative, the locative, the instrumental, the final, and the resultative (for an illustration, see chapter 9, 83–6).[20]

Thematized graphs can be used in three ways.

(i) Taken independently of the labels of their nodes (which represent variables), they are reduced to case frames. The study of these frames and of their combinations belongs to *dialectics*; see chapter 5).

(ii) If one or several variables of a graph are linked to semic molecules, with at least one variable remaining free, a matrix of homologation is obtained. Matrices of homologation play an eminent role in the methodology of the social sciences (in Dumézil and Lévi-Strauss, for example): they found in fact qualitative analogical reasoning. I use them later to describe the relations between generic isotopies, and to build narrative sequences. They remain the principal means of (re)discovering idiolectal semantic classes.

(iii) Finally, when all the variables represented by its nodes are linked, a thematized graph can be used in two main ways. If it was obtained from the described text, one can look for its other occurrences.[21] If this graph represents a normative and socialized maxim, it is given the name *topos* (see Rastier, 1987a).

IV. Topics

Topics is the sociolectal sector of thematics. The occurrence in a text of a topos can be noted as an indication of genre. A topos where no occurrences are noted is implicit, but if it upholds entymematic reasoning[22] it is required by the description. Let us take as an example of a topos rendered explicit, the one Riffaterre calls 'the flower on the brink of the abyss' (1983, 60). It can be represented as follows:

[A] - - - - → (LOC) - - - - - → [B]

LOC: locative

A = /prominent/, /fragile/, /attractive/, /alive/, /coloured/.

B = /hollow/, /powerful/, /repugnant/, /mortal/, /sombre/.

Here are some occurrences: 'I planted *flowers* for her at the edge of the *precipice*' (Racine); 'Beneath the *flowers* that I know, there is no prairie / But the black milk of the unknown *abyss*' (Tardieu); 'this *gulf* of *flowers*' (Balzac); 'Poor *flower*, from the height of this summit / you had to go into that immense *abyss*' (Hugo).[23]

In fact, the lexicalizations *flower* and *abyss* are misleading; other lexicalizations fit just as well, as long as they have the same semic molecule: thus *precipice* or *gulf* can be substituted for *abyss*. Moreover, these lexicalizations can admittedly be metaphoric; for example, *flowers* and *gulf* can (respectively) designate the appearance and the reality of a dangerous mistress, dangerous because seductive (see Balzac, *Massimilia Doni*, Paris, Gallimard, Bibl. de la Pléiade, IX, 237).

Every topos can be transformed, by a modification of invested themes, or of the structure of its graph. Hence, Tardieu writes: 'then oh *flowers* in you, in turn / does the *abyss* nestle'; and therefore transforms the topos as follows:

[B] - - - - → (LOC) - - - - - → [A]

Whether they are made explicit or not, topoi are the raw material of textual creation. 'The pitcher goes so often to water, that, in the end, it gets filled ...'[24] A topic characterizes not only a discourse, but also the genres associated with it. Without being rigorously structured (each topos stems from a suitable story), topics none the less carry negative or positive prescriptions that exclude or impose the use of such and such a semantic class, or even such and such a sememe. The semantic domains that characterize a discourse and even a genre can then be delimited. For example, regarding the imperial anthologies of the Heian age, Shuichi Kato notes: 'There are innumerable poems about the moon, but almost none about the stars (with the exception of the Milky Way and the *tanabata*). Unanimously or almost unanimously, poets of the period neglect the stars and the violets in their poems.'[25]

V. Archthematics

This name shall be given to the part of thematics that deals with the division of the semantic universes into value-assigned spaces. It focuses on the most general of generic themes that stem from the semantic dimension (see above, 34). Outside of linguistics, these dimensions have been studied in anthropology (see Lévi-Strauss' *nature/culture* opposition) and in semiotics (see Greimas' *life/death* opposition). Dimensions oppose each other in pairs through qualitative oppositions (A vs B). Combined with privative oppositions (A vs not A, B vs not B) they are defined with respect to the contradictory classes (not A not B) or neutral (not A and not B). In this way, the quatern – later called the *semiotic square* – formerly presented by Greimas and Rastier (1968) can be considered as a first representation of an archthematic structure. However, as later works demonstrated, semantic universes fortunately cannot be reduced to a quatern[26] (see Rastier, 1971, 1972).

The typology of archthematic structures remains an open question. The thematics whose contours I have sketched belongs to textual linguistics, and not to literary criticism. But it cannot by itself take the place of a theory of the text. It is only one of the necessary components of a textual semantics. Its relations with the other components open, it seems to me, some promising directions for research.

5

Dialectics

This semantic component accounts for the succession of intervals in textual time, as well as for the states that occur and the processes that take place. Most notably it deals with aspectual phenomena. The construction of thematized graphs at the mesosemantic layer is a precondition for describing the dialectic component of a text. Indeed, their nodes represent *actants*[1] and *processes*, and their connections, the case relations that articulate them. Sememes or semic molecules originate in the nodes of these graphs. By this, thematics is articulated along with dialectics at the mesosemantic level: the semantic features of the actant are obviously linked to its case valencies. The dialectic component accounts for the relationship between graphs in three respects: it recognizes their sequences, their homologations, and interprets them as strings of operations on classes of contents.

I. Sequences

In spite of appearances, sequences do not fall within the scope of syntagmatics in the ordinary sense of the term. Thematized graphs are in effect (re)constructed mesosemantic units, without any necessary connection to the linear order of signs in a text.

> *Note*: The linguistics of the sign has certainly insisted on the linearity of the signifier. It does not follow that the signified is organized according to the same order relationship. Even on the most superficial level, a linearity of the signified could not be postulated (see chapter 7).

A: An Inventory of the Graphs

Graphs that do not explicitly appear are provided by catalysis (in the Hjelmslevian sense). For this, one can have recourse to presuppositions independent of the field and stemming from the inherent contents of signs (for example, an utterance like *he started again* obviously authorizes reconstructing a first attempt); or, even more, of the inferences allowed by knowledge of the field. Once this is done, distinct inventories are established (i) for each universe (if the text includes several that are, for example, relative to narrative actors); and (ii) in each of these universes for each of the worlds.[2]

B: Setting into Order

The order relationships arising from dialectics are then introduced in the following way:

(i) The aspectual features are designated so as to arrange the phases of the process (inchoative, durative, terminative, etc.) and their type of occurrence (singulative, iterative, etc.).
(ii) The temporal features are selected in order to situate the intervals within and between processes. Aspectual analysis governs temporal analysis, as can be demonstrated by a simple experiment: a French text in the imperfect may not allow for the ordering of the graphs corresponding to it; rewritten in the past historic, it will allow it (see Nef, 1983, 279–80).

Occasionally, and notably in literary texts, it is impossible to give a total order to each of the worlds. Series of graphs can be situated in intervals that cannot be arranged into an order. One must then adopt an arborescent representation of time, by graphs that are not necessarily connected.

C: Typical Syntagms and Their Sequences

The stereotyped sequences of thematized graphs are generally specific to a genre. For example, in our tradition, at least since the time of Apicius, the kitchen recipe has sequences that follow each other: collecting the ingredients, preparation, seasoning and sauces, serving suggestions.

In addition to practical texts (like recipes), mythical texts also have such sequences: narrative functions can in fact be defined as typical syntagms, and tests, as sequences of these. The study of typical syntagms and of their sequences is crucial for methodology and interpretation. In fact, their stability in a genre or in a given text allows us to detect ellipses and supply them by catalysis. The *scripts* used in the automatic analysis of narrative have no other mission than to authorize these processes of supplying. Typical syntagms cannot be classed a priori by a universal praxeology. They are basically relative to discourses; secondly, to genres, that codify evenemential schemata.

II. Questions on the Narrative

Since in what follows we shall study mostly narrative mythical texts, let us pause to consider for a moment the problems of narrative. For the past thirty years, they have elicited unprecedented research efforts in three fields distinct from folkloristics.[3] Narratology has developed in the domain of literary studies and particularly in poetics (see, for example, the works of Genette, Todorov, Mieke Bal, Gerald Prince). It has for the most part confined itself to literary texts as defined by our tradition. Reflecting contemporary aesthetics of the novel, it has especially focused on the problem of narration, without attempting to work out a universal grammar of narrative. Narrative semiotics, developed especially on Greimas' initiative, has taken as its point of departure Propp's *Morphology of the Folktale*. He simplified, systematized, and generalized Propp, drawing from his work a narrative grammar that constitutes what is generally considered to be the core of this semiotics. This universal grammar is called upon to describe all the narratives of all societies[4] and even of all texts, since 'the semio-narrative structures ... constitute the most abstract level, the *ab quo* instance of the generative trajectory' (Greimas and Courtés, 1979, [1982] 153), which is supposed to be able to engender all semiotic manifestations. This semiotics recognizes narrative structures in every text, even in a recipe for basil soup (see Greimas, 1983, 157–70). However, its theoretical ambition is hindered by its descriptive weakness: prevented by its universalism from ascertaining the specificity of texts, narrative semiotics projects the same a priori grid onto everything, feeling proud when discovering it everywhere.[5]

In Artificial Intelligence, the main research on narrative was carried out in the decade between 1974 and 1984. The rise of computational linguistics allowed the problem of the automatic 'comprehension' of narratives to be raised. Innovative research in Europe (cf. Sabah, 1978) did not turn attention away from the systems realized in the United States (see especially Schank et al., 1975; Dyer, 1983). These systems, which answer questions on short narratives, are unfortunately ad hoc and cannot be transported: work done on them, however, created some interest in narrative grammars. The main debate centered on the concept of *grammar*: regarding narratives, though, one cannot speak of grammars in the Chomskian sense of the term.[6] So be it, but this rather weak criticism was sufficient to discredit for a long while research in this field. Rather, it would have been better for debate to be centred on the concept of narrative, a concept that remained regrettably intuitive.

All in all, these three fields of research have much to offer, but the situation of the narrative within a typology of texts has not been worked out sufficiently in any of them. In fact, from the outset narratology limited itself to literary texts; narrative semiotics set up a certain form of narratives as a universal category, whereas Artificial Intelligence hardly concerned itself with textual typology that, in fact, should have been formulated by linguistics. One might object here that the narrative is a semiotic structure (in Greimassian terms) or a conceptual structure (according to Schank),[7] and that separated from natural languages it falls out of the domain of linguistics. Let us admit, for example, that mime or silent film can display visual narratives. However, especially from an interpretative perspective, it is necessary to construct the narrative from linguistic units of the lower level. There admittedly exists a difference in complexity between thematized graphs (directly articulated from mesosemantic units belonging to the level of the utterance) and large narrative units that are attributable to the level of text; but this does not make for a difference of nature, such as, for example, that linguistics should confine itself to the utterance, and let semiotics look after anything concerning the text. Moreover, the 'conceptual level' in Artificial Intelligence is generally only a semantic level whose specificity is not recognized.[8] Narrative is not for me an abstract form, just as languages or images would only be variable and inessential substances in which that form would appear.[9] Researchers in visual semiotics must formulate specific methods of narrative analysis. Within the scope of linguistics, narrative remains a textual structure and it would be at the very least risky to separate the study of this semantic structure from that of the text.

I shall now attempt to situate the narrative – considered as a narrative text – within a typology of texts; and secondarily, determine whether or not the narrative status of a text stems from its dialectic component alone. Beyond traditional definitions, structuralists sought to define the elementary structure of the narrative. Starting from the works of Lévi-Strauss and Dumézil, Greimas suggests the following proportion:

$$\frac{A}{\text{not } A} \approx \frac{B}{\text{not } B}$$

According to him, it defines the narrative.[10] This formulation has often been interpreted as:

$$\frac{\text{before}}{\text{established content}} \approx \frac{\text{after}}{\text{inverted content}}$$

Here one again encounters the newly formulated Aristotelian *metabole* (see

Poetics, chapter 18); but with a loss of some precision, as such a formula could also account for a cooking recipe (see Rastier, 1974, 163).

Another complementary but unpromising way consists of formulating the minimal narrative that would feature the elementary narrative structure. Genette suggests *I walk* or *Peter came*; Greimas and Courtés cite *Adam ate an apple*; Gerald Prince tells us *John was rich, then he gambled, then he was very poor*; one could add *veni, vidi, vici*, or *I come, I shoot, and I return* (the title of an Italian western movie). I shall not take either of these two ways. Hypostasiating the narrative will not enable me to transform this intuitive notion into a scientific concept. I prefer to doubt, on the one hand, that it is *one* textual genre (common usage would have one speak in terms of narratives that are mythical, romanesque, historical, etc.) and on the other hand that it is a universal of textual linguistics.

III. The Evenemential Level

Let me then formulate some other propositions.[11]

a) On the macrosemantic level, an *actor* is represented by a node in a thematized graph. It is constituted by a semic molecule. This molecule is constructed by analysing the denominations, defined descriptions, defining syntagmas constituting an anaphoric string, without conditions of coreference.[12] This molecule has the status of a type. It 'summarizes' a class of *actants* that can be considered as its occurrences on the lower (mesosemantic) level. In the same interval of dialectic time, this type is not modified, no matter how varied its occurrences. However, between two intervals of dialectic time, this type can be modified by the addition and/or deletion of semes. In this, the actor remains endowed with relative stability, even if at the last interval of dialectic time all its constituent contents have changed. The actor is thus endowed with rigidity.[13]

However, one restriction: the denominations, descriptions, or definitions of an actor that come from a semantic field other than the dominant one are not restored to the latter by rewriting. When, for example, Balzac's cousine Bette declares she is a 'vraie lionne' (real lioness and high-society woman), it is necessary to be able to preserve the codified polysemy and maintain the possibility of reading 'elegant' just as well as 'beast.'[14] In short, allotopic denominations, descriptions, and definitions allow for the construction of homologous actors on diverse isotopies. Defined in this way, the actor is not to be confused with the established but intuitive notion of *character*.[15] It is not necessarily human, anthropomorphic, or animate. It does not necessarily correspond to a naive ontological entity: a process like 'the fall of the dollar' can be a very presentable, indeed all too real, actor.

b) A *role* is a type of interaction between actors within thematized graphs. It is defined relative to an actor, to whose characterization it thus contributes. For example, Dom Juan assumes the role *a* in:

[DOM JUAN] <--(ERG) <--[OUTRAGE]--> (OBJ)--> [THISBÉ]

and Thisbé the converse role *a'*.

The set of an actor's roles defines its interactional sphere; their succession, its interactional history. When examining roles one notes stable groupings that result from the stereotyped character of dialectic linkings, for a given discourse. In a given dialectic interval the actor's roles are correlated with the semic molecule that individualizes the actor in that same interval. Each seme of that molecule can determine the valences with respect to other actors. We can now fine tune our definition of the actor. It is made up of two sets of semes (even if they only contain one): its semic molecule, and its case semes, such as they are described in the inventory of its roles (relative to other actors and not *in abstracto*). Even though they are connected by applicative relationships, these two sets are disjoined for methodological reasons.

c) *Functions* are typical interactions between actors. One cannot dispense with the idea that they are relative to a discourse, indeed to a genre.

In Artificial Intelligence or in semiotics, universal grammars retain a small number of primitive actions.[16] However, they all encounter a methodological dilemma, from which it seems none can escape. Either one tries to code all the sentences of the text and then has to combine the primitives in a happenstance way, or one codes only the sentences that lend themselves to this and then one is resigned to reading into the text only the predefined narrative. In general, coding procedures remain annoyingly implicit. Although a muffled silence seems appropriate, this hinders the development of narratology in all of its applications, from pedagogy to Artificial Intelligence.

Rather than hastily establishing a list of functions, I shall explain those criteria that can be used to create a typology of functions:

(i) Position in dialectic time,[17] equally relative to absolute indicators (notably the beginning and end of the narrative) as to the indicators, themselves relative (for example, contiguous functions).

(ii) The existence of stable functional syntagmas allows one to class functions into presuppositions and presupposants, and to identify and, if need be, to supply the missing functions in description. We notice in certain genres presuppositions between functional syntagms.

(iii) Correlatively, certain functions initiate (for example, the *mandate*), others terminate (for example, *acceptance*). Actors in interaction must be typified accordingly.

(iv) Certain functions are grouped into syntagms (for example, *contract, exchange, conflict*); others are not (for example, *displacement*, which often establishes a demarcation between syntagms).

(v) Certain functions fit into others that are indexed by the modality of the possible (for example, *challenge, contract proposal*).

(vi) One can categorize functions and functional syntagmas into two modes: *irenic* and *polemic*. This opposition seems necessary for a semantics of interaction (it proceeds from its own ethological foundations).

Here, in short, is the table of functions that I have used in this work:[18]

irenic syntagms	irenic functions	polemic functions	polemic syntagms
contract	*proposal* (possibility of t_1)	*challenge* (possibility of a_1)	*confrontation*
	acceptance (possibility of t_2)	*counter-challenge* (possibility of a_2)	
exchange	*transmission* (t_1)	*attack* (a_1)	*conflict*
	transmission (t_2)	*counter-attack* (a_2)	
consequence	*retribution*	*sanction*	*consequence*

Displacement is added to these ten functions (eight of which can be grouped into four couples). Each function's name designates a semantic graph. For example, *gift* is transcribed:

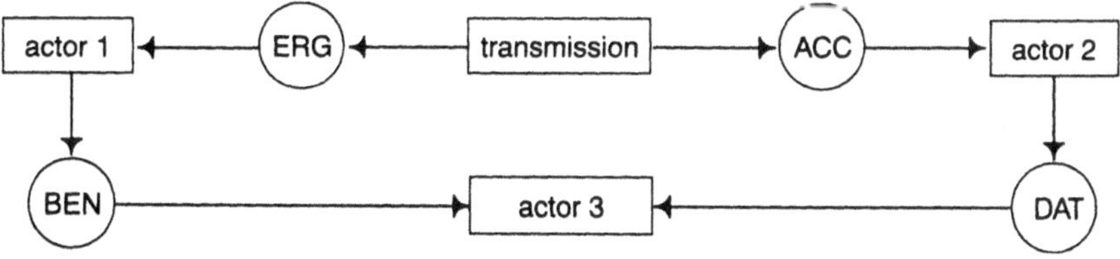

And the *proposal* graph would contain the *gift* graph.

The graphs of the functions of the same pair are incorporated into more complex graphs (see, for example, Sowa, 1984, 110). The irenic functions include at least three actors, and polemic functions at least two. In addition to differing in terms of the number of actors they contain, the functions clearly differ in terms of the number and nature of links: for example, displacement may include at least three actors, but two of them are the starting and arrival points of the locative links (LOC). Since function graphs are types, they can be 'deformed' as they occur.

Note: The other specifications stem from thematics. The same holds true for the distinction between semiotic, parental (alliance and filiation), and economic exchanges.

Solidarities within a pair of functions (between *proposal* and *acceptance*, for example), and relations of modal transformations between pairs of functions (thus, exchange is first of all *virtual* in the contract), and finally, relationships of presupposition (between *sanction* and *conflict*, for example) all contribute to establishing narrative *tension*. The factual morphologies codified by narrative genres create a suspense that results from the relationships between functions, independent of the psychological phenomena of identification between the real reader and the fictitious actors.

From an interpretative perspective, coding functions can nevertheless take complex paths. The analyst can certainly make use of the syntagmatic relations between functions from the same column (see the preceding table) to locate, for example, the 'missing' functions. However, the analyst in question must also take into account the relations between columns, in particular, when narration (see below) stems from a deceptive strategy: for example, a false contract is equal to a real confrontation; it can be followed by a false exchange and a real conflict; a false retribution and a real sanction, etc.[19] We can see a study of interpretative manipulations emerging here. In this way, *ruse* can be defined as the transposition of *polemic* functions into *irenic* functions, and the converse transposition as *game*. Actors, roles, and functions are the units that define the *evenemential* level of dialectics. Whether narrative or not, every text having a dialectic component can be analysed at this level.

IV. The Agonistic Level

The following concepts will allow us to define the agonistic level and to specify how it is superimposed on the evenemential level by supplementary rules and prescriptions.

a) An *agonist* is a class of actors (even if only one actor) defined by their molecular type (according to their semic structure) and by a type of roles (according to their interactive structure).

The actors subsumed by the same agonist can be indexed on different generic isotopies (see below, chapter 11, the human, animal, and topographic actors subsumed by three of the agonists). Moreover, they can be indexed in different worlds, and even in different universes (cf. below on dialogics). The classification of agonists has sometimes been assimilated to that of semantic cases.[20] Now, even when the hypothesis that case primitives operate on all semantic layers (micro-, meso-, and macro-) is maintained, this assimilation remains invalid for three complementary reasons, which allow us to comprehend the specificity of the agonist:

(i) An actor generally occupies various actantial positions throughout the text. However, an agonist is not in principle linked to a determined actantial position.[21]

(ii) Agonists become types through evaluations stemming from archthematics. For example, in order to identify agonists as the *hero*, the *helper*, or the *traitor* in the Russian folk-tale, one must obviously have at one's disposal at least an implicit model of the values of Russian society of the past, and be able to distinguish the 'good' from the 'bad.'[22] For all that, every text does not grow out of a single set of values. And value systems are not necessarily binary, they do not necessarily cover the entire text, and they can vary within the text. So much so, for example, that the categories such as *hero* and *false hero*, enumerated by Propp, are theoretically inadequate to describe most good contemporary novels.

(iii) Even if subsequently some have tried to universalize the inventory of agonists established by Propp, none the less, according to him, it remained specific to the *genre* he was describing. With an exemplary scientific rigour, he resisted any extrapolation from it.

Let us then acknowledge that the concept of agonist is a methodological universal; but that the number and the nature of agonists depend upon the genre of the text; and, beyond this, upon the discourse from which the text originates and upon its social surrounding. This proposition translates the more general affirmation that a general and comparative narratology prevails over universal narratology, and that in textual linguistics as elsewhere, the ruling dogmatic rationalism leaves room for an empirical rationalism. This will not prevent, however, the in-depth examination of anthropological, and even ethological hypotheses on actancy.

b) *Sequences* are units of a level that is superior to the narrative function. They homologate isomorphic functional syntagms. The following chart, for example, shows the first sequence of Molière's *Dom Juan* (taken from my 1971 study, 307).

Sequence 1	A and C are linked by a contract not recognized by B	B proposes to A who accepts it, another contract	B breaks it or does not fulfil it	B departs
A = Elvire B = Dom Juan C = Heaven	f.5	f.6	f.8	f.9
A = fiancée B = Dom Juan C = fiancé	f.24	a	f.25	f.27
A = Charlotte B = Dom Juan C = Pierrot	f.29	f.32	f.39	f.45
A = Mathurine B = Dom Juan C = aunt	b	f.37	f.38	f.45

(i) We know (act I, scene 2) that Dom Juan always seduces using promises of marriage: 'he uses no other traps to catch the ladies.'
(ii) Of Mathurine's situation we know only that she must account to her aunt for her actions (see act II, scene 2).

From the 117 functions noted in this text, I constructed 34 syntagms, and then 13 sequences containing all of them. This illustrates in a way what Lévi-Strauss – referring to myth – called the narrative's *overlaid structure*. Agonists and sequences are the constituent units of the *agonistic* level of narrative.

V. Archdialectics

Archdialectics accounts for the dialectic relationships between the space values defined by archthematics. More precisely, it identifies the correlations between space values and dialectic intervals: initial state, mediating intervals, final state. 'Happy endings' and 'morals of the story' fall under its jurisdiction. These correlations cannot be reduced to simple applications: for example, a space value can be included in another in a modalized form (as a promise, a prophecy, etc.). Relative to the evenemential and agonistic level, archdialectics allows one to classify actors and agonists into 'camps,' and to evaluate the assessment of functional syntagms and sequences (by defining improvements and deteriorations). Does this mean that every function, syntagm, or sequence can be translated into an archdialectic formula? I attempted such a thing by using the operators of modal logic (1971), but it was necessary to further my theoretical understanding of this, and Ricoeur (1980) correctly reminded me that narrative functions cannot be reduced to logical operations. Admittedly, the text can emanate from several archthematics and, therefore, from several archdialectics. Describing the agonistic level becomes very complicated, as one can then produce several internal versions of the narrative (see chapter 11, the analysis of *Toine*).

VI. Elements of Dialectic Typology

I can now propose these typological outlines:

Level / Types	Evenemential	Agonistic	Archdialectical
I	+	–	–
II	+	+	+
III	+	–	+

(i) Actors and functions are the characteristic units of the evenemential level; agonists and sequences those of the agonistic level; series of operations that induce content values to follow each other in textual time.

(ii) In our society, for example, scientific and technical texts have the first type of dialectic structure. Mythical narratives have the second type of dialectic structure, whereas certain religious texts and some modern poems have the third type of dialectic structures.[23]

(iii) By reformulating earlier proposals, I could suggest that the opposition between *practical* and *mythical* separates the two first types, and the distinction between *ideology* and *axiology*, the last two. Hence the following:

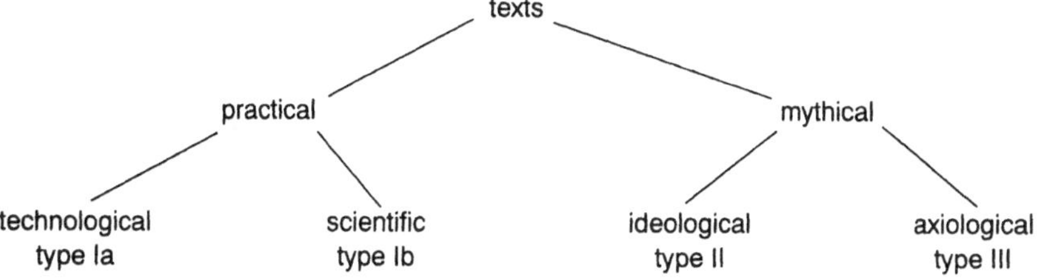

However, I should acknowledge that this typology still needs to be worked out in more detail. As it is, juridical texts could be called technical and axiologic at the same time. Moreover, I have given only a few examples, and we must guard ourselves against setting up genres linked to a culture in metalinguistic categories.

(iv) Except for the texts that are devoid of a dialectic component[24] – and that admittedly do not figure in this table – I have not noted texts not having an evenemential level. From this can be induced the hypothesis that every text with a dialectic component has its structure at this level, even though not necessarily at the other levels.

(v) The levels identified here are not therefore superimposed strata, that an algorithm of generative or interpretative rules 'would traverse' one after the other; but rather, as with the textual components themselves, subsystems in optative cooperation.

As with all syntagmatics,[25] the three levels identified in the dialectic component articulate textual signification through transformations. The dialectical method of analysis takes this into account, and thus, the segmentation and coding of the text are only preliminary steps, which the analysis of transformations can regulate through retroaction.

The theory of dialectic transformations that comparative mythology has worked out seems quite strong. Clearly, it is useful to distinguish the external transformations between texts from the internal transformations within a text. The former are diachronic or synchronic. They are brought to the fore by the same historical and comparative method that presided over the constitution of linguistics. The latter segment internal temporality of textual content (and can even be called *chronicals*). As with external transformations, they cannot be studied without taking the thematic component into account. If the typology of dialectic structures presented above is accepted, the notion of narrative, which is too vague, must be abandoned because of its descriptive inadequacy. Even if it were restricted to texts that include an agonistic level, it would not be sufficient for defining a genre.

6

Dialogics

Whereas dialectics was based on the succession of temporal intervals, dialogics is based on modalities. Without favouring any in particular, I retain all of the semiotic modalities: ontic, alethic, epistemic, deontic, boulestic, and evaluative (*de re, de dicto*).[1] These general semantic categories do not merge with the modal systems of natural languages, even though they make it possible to describe them. They are the universals of the theory.

Modal logics that have proliferated since the twenties are extremely interesting for linguists (see, for example, Martin, 1987), for whom Boolean logic readily loses its fascination. However, to my knowledge, except in partial or contrived examples, none of them can be applied systematically to the description of languages. This is because the plasticity of natural languages makes it impossible to reduce them to formal languages. Their signs are neither constants nor variables, and they are modified unpredictably as they occur, both at the level of expression and of content. It is up to logic to accommodate itself to language if it can, and not for linguistics to set its descriptions on existing logics.

I. The Fundamental Concepts of Dialogics

Every modality is connected to a *universe* (an autonomous set of semantic graphs) and to a *world* (a set of graphs modalized in the same way within a universe). Moreover, every universe and every world is connected to at least one actor. In other words, every modality is connected to a site and to a mark: thus the true, the possible, the known can be defined only *in* a universe (U) and for an *actor* (A). From this relativistic perspective, a true proposition is not defined as such by its analytic character (or even by its synthetic character): it is simply true in all the universes of the text and for all its actors. Let me specify.

A. Every actor is situated in at least one universe, if only because its occurrences belong to thematized graphs that all have a modalizer,[2] even a minimal one. On the other hand, each actor does not necessarily have a universe. Actors without a universe can be situated in the universe of other actors, without, of course, the converse being true. In the semic molecule that defines the actor, no feature is required a priori for a universe to be associated with the actor. Notably the features 'human' or 'animated' are neither necessary nor sufficient, and on this point textual semantics plays a part in freeing us from the anthropomorphism that dominates our cultural tradition. Finally, several actors can be associated with identical or simply analogous universes. This is the case, for instance, of La Violette and La Ramée in Molière's *Dom Juan*. This must be ascribed to their semic molecule and to their roles.

B. A universe is the set of thematized graphs associated with an actor in a determined interval of textual time.

Note: Here and below I follow Martin (1983, 1987). Without diminishing my debt towards him my views diverge from his on two important points. The universes are not ascribed to real speakers, but only to the actors of the utterance or of represented enunciation, and I do not adopt a vericonditional perspective.[3]

Each universe can be divided into three types of graphs (uttered, or inferable), or *worlds*:

1. The *factual* world, composed of graphs that include an assertoric modality.
2. The *counterfactual* world, composed of graphs that include the modalities of the impossible or the unreal.
3. The *possible* world, whose graphs include the corresponding modality.

Note: Possible worlds theory, invented by Leibnitz and formalized by Hintikka and Kripke, has undergone stimulating developments over the past thirty years; in textual semiotics see, for example, works by Doležel, Vaina, and Ryan. In order to avoid Pangloss-like optimism, it should be noted that the mathematical theory of possible worlds is not technically applicable to the domain of linguistic description (see Grunig's arguments, 1982).

The theory of models creates an infinite number of possible worlds. Here, I have reduced these worlds to a finite number, drastically limited to three. Correlatively, in each world I accept graphs that can be translated into contradictory propositions. Indeed, languages and many texts are not subject to the so-called laws of thought that are the principle of identity, the excluded third and non-contradiction. With certain exceptions, textual worlds are open worlds, that is to say the denotation of their graphs can be undefined or inconsistent. Besides, at least for a given interpretation, these worlds are *finite*. But the number of graphs that these interpretations create by inference is neither fixed nor predictable. Finally, the worlds of a universe are not always open to each other. For example, a graph whose denotation is true in the counterfactual world is not necessarily false in the factual world: it does not necessarily have an image in it,[4] or the denotation of its image can be undecidable.

Let us consider the issue of the relationships between universes. In each of its worlds, a universe can contain several graphs that are the image or the duplicate[5] of graphs situated in another universe. A universe can be included totally in another; this is the case, for example, with narrative embedding. Thus, in *The Story of the Little Hunchback* (*One Thousand and One Nights*), the universe of the barber of Baghdad's third brother is included in the barber's, whose universe is included in the tailor's, then in Scheherazade's, then in the narrator's.

The duplicates of true propositions[6] in the factual worlds of all the universes of the actors of a text make up the factual world of the universe of reference. This universe also includes a counterfactual world and a possible world, organized in an analogous way. Even if absent, the universe of reference is associated with the represented enunciator.[7] In the final analysis, it is with respect to the universe of reference that the reader can attribute a truth value to the propositions of all the other universes. Here is how.

First of all, the decidable propositions of a universe take on their value with respect to the true propositions of the factual world of this universe. Next, whether true, false, or undecidable, the propositions of a universe can include images or duplicates in other universes of the same text (outside the universe of reference). Finally, other duplicates or images can be constructed or discovered in the universe of reference. Thus a proposition can be evaluated in three ways: (i) in its universe; (ii) relative to duplicates or images in the other universes outside the universe of reference; (iii) in the universe of reference.

(i) In *El Burlador de Sevilla*, Dom Juan's victims maintain that he does evil (*daño*); Dom Juan admits it (act III, l. 109). By simplifying, let us say that the proposition 'Dom Juan does evil' is true in every universe including the universe of reference. In the same way, in Molière's *Dom Juan*, Sganarelle and his master both speak of being shipwrecked (act II, scene 2). This shipwreck is therefore[8] true in the universe of reference. On the other hand, contrary to Dom Juan, Sganarelle interprets this as a sign from heaven. 'The shipwreck is a sign from heaven' is hence a true proposition in Sganarelle's universe, but undecidable or false in Dom Juan's, and undecidable in the universe of reference. In a comparable way, Dom Juan's crimes are labelled as such by his 'victims' but not by him, and that truth value of his moral judgments remains undecidable in the universe of reference. Only Dom Juan's hypocrisy is recognized as true in the universe of actors subsumed by opposed agonists (see act V, scene 2). His hypocrisy is therefore true in the universe of reference, where it is the absolute[9] crime.

(ii) Let us return to the third brother of the inexhaustible barber of Baghdad. A blind man called Bakbac is defending himself against a thief when the police arrive. The thief imitates the blind man, but upon receiving a drubbing, he consents to open his eyes and then accuses Bakbac of being a false blind man, an accomplice who has robbed him. And the poor wretch is in turn beaten so that he opens his eyes.[10] The proposition 'Bakbac is blind' is true in the thief's counterfactual world and in the policeman's factual world, but false in Bakbac's factual world, and in the universe of reference.[11] This example raises the issue of access between universes having the same hierarchical rank.

Now to illustrate access between hierarchically subordinated universes, all we have to do is to ask how we know that Bakbac is blind. Because the immediate narrator, the loquacious barber, affirms it without its being refuted by any of the narrators of a superior rank (the tailor, Scheherazade, and the narrator of the *One Thousand and One Nights*).

The inclusive universe of reference is presumed to be coherent, including the universe of reference. This presumption appears to be general. Sometimes, in texts that include parables, apologies, authoritative citations (judicial, religious, scientific, etc.), the sections of the text included or presumed to be, impose the truth values of their universe of reference to those of the inclusive text.[12] Sometimes, on the contrary, as in the case of embedded narratives, the included universe *inherits* the truth values from the inclusive universe.

In any case, this presumption stems from norms, and not from laws. In the case of embedded narratives, we can talk about an implicit *contract of veridiction* that normally is revealed only when it is broken. In the case above, the tailor tells the story of the barber to charm the Sultan of Casgar and to save his own life. He is accused, convicted and convinced of having killed his buffoon. Curious about seeing this extraordinary barber, the sultan summons him: and he revives the buffoon. Scheherazade had therefore lied when she claimed he was dead.[13] The anonymous narrator of the *Nights* denounces the veridiction contract in this way.

Note: I mention truth values without nevertheless siding with vericonditional semantics as such. Extensional semantics is only remotely concerned with linguistics: the problem of reference in the strong sense of the term belongs to the domain of the philosophy of language and that of truth to the sciences. Strictly speaking, linguistics need only be concerned with the truth of its own propositions.

Having relinquished extension, semantics becomes so intensional that it no longer warrants this qualifier (since *intension* and *extension* are interdefined). The truth it is dealing with has to refer to the internal referent of the text, that is to say, in the final analysis, to textual cohesion that elicits a referential impression (see chapter 13). If, in the *Odyssey*, it is true that Ulysses is Penelope's spouse, this truth in the weak sense[14] has nothing in common with a truth in the strong sense that, for example, would state that Aristotle was Alexander's tutor. Once this truth in the weak sense has been recognized as such, it does not follow that logic can account for it. If, one day, it is constituted, it will have to deal with lie and illusion, non-trivial problems (from a technical point of view). If, for example, in simple binary logic the negation of negation is identical to assertion, when Blaise in *Les comédiens sans le savoir* (Marivaux) cries out: 'they are pretending to be pretending,' this is not simply the equivalent of 'they do it!'

C. I previously mentioned *universes of assumption*. This expression may have caused some confusion, and it is necessary to define further the concept of assumption. All that enables (i) including a proposition in a universe and (ii) associating a universe with an actor, falls under it. In order to determine what propositions are assumed by an actor (or by an enunciative focus) one must consider:

(i) Prosodic or graphic demarcative signs (for example, quotation marks, italics, changes in tone).
(ii) Marks of represented enunciation: anaphors, deictics, tense, mode, aspect, inherent, or lexical evaluations – in short, everything that directly or indirectly refers back to an *ego* and a *hic et nunc*.
(iii) Inferences conforming to topoi of the text or compatible with them, and bearing on propositions already assumed by the actor; plausible inferences made from the dialectical roles; inferences from propositions assumed by other actors but attributed to the actor studied (without their necessarily having spoken lines in the latter's universe).

Of course, in one's descriptive practice one encounters all sorts of propositions whose domain of assumption is not localized, or whose domain can be localized simultaneously in different universes. So-called 'indirect free style' is filled with these indeterminations and ambiguities. Moreover, the same syntagms can juxtapose sememes from different universes, and sememes that are opposed, namely by their evaluative features. In this case,[15] contradictions are often interpretative instructions that lead to dissimilation of the universe. When, for instance, in Balzac's *La cousine Bette* Judge Rivet 'feels the satisfaction that the certainty of having accomplished a good bad action must cause' (chapter 18), *bad* belongs to Steinbock and the narrator's universes, *good* to those of Lisbeth and the judge. Finally, descriptive practice must account for the dynamics of the worlds and the universes: at each interval of narrative time, their content can be modified by changing the modality of the propositions, as well as by the 'beginning' or the 'ending' of the propositions. Consequently, the groups of universes[16] also change; a universe can, for example, be modified to the point of passing from one group to another. Here, dialogics is articulated at the agonistic level of the dialectic – and not only at its evenemential level.

II. From Narration to Represented Communication

From the outset narratology has chosen not to work out a typology of texts; or, more precisely, it presupposes a typology in which the narrative would be a 'natural' category. Its favourite object of study is the modern literary narrative, and notably the novel. Now, characteristic narrative techniques[17] affect represented communication and take precedence, so to speak, over narrative grammars.

Note: Here I am not dealing with 'real' enunciation defined as the production of a text. The 'enunciative operations' have been the object of numerous theories that have remained programmatic, since they have no experimental basis. The development of cognitive research may enable them to progress. But even a superficial study of fiction shows that anaphoric or pronominal deictic signs, in spite of what has been said, can pass for certain indices of subjectivity in language. At best they help in the construction of the referentials that these universes happen to be. In the past, enunciation was favoured to the point of the neglect of reception (or the situating of it entirely in enunciation). Now, the subjectivity expressed in language is as much the receiver's as the sender's. Nevertheless, both in linguistics and in semiotics,[18] the privileged role of the speaker has been strengthened by the success of the generative enterprise.

Within the conceptual framework established here, narrative belongs to dialectics and narration to dialogics. Their relations activate the interactions of these two components. The notion of narrative covers very diverse textual structures and, we shall see, the same holds true for narration.

The effect of dialogics on evenemential dialectics should be defined. At this level, one must take into account intrinsic dialogics. It appears in the modalization of the functions. For instance, the function *contract* consists in an exchange of transmission graphs situated in the possible world[19] of the contracting actors. Moreover, dialogics and dialectics clearly interfere when the poles of represented communication are also actors, or even agonists. Hence in the *Story of the Little Hunchback*, the five narrators and their principal listeners (the Sultan of Casgar and the Caliph of Baghdad) are actors, just as the hierarchically superior interlocutors are (Schahriar and Scheherazade). As such, they are defined by a semic molecule and by roles; in addition, specific universes are associated with them. When the poles of represented communication are not associated with dialectic roles (and are not therefore actants of the utterance, nor actors), it is necessary to take into account the following alternative.

a) In the first case, the categories proper to enunciation remain: the anaphoric and pronominal deictics enable one to localize at least one enunciative focus[20] and one interpretative focus. They can neither be named nor described, but have a semic molecule (marks of gender, sex, number, spatiotemporal position).[21] Moreover they are associated with universes, or are associated to universes by inference.

b) In the second case, interlocution itself is no longer represented. The paradox of communication without interlocution now appears, frequent in gnomic genres (for instance, proverbs or scientific résumés) that attempt to create the impression of objectivity. The enunciator and receiver have become implied.[22] We cannot construct a semic molecule defining them. All that we know, for example, about the narrator of the *One Thousand and One Nights* is that he has knowledge about 'chronicles of Sassanians, the ancient kings of Persia,' and that from the very first line he fades and disappears forever from the work.

None the less, in certain cases a universe can be associated with an implied enunciator: the propositions constituting her or him are then obtained by inference, from evaluations contained in the text. Debates on objectivism in the *nouveau roman* and the so-called School of the Gaze has at the very least shown that the implied enunciator is as objective or as subjective as the others; and outside of literature, implied enunciators uttering instructions have accustomed us to their lack of objectivity.[23] Even by conjuring up Occam (as Genette did, 1983, 96–7), I maintain the distinction between real enunciator and implied enunciator, real receiver and implied receiver.[24] In poetics at least, there exists today a wide enough consensus on this point (notably with Chatman, Bronzvaer,

Lintvelt, Hoek). The two dialogical systems (*a* and *b*) that I have just described are insufficient to define types of texts and also constituted genres. A text can moreover juxtapose these two systems: for instance, the first chapter of *Madame Bovary*, then the following ones, successively illustrate these two modes.

Note: I set aside here the Platonic theory of genre (see *The Republic*, 392–4), which has preoccupied many poeticians from Aristotle to Genette. Diomedes formulates it as follows:[25] (i) in the *genus activum vel imitativum*, there are no interventions of the poet in the poem; (ii) in the *genus enarrativum*, only the poet speaks; (iii) in the *genus commune* the characters and the poet speak in turn. Hence the classical division:

	Dramatic	Lyrical	Epic
Diomedian genres	*activum*	*enarrativum*	*commune*
Examples	first	first	
	Bucolics	*Georgics*	*Aeneid*
Dialogic systems	*a*	*b*	*a/b*

But we see the difficulty. Diomedes' schematism forces him to class the first and ninth *Bucolics* under the dramatic genres, with tragedy and comedy; and the eight others must be classed under the epic genre! Servius even goes so far as to spread the *Bucolics* over the three Diomedian genres.
Let us at least keep in mind that a descriptive theory of genres must account for textual cohesion, and not break it up in order to ensure its own cohesion.

I now propose a typology of represented communication. The enunciator and the receiver are said to be *intra-* or *extradialogical* according to whether or not they are associated with an explicited universe.[26] The enunciator and the receiver are said to be *exclusive*; if not, I distinguish between *inclusive* interlocutors (which encompass other enunciators and receivers) and *included* interlocutors (encompassed in the universe of other interlocutors).[27] Hence the following:

Enunciators

- intradialogical
  - exclusive: e.g., Jodelle, in *Amours*
  - inclusive
    - embedded enunciations: e.g., *The Story of the Little Hunchback*
    - interlaced enunciations: e.g., *L'Assommoir*

- extradialogical
  - inclusive

- alternating enunciations: e.g., *Dom Juan*
- exclusive: e.g., Denys of Thrace, *Technè Grammatikè*

The same criteria can be used for a typology of receivers:

Receivers

- intradialogical
  - exclusive: e.g., Baudelaire, 'Au lecteur'
  - inclusive
    - embedded receptions: e.g., *The Story of the Little Hunchback*
    - interlaced receptions: e.g., the end of Joyce's *Ulysses*

- extradialogical
  - inclusive
    - alternating receptions: e.g., *Dom Juan*
  - exclusive: e.g., Denys of Thrace, *Technè Grammatikè*

Because of the privileging of enunciators (such as in the Diomedian classification), a typology of receivers was overlooked for the longest time. Modern theories of art as personal expression, the reduction of poetic genres to lyrical genres, biography from Sainte-Beuve to Lanson, all encouraged confusing the real author (as a historical person), the implied author (as an interlocutory centre), and the intradialogical interlocutor. Through this the receivers appeared as creations of enunciators and were subordinate to them. On the other hand if, by a necessary methodological reduction, one separates the three instances of communication, the represented[28] receiver does not become less fictive than the represented enunciator; and the implied receiver acquires a status comparable to that of the implied enunciator. Finally, the real receiver raises as many problems as the real enunciator: both can adopt different strategies of assumption and choose to occupy various enunciative foci. Moreover, for an interpretative semantics, the reader is as creative as the author is, even if it is in another way.

As comparable as they may be, the typologies of enunciators and receivers I have presented do not merge. For example, an extradialogical receiver can be associated with an intradialogical receiver (for example, Baudelaire in *Les Fleurs du Mal*, LXXVII) or intradialogical (Mallarmé in 'Salut'). In a word, in order to describe more subtly the varieties of interlocution, it is necessary to characterize the enunciator and receiver in relation to other components. For instance, whether they coincide or not with an actor (or agonist), they have an intra- or extradialectic status. In addition, one could characterize the interlocutors according to whether or not they are thematized, that is to say, associated with a sememe or a semic molecule.

7

Tactics

The tactic component accounts for the linear organization of the semantic units. Tactics is concerned with the planes of expression and of content, considered either separately or together. But since the units of these two planes do not correspond necessarily term for term, they are organized in differentiated linearities. I shall now examine the tactics of content.

A. Although the Saussurian tradition has established the idea that a language is a system of signs, it does not follow that linguistics needs to be constructed around the concept of sign.

By declaring the test of commutation to be fundamental, structuralism has reinforced the prejudice that signifieds and signifiers can be joined together indissolubly term for term: a famous Saussurian image compares the two faces of the sign to both sides of a sheet of paper. Moreover, Hjelmslev also acknowledges the existence of isomorphism between the two planes of language[1] (hence the phonologism that marked the beginnings of componential semantics).

These positions must be qualified.

(i) The relation signifier/signified is *determined* by the relations between signifieds. The phenomenon of dissimilated meanings illustrates this perfectly well.[2] For example, in 'A father who punishes, Madam, is still a father' (Racine), the sign *father* in both cases maintains the same relation signified/signifier (that defines their class of equivalences). And nevertheless the signifieds of these two occurrences modify each other reciprocally through dissimilation, so that in the first, the feature /educator/ is activated, as well as the feature /benevolent/ inhibited, whereas it is the inverse in the second.

The relation signifier/signified is therefore fixed for sign types; for sign occurrences, it varies indefinitely with respect to contexts. This would have to be taken into account in order to characterize the linearity of the signifieds.

(ii) Is the signified (phonic or graphic) subject to sequential processing? From the point of view of generation, this sequentiality is undoubtedly simply local. From the point of view of interpretation it is perhaps simply global. Locally, the treatment of the signifier is first of all overdetermined by semantic anticipations and retroactions – so strong that they can produce ordinary perceptive 'hallucinations' that lead for example to hear in good faith what has not been said, as well as not hear what has been said.[3] In any case the interpretative pathways are undoubtedly not simply linear, and even less deterministic.[4] For instance, studies on ocular ballistics[5] that examine in detail the trajectory of the gaze during the reading of sentences are proof of this. In short, though vocal signifieds are articulated successively, and graphic signifieds generally set out linearly, the 'linearity' of the signifier[6] is a constraint of the interpretative paths, albeit an important, but not an invalidating one. None the less, even if it is only when breaking linearity, the interpretative paths have to take it into account.

B. Our work in semantics cannot examine in detail the tactics of expression, except for mentioning its relations with the tactics of content.

At the level of the first articulation, the following are the concern of the tactics of expression: at the sentence level, the order of words[7] in the syntagm, the order of the syntagm and the groups separated by punctuations or pauses; at the transphrastic level, paragraphs, sections, and chapters of the written; the sequences and sessions that are part of the oral component.

On these two levels the position of the expression acts as an interpretant. At the first, it permits for instance the selection of meanings (for example, the place of the adjective in French); or again it enables the afference of casual semes (in languages without morphological cases); finally it can mark emphasis (focalization, topicalization) or various modalizations (for example, the interrogative inversion in written French). At the textual level, the position relative to the transphrastic units plays of course an eminent role in the interpretative paths, be they linear or not. For example, chronology proper to the dialectic structures of the text is often only marked by succession. At the second level of articulation, prosody and metrics involve diversely the three levels of word, sentence, and text. Here again, position acts as an interpretant of the semantic relations. For instance, contents containing contrary or contradictory features are often readily put in the same position (cf. the rhyme *beau/tombeau* in 'Victorieusement fui ...' where Mallarmé develops the topos of beautiful erotic death). In addition to the position of the syllables, that of the phonemes and letters can be codified to converge toward signification (cf. Villon and Molinet's acrostics, the *alphabetical* Psalms, etc.).

C. On both planes of language, the position relative to the units is codified by norms that are at the same time part of the functional system of language and of other instances. I do not attempt here to untangle one from the other, as distinguishing them is not necessary for the demonstration, in so far as no text can exist without genre.

Moreover, in my analysis I distinguish: a) the position relative to the signifieds; b) the position of the signifiers; and c) phonic, graphic, or semantic investments realized in these positions. The relations between positions and investments establish the interplay between tactics and thematics.

A still badly explored domain of research, that of *semantic rhythms*, opens up here. The easiest ones to isolate are those resulting from the intermingling of isotopies. For instance, these three verses from Jodelle (*Œuvres*, I, 397) that have the rhythm ABC/ABCABC/ABC:[8] 'Oncques traict, flamme ou lacqs d'amoureuse fallace / n'a poingt, bruslé, lié, si dur, froid, destaché / Coeur comme était le mien blessé, ars, attaché' / (Never has arrow, flame, or knot from deceitful love / burned, tied, so hard, cold, detached / as was my Heart wounded, burned, attached).

Note: Often, on the plane of expression, semantic rhythms are correlated with accentual rhythms. Here the semantic oppositions between the two last hemistichs of the second and third lines ('dur' vs 'blessé,' 'froid' vs 'ars,' 'destaché' vs 'attaché') are underscored by an identical accentual structure.

Naturally, semantic rhythms put all sorts of features into play. Take a verse of Psalm 114:[9] 'The mountains leap like rams / The hills jump like lambs ...' Here the taxemes //relief// and //ovines// are linked in such a way that we have a succession of generic features: *a b a b*. But if we consider the specific /inferative/ and /superative/ features that oppose 'hills' to 'mountains' and 'rams' to 'lambs,' another rhythm is superimposed on the first: *a a b b*. The superimposition of different semic rhythms could be called *semantic polyphony*.[10] The positive and negative parallelisms, studied notably by Jakobson,[11] constitute one of the forms of semantic *counterpoint*. By some of their semes they unite and oppose sememes. In classical Chinese poetry, they are strictly codified. For instance, in his 'Song of eternal regrets,' Po Kiu-I writes: 'Spring wind peach tree pear tree flower formerly open / Autumn rain ou-t'ong[12] leaves fall now' (literal translation). Each sememe of the first line is counterpointed by the one that occupies the same position in the second: It is opposed to it by at least one specific seme, although it has the same generic semes (since it is in the same taxeme).[13]

The distinction between inherent and afferent semes is also important for semantic rhythms. In this description of Fritz Brunner: 'This young old man [*vieillard*], this premature philosopher ... '(Balzac, *Le cousin Pons*, chapter 16), I consider only the evaluative features. The /pejorative/ feature is inherent to 'old man' and 'premature'; the /meliatory/ feature is afferent to 'young' and 'philosopher' where it is actualized by dissimulation. The following are the afferent features between parentheses:

	'young man'	'old man'	'philosopher'	'premature'
specific features	/anterior/	/ulterior/	/ulterior/	/anterior/
generic evaluative features	(/meliatory/)	/pejorative/	(/meliatory/)	/pejorative/
	actualization		inference	actualization

This designates the familiar figure of a chiasmus,[14] but counterpointed with evaluative features ('old man' and 'premature' are pejorative, for they go beyond a level of acceptability: too ulterior or too anterior). Undoubtedly, the notion of chiasmus is too simple here, for it applies only to a semic line, but not to the two we have identified. Counterpoint can be more complex still, even in the cursory alternatives that J. Gracq juxtaposes: 'Writer or pen-pusher, percheron or purebred' (*Lettrines*, Paris, Corti, 1986, 38). This gives:

	'writer'	'pen-pusher'	'percheron'	'purebred'
macrogeneric features	/human/	/human/	/animal/	/animal/
generic evaluative features	(/meliatory/)	/pejorative/	(/pejorative/)	/meliatory/
	actualization		actualization	

Three rhythmic forms are superimposed: *a a b b* on the first line; *a b b a* on the second; and, if we take into consideration the distinction between the afferent and inherent features, *a b a b*.

These three forms are obviously of a general nature. They are found in the tactics of the expression: rhyming couplets, *a b b a* rhyme scheme, and alternate rhymes, respectively. They also structure the transphrastic level of the tactics of content, particularly, as can be imagined, in texts where the thematic component is organized in quaternary structures. If, for instance, we reread texts describing the seasons, such as Hesiod's *Works and Days*, Virgil's *Georgics*, Thomson's *The Seasons*, we shall see the three quaternary semantic rhythms appear between the major textual units.

Note: For want of space I leave this to the reader. These observations are valid – as far as the examples are concerned – only in our cultural tradition: for instance, Japanese poetry identified five seasons (including New Year's Day). Moreover, in spite of the real interest of research on the 'good perceptive forms,' we cannot affirm that quaternary rhythmic forms are universally appreciated. For example, classical Japanese poetry privileges uneven lines and stanzas.

The study of semantic rhymes would require a monograph. To finish with the relations between the thematics and tactics of expression, we should note that genres sometimes codify them very strictly. Thus, in the first treatise of the *Sanzôshî*, Hattori Tohô quotes the following words of Bashô as an example: 'We shall respect the ancient rule of ten verses on the first page ... The *renga* disapproves of using verses devoted to the dragon, the tiger, the demon, women and other subjects that hold one's attention. Although the *haïkaï* rejects both the demon and women, it nevertheless admits the dragon and the tiger.'[15] The intervals between recurring themes are equally codified: 'where [the renga] imposes an interval of seven [in a same grouping] the haïkaï reduces it to five.'[16]

D. Regarding the relations between the tactic component on the one hand and the dialectical and dialogical components on the other, I mention first the dialectical and dialogical rhythms.

The first concern particularly what is called narrative technique. They are defined by the number of dialectical intervals in relation to the quantity of tactic units with which they are correlated. With respect to the norms of a genre, a narration is rapid if it establishes many dialectical intervals in a few tactic units. This relative speed can be distinguished from 'tempo,' which is determined by the temporal quantification of the intervals. Take, for example, the sudden acceleration of tempo at the beginning of the sixth part of Flaubert's *L'Education sentimentale*: nineteen years go by in twelve lines.[17] On the other hand, in the *Chronique séculaire des Hankoni* (translated in *Invitation à un concert officiel et autres récits*, Paris, Fayard, 1985), Ismaïl Kadaré adopts a rapid rhythm but a regular tempo: seventy-eight chapters in sixty-eight pages cover a period from 1713 to 1901.

As far as dialogical rhythms are concerned, they are defined by changes of universe and, secondarily, of worlds, with respect to the number of tactic units to which they are correlated. Of course, in the theatre these rhythms are the easiest to study. In the novel written in the indirect free style, dialogical rhythms indicate, in their variation, displacements of the enunciative and interpretative foci.

The relative *position* of the dialogical and dialectical units has a primary impact on the interpretative paths. For example, the disparity between the tactical order and the succession of dialectical units is one of the means used to create *suspense*. Genres codify these sorts of disparities. Thus, the traditional detective novel prescribes a 'stringing backwards,' backtracking from the conclusions (presented at the beginning) to the premises (presented at the end). It imposes a retrospective trajectory on unknown premises. By contrast, tragedy has a path that goes from prospection to known conclusions. In all cases, the separation of the successive dialectical units, as well as the juxtaposition of the units separated by dialectical time, constrain the reader to construct and destroy hypothetical intermediary representations. In the best of cases, the reader takes pleasure in doing this.

With respect to dialectics, tactics enables the dramatization of the construction of the interlocutors, especially if they are intradialectical (in Balzac's *Memoirs of Two Young Married Ladies*, for example). One can notably defer the construction of the narrator by revealing belatedly his or her dialectical roles (as Agatha Christie does in *The Murder of Roger Ackroyd*) or again certain elements of its semic molecule (see 'Did I Say I Was a Hunchback?' in *The Mill of Poland* (Giono), in which the narrator reveals the reason for his bitterness on the last page). In both cases the reader is forced to reshape the representations he/she had until then constructed of the narrator and his or her intentions.

E. Although the linearization of the signified is sometimes considered a surface phenomenon, I do not necessarily conclude that the tactic component happens to be subordinated to the other three. That notwithstanding, for interpretative semantics, nothing is deeper than the surface.[18] A long tradition has accustomed us to reduce the signified to the concept, and to think that the 'thing to say' could have some autonomy with respect to the way it is said. As soon as we deal with a corpus, this 'conceptualist' illusion should disappear by itself.

8

The Interaction of the Semantic Components

A. Let me specify briefly how the semantic components interact.[1]

Two of them have to be present in every text: thematics and tactics. A text having a minimal semantic structure, which could be reduced to a simple enumeration, even to the simple repetition of a word,[2] would still be the result of interaction between these two components.

In addition to this extreme case, five other types of binary interactions between components must be identified.

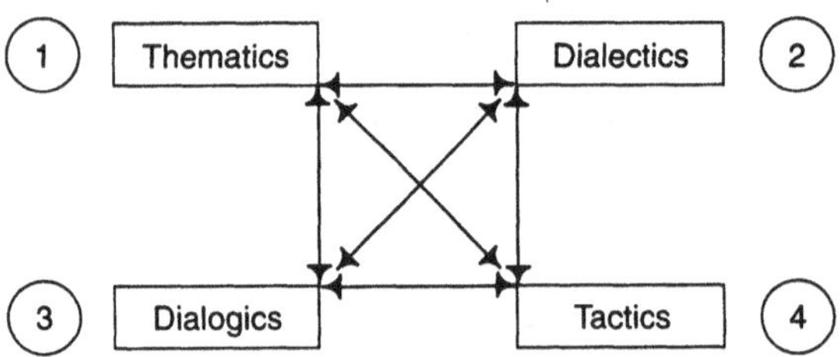

But also, three types of ternary interactions: 1-2-4; 1-3-4; 2-3-4.

In the case of a text organized in terms of these four[3] components, it is questionable whether all the types of predictable interactions necessarily would be present. As we shall see, this opens up the possibility for a textual typology founded on the types of interactions of the components. Without attempting to predict their presence *in abstracto*, I illustrate in the second part of this book different examples of interactions. These modes of interactions vary for two reasons. Unlike the stratified components of generative grammars, the semantic components are neither ordered nor hierarchized a priori. Therefore my presentation of them remains neutral with respect to the opposition between generation and interpretation; or rather, their hierarchical organization can serve as the starting point for working out models of generation as interpretation. Since they are not ordered with respect to one another, the semantic components can be in constant interaction.[4]

These properties break with modularism and sequentiality, which have been dominant in many linguistic and semiotic theories over the past few decades, and which are still solidly ensconced, especially in cognitive research. Classically, they suppose that languages (according to Chomsky) and mind (according to Fodor)[5] are regulated by the successive actions of autonomous modules activated in a strict order, the output of the first becoming the input of the following one, etc. Hence these modules do not interact during their processing[6] (they are 'encapsulated,' according to Fodor). In linguistics, modularism has ensured Morrisian tripartition between syntax, semantics, and pragmatics – which has led to the impasse that we know (see Rastier, 1988a). In generative semiotics, the sequentiality of the generative trajectory has forced the layering of multiple levels, linked by conversions that remain problematic. Finally, contrary to cognitive fundamentalists, I do not formulate realistic hypotheses (in the strong sense). I am careful not to postulate that languages – and the human mind – are structured by the semantic components presented here.

If the concepts used can be considered as universals, it is only as universals of method. They constitute criteria for a textual typology, and not textual invariants. Hence my undertaking falls within the domain of general and comparative linguistics and not within that of universal linguistics. For instance, categories from thematics, such as the concepts of seme, domain, and semic molecule, are universals of method; on the other hand, semes, for example, are units specific to each language. These precautions seem necessary for anyone who fully wishes to take into account the cultural nature of languages and of texts. Since the object of linguistics is languages and not language,[7] the object of textual semantics is texts and not *the* text in itself.

B. The relationships between components vary with respect to occurrences of systematicity. Each of the components can in fact be regulated by three types of systematicity: the functional system of language; sociolectal norms (including the norms of genre); idiolectal norms (that are optional). A continuum of thresholds stretches from the first to the third.[8] Generally, the prescriptions of the first prevail over those of the second, which prevail in turn over those of the third. However, under favourable conditions, an individual's usage can become the group's norm; and the group's norm can prevail over the standard norm called language.[9] For the constituents of language, including the rules of syntax, contradictions between types of systematicity are powerful factors of diachronic evolution. In a text, they account for discordances between standard usage. For example, in this line by Jodelle, 'Luy moi, prend moy, tien moy, mais hélas ne me pers' (Make me glow, take me, hold me, but alas do not lose me) the transitive construction of *luire* 'glow' (literally 'glow me') can be related to a sociolectal tactic norm (iambic rhythm) and especially to an idiolectic dialectical norm that compels the masculine narrator-actor to be the object of processes in which a feminine actor has an ergative role.[10]

C. In addition to the fact that they can be regulated by three types of systematicity, the semantic components can be generalized since they interact at three levels of linguistic description – word, sentence, and text.

At the level of the sentence, the components fundamentally interact in the same way as at the textual level, but in a less complicated way. Tactics and thematics are also necessary here, whereas dialectics and dialogics are optional. Notwithstanding, the sentence is not an insurmountable frontier,[11] and the occurrences of numerous textual genres can consist of a single sentence (epigrams, haiku, maxims, landays, etc.). At this level, within the tactic component, language generally dominates the other socialized norms (whereas at the textual level, this dominance is reversed: if locally the former dominates the latter, globally this dominance is reversed). At the level of the word, the prescriptions of the functional level of language acquire a supplementary degree as far as the two necessary components are concerned. As for tactics, the distribution of morphemes in the word is strictly regulated. Regarding thematics, the inventory of the contents that can occupy a given position can be very closed (in the case of affixes, for example).[12] The optional components can also work at the level of the word. Thus, a thematized graph can be constructed starting from a word such as:

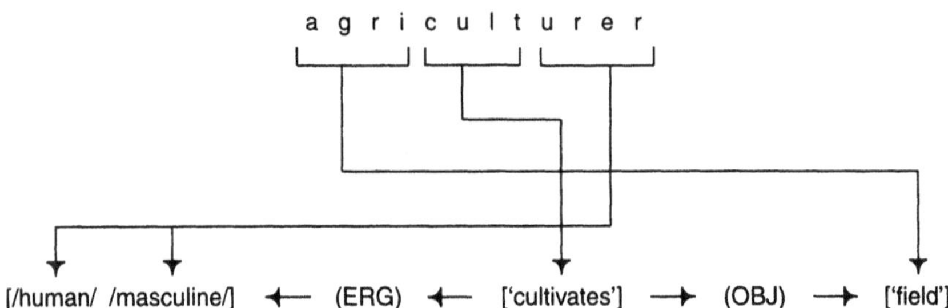

Such a graph can also contain temporal intervals (for example, an *ex-president*) or modal changes of levels (for example, a *pseudo-colleague*).

In short, the four semantic components can interact at the three levels of description. Of course, this interaction becomes more complex as we pass from word to text. Correlatively, the dominance of the types of systematicity differs according to levels. As we get away from the word, the dominance[13] of the functional system of language decreases. It generally accounts for the semantic structure of the word, but is unable to account for that of the sentence. At the level of the text, sociolectal and/or idiolectal norms dominate in general. This variation appears clearly for the part of syntax that is governed by the functional system of language. From my perspective, syntax appears as a privileged means of regulating the interaction of the semantic components. Now, the internal syntax of the word obeys stricter rules than those of the simple sentence; and at the textual level, syntactic rules (of anaphorization, concordance of tense, etc.) become so weak that they are generally confused with sociolectal norms.

Note: Naturally a continuum stretches between these three levels. A sentence can consist of a word; a text can consist of a sentence.[14] Moreover, the status of the complex sentence is not unanimously agreed upon.

The question of genres can now be treated in a new light. At the three levels identified, and especially at the last one, a genre is defined by the interaction of socialized norms, with several linguistic components (of content as well as of expression).[15] For example, a haiku is defined by tactics of expression (two lines of five syllables framing a line of seven) and by thematics (it contains a topical 'word about the seasons'); the Pashtoun *landay*, by tactics of expression (two lines of free verse of nine and thirteen syllables, without obligatory rhymes, but with solid internal scansions), by the media component (orality, with different vocalizations according to the regions), by its topic of love, by its dialogic (the represented narrator must be of the same sex as the speaker). In a given social state, these interactions can, in fact, be exclusive. For example, Zumthor notes regarding the dialectical structures of the *chanson de toile*: 'Theoretically the same narrative schema can be developed in an independent way, as a tale. The fact that it is not, is remarkable in itself' (1972, 166). The evolution of genres can be described by the evolution of the interaction between components. Take, for example, the thematic evolution of the *landay*. As the late Sayd B. Majrouh noted, its topic has changed over the past years in the refugee camps of Pakistan. Erotic themes have been replaced by the theme of the holy war (in the masculine *landays*) or by that of exile (in the feminine *landays*).[16]

From the 'classical' perspective of stylistics, a genre could be defined by the interaction of different levels of language. This type of definition seems sensible, but in addition to the fact that the levels of language, except for the two planes, are difficult to isolate, one has to acknowledge the possibility that a genre is defined by the interaction of components belonging to the same level.

Notwithstanding, the notion of genre still has to be relativized. This is not only because a genre is relative to a culture – without for all that being reduced to an 'ideological formation' unworthy of attention. Textual linguistics must be able to describe such formations. But, in addition, it must be able to treat in the same way genres that are not identified as such or, at least, that are not specified. Moreover, it is doubtful that any genre is universal. Let us examine the most favourable case, that of minor oral genres such as riddles and proverbs. Their analogues can be found in many societies, but is this to say they play the same role? Not at all, since the codified situations of communication differ invariably,[17] even with lullabies or funeral orations. Now, as we have seen, the interactions of components that define a genre are linked to the conventions of communication. These conventions constrain enunciation, enabling (and this is very important) the fixing of references[18] and the orientation of interpretation. Specific interpretative strategies that assume the status of intrinsic instructions are hence associated with each genre. In attempting to neutralize the traditional rules of narrative understanding, modernist novelists have proven this *a contrario*. When the descriptive categories proposed will have made it possible to describe genres, which are recognized or not as such, they should lead to the relativization of the notion of genre. According to the number and the type of interactions between components, one must indeed recognize *degrees of genericity* (for textual types), and of *typicality* (for textual occurrences).

PART TWO

ESSAYS IN TEXTUAL SEMANTICS

The term *essays* corresponds to the tentative nature of the following chapters. Each chapter in its own way extends the propositions contained in the first part of this work and is not a simple application. In addition to its descriptive intent, each chapter indeed pursues its own theoretical objective, either by explaining in detail the interaction of the two textual components, or by illustrating a problem mentioned in the first part, for example, that of the referential impression.

The five chapters follow one another in the chronological order of the texts studied.

9

Moon, Diana, Hecate

This is not a representation of your nature, or of that of the gods, exclusively; it is a representation of this entire treble world.

Nâtya-çâstra

A few days before his death, Etienne Jodelle (1532–73), a notoriously unrecognized poet, dedicated this sonnet to Maréchale Claude-Catherine de Retz:

> Of stars, forests, and Acheron honour,
> Diana, on high, middle and lower World presides,
> And her horses, her dogs, her Eumenides guides,
> To enlighten, hunt, cast death and horror.
>
> So great is the brilliance, the hunt, the consternation
> One feels under your beauty bright, fleet and deadly,
> That lofty Jupiter, Phoebus, and Pluto readily
> Deem diminished, lightning, bow and terror.
>
> Your beauty through its rays, snares, and frights
> Enchants the soul, captures, grips, and torments:
> Make me glow, take me, hold me, but alas do not lose me.
>
> Forceful harmful flares, fires, nets, and ambushes,
> Moon, Diana, Hecate, in the heavens, earth and hell
> Adorning, pursuing, tormenting, our Gods, ourselves, our shades (my translation)[1]

The methodology of semantic analysis cannot be fixed once and for all *in abstracto*.[2] In fact a text cannot be reduced to a hierarchy of levels harmoniously superimposed and accessible according to a fixed order (whether the perspective adopted happens to be generative or interpretative). It results from the sometimes conflictual interaction (but always governed by a genre) of several orders of autonomous, albeit interdependent, structures.

The method adopted naturally depends on the objectives pursued and the hypotheses to be verified. Here, I hope to highlight the specificity of the text, especially regarding its thematics and its tactics, and secondarily, to illustrate the theoretical propositions presented above.

I. Thematics

1. Generic Isotopies

The text links three semantic domains in a remarkable way. Table I is a list of the sememes indexed.

I

Domains	A //heavens//	B //earth//	C //hell//
line 1	'stars'	'forests'	'Acheron'
line 2	'high'	'middle'	'lower'
line 3	'horses'	'dogs'	'Eumenides'
line 4	'enlighten'	'to hunt'	'death'
			'horror'
line 5	'brilliance'	'the hunt'	'consternation'
	'great'	'fleet'	'deadly'
line 6	'bright'		
line 7	'lofty'		
	'Jupiter'		'Pluto'
	'Phoebus'		
line 8	'lightning'		
	'bow'		
line 9	'rays'	'snares'	'terror'
			'frights'
line 10	'enchants'	'captures'	'grips'
			'torments'
line 11	'glow'	'take'	'hold'
			'do not lose'
line 12	'flares'	'forceful'	'harmful'
	'fires'	'nets'	'ambushes'
line 13	'Moon'	'Diana'	'Hecate'
	'heavens'	'earth'	'hell'
line 14	'adorning'	'pursuing'	'tormenting'
	'Gods'	'ourselves'	'shades

Without going into excessive detail, I point out that the reasons leading me to list sememes in such and such a class differ as to their plausibility. For example, the generic feature /heavens/ is inherent to certain sememes, but afferent to others. Thus, it is inherent to 'stars'. On the other hand, it is afferent to 'fires' [because of the phraseology: in poetry the 'fires of the sun' abound; for example, Lamartine: 'Let me fly off on the fires of the sun' (*Harmonies*, I, 2)]. This socially normed afferance is confirmed by the context ('Phoebus'). Finally, certain sememes are indexed by locally afferent features. 'Horses' can appear in class A because of the feature /positive evaluation/ (contrary to 'dogs' and 'Eumenides'). The moon ('Selena') as we know travels the length of the nocturnal sky on a silver chariot pulled by white horses. The recurrence of contents belonging to the three domains, //heavens//, //earth//, and //hell//, enables us to induce three symmetrically interwoven generic isotopies.

2. Specific Isotopies

Table II highlights the semic recurrences on which the cohesion of class A is founded:

II

A	/luminosity/	/intensity/	/altitude/	/positive eval./
'stars'	+	(+)	+	+
'high'			+	(+)
'horses'	(+)		(+)	(+)
'to enlighten'	+		(+)	+
'brilliance'	+	+		+
'great'		+		(+)
'bright'	+	+		+
'lofty'		+	(+)	
'Jupiter'	+	+	(+)	+
'Phoebus'	+	+	+	+
'lightning'	+	+	+	
'bow'	(+)	(+)		
'rays'	+	+	(+)	(+)
'enchants'		+		(+)
'glow'	+		(+)	
'flares'	+	+		
'fires'	+	+	(+)	
'Moon'	+	(+)	+	
'heavens'	+	+	+	
'adorning'				+
'Gods'	(+)	+	+	+

The parentheses signal afferent features, whether or not they happen to be socially normed and/or propagated by the context.

The recurrence of these four (specific) features establishes a network of generic isotopies in the text that parallels the generic isotopy /heavens/, and justifies the constitution of class A.

This class contains 21 sememes.[3] The number of occurrences of each feature is respectively 16 (of which 3 are afferent), 15 (3), 14 (6), 15 (6), for a total of 60 and an average of a little less than 3 features per sememe.[4] The first number enables us to evaluate the *weight* of the network of specific isotopies; the second the *density* of the network, defined by the average number of recurrent features for each sememe.[5]

Let us analyse class B in the same way in Table III.

III

B	/average position/	/pursuit/	/capture/	/negative eval./
'forests'	+			
'middle'	+			
'dogs'		+	(+)	(+)
'to hunt'		+	(+)	
'the hunt'		+	(+)	
'fleet'		(+)		
'snares'			+	+
'captures'		(+)	+	(+)
'take'			+	(+)
'forceful'			+	(+)
'nets'			+	(+)
'Diana'	+	(+)		
'earth'	+			
'pursuing'		+	(+)	(+)
'ourselves'	(+)			

The number of occurrences of each feature is respectively 5 (1), 7 (3), 9 (4), 7 (6). Hence a weight of 28 for the entire network; this number, related to the number of sememes (15), gives an average density of less than 2.

Finally for class C, see Table IV.

The descriptive features have respectively 7 (3), 17 (1), 7 (3), 20 (5), 9, and 17 (5) occurrences. Or, for the entire network, a weight of 77 and an average density near 4.

The choice and the labelling of the descriptive features are open to criticism, and anyone can always propose a more efficient description.[6] To give an idea of possible areas of research, one could study the relations between the features of each network. Some of them can be related to anthropological constraints: for

IV

C	/obscur./	/intens./	/low pos./	/neg. eval./	/death/	/fear/
'Acheron'	+		+	+	+	+
'lower'	(+)		+	(+)		
'Eumenides'	(+)	+	(+)	+	+	+
'death'		+	(+)	+	+	+
'horror'		+		+		+
'consternation'		+		+		+
'deadly'		+		+	+	(+)
'Pluto'	+	+	+	+	+	+
'terror'		+		+		+
'frights'		+		+		+
'grips'		+		(+)		(+)
'torments'		+		+	+	+
'hold'		+		+		
'do not lose'		+		(+)		
'grievances'		+		+		(+)
'obstacles'		+		+		(+)
'Hecate'	(+)	(+)		+		+
'hell'	+	+	+	+	+	+
'tormenting'		+		+	+	+
'shades'	+		(+)	(+)	+	(+)

example, the negative evaluation of obscurity is due to the preeminence of vision in humans; the association between luminosity and altitude is also not surprising. Others are more easily related to cultural traditions: thus, the link between the low situation (chthonian) and death is established by societies like our own that practice burials.

3. Interaction between Classes

The semantic classes A, B, and C show remarkable cohesion, through both the recurrence of generic features and the recurrence of specific features combined into networks.

Let us now examine the interrelations between these networks, by first of all focusing on qualitative data. Several descriptive features share the same semic categories.

categories / classes	position	evaluation	lighting	polarity
A	/altitude/	/positive/	/luminosity/	/intensity/
B	/average/	/negative/		
C	/low/	/negative/	/obscurity/	/intensity/

Classes A and C are polar classes: their descriptive features are in a relationship of identity (/intensity/) or contrariety /high/ vs /low/, /positive/ vs /negative/, /luminosity/ vs /obscurity/.

Two descriptive features of class C, /death/ and /fear/, have no corresponding terms in class A (as would be the case with the contrary features /life/ and /hope/, conventionally associated with //heavens// in Christian tradition).[7]

The descriptive features proper to class B and that have no corollaries in the other classes, /pursuit/ and /capture/, are linked by relations of implication, not only among themselves (if /pursuit/ then /capture/), but also with /fear/ and /death/ in class C: if /pursuit/ then /fear/; if /capture/ then /fear/; if /capture/ then /death/.

Let us now examine the quantitative data:

	Weight	Density
A	60	≈ 3
B	28	≈ 2
C	77	≈ 4

For each of these criteria, we obtain the relation C > A > B. By relating these data to the content of classes, we conclude that hell dominates both heavens and earth.

Let us now specify the relations established between the homologous members of the three classes, first of all at the semantic level. The sememes indexed to the three generic isotopies belong to the same taxemes (as is often the case in enumerations). Three cases arise:

(i) The taxeme is formed by language, such as: 'high', 'middle', 'low'. In this case the mention of its polar terms and of its threshold ('middle') is sufficient to induce the feature /totality/ (cf. *from A to Z, urbi et orbi*, etc.).

(ii) Other taxemes are socially codified by literary norms. Hence, 'heavens', 'earth', 'hell' is a mythological reformulation of the taxeme 'sky', 'earth', 'hell', which is well established in the phraseology. The same can be said for 'Gods', 'ourselves' → ['humans'], 'shades'.

(iii) Finally other enumerations do not correspond to taxemes codified by language or by other social norms, and we have not noted in Jodelle's work the recurrences that would permit us to consider them as manifestations of idiolectal taxemes. The same holds for 'stars', 'forests', 'Acheron'; 'horses', 'dogs', 'Eumenides'; or 'bright', 'fleet', 'deadly'.[8]

Further on we shall examine in detail the remarkable fact when studying *tactics* that the expressions containing these taxemes or groups are always situated in the same line of poetry, and even in the same hemistich.

Let us now turn to the relationships between the three semantic classes and their expressions.

a) The *morphological categories* of the words in which the sememes of the three classes appear (through one of the signs constituting them), reoccur regularly. If we designate with the letter *N* nouns (and *NP* 'proper' nouns), with *Ad* adjectives, *V* verbs, *Pa* participles, and *P* pronouns, line by line we get:[9]

Verses			Line			
Q1	1:	N, N, Np	2:	Ad, Ad, Ad	3:	N, N, Np
					4:	V, V, V, N, N
Q2	5:	N, Ad, N, N	6:	Ad, Ad, Ad	7:	Ad, Np, Np, Np
					8:	N, N, N
T1	9:	N, N, N	10:	Pa, Pa, N, Pa	11:	V, V, V, V
T2	12:	Ad, Ad, Ad, N, N, N	13:	Np, Np, Np, N, N, N	14:	Pa, Pa, Pa, N, Pr, N

Each line contains at least three words from the same morphological class, in which a sememe belonging respectively to one of the three semantic classes A, B, C[10] is found. This arrangement reoccurs in lines 12 and 13, but less rigorously in line 14, since a noun is replaced by a pronoun: it is hence extended to each of the two hemistiches. This corresponds to the norms of the genre, that prescribe the final intensification.

The morphological data confirm the term-by-term relations noted between the homologous sememes of the three classes A, B, C. Let us now turn from morphology to semantics. The words whose morphological recurrences we have just noted are made up of several signs: a lexeme and several linked grammemes. This is the content of the lexeme whose inclusion we noted in classes A, B, and C.[11] But the grammemes also have sememes as their content (those of genre, number, person, etc.) and they define what Coseriu has called the *categoric signified* of the lexeme.

If therefore in each line at least three lexemes contain sememes belonging to the opposite classes, these sememes are also linked to grammemes whose content is all or in part identical. Examples: adorn-*ing*, pursu-*ing*, torment-*ing*.

A B C

b) These recurrences of the signifieds are obviously paralleled by recurrences of the signifiers. Let us now leave the plane of morphemes for that of phonemes. Without trying to be exhaustive, since we are only attempting to corroborate the initial thematic analysis, let us simply note the most obvious isophonies.

They establish between signifiers terms that are homologous to the three classes; for example:

A	B	C
*ch*evaux (horses)	*ch*iens (dogs)	
*ra*is (rays)	*rets* (snares)	
*f*eux (fires)	*fil*ets (nets)	
éprise (*en*ch*an*ts)	*prise* (*en*tr*an*ces)	mart*yre* (torments), *étreinte* (grips)
*fl*ambants (flares)	*f*orts (forceful)	grie*f*s (grievances)

And again, for the sake of memory, by the repetition of associated grammemes, whether linked or free:[12]

A	B	C
éclair*er* (enlighten)	chass*er* (hunt)	donn*er* (give)
luis *moi* (make *me* glow)	*prends* moi (take *me*)	tiens *moi* (hold *me*)
orn*ant* (adorn*ing*)	quest*ant* (pursu*ing*)	gên*ant* (torment*ing*)
nos dieux (*our* Gods)	*nous* (*our*selves)	*nos* ombres (*our* shades)

To sum up these correlations between sound and meaning, let us take up once more the tattered but useful image of weaving that determined the etymology of *text*. If one calls *weft* the 'vertical' relations internal to classes A, B, and C, and *warp* the 'horizontal' relations established within each line between their homologous terms, we note that the semantic and phonetic 'weavings' are superimposed and complement one another:[13]

	weft	warp
semantics	close	loose
phonetics	loose	close

When I specified this, my intent did not simply originate in a 'structuralist' imaginary universe that constantly grids its object, or even the quadrangular form of the sonnet. Instead I intend to explore the possibility of a much broader activity.

Studies on the parallelism between sound and meaning often neglect the linguistic constraints proper that govern every stylistic interrelation between the two planes of the text.

Even if, following Hjelmslev, we admitted that the seme is homologous to the pheme, the sememe to the phoneme, and the content of the word homologous to the syllable,[14] the fact remains that the combinatory possibilities within each of the two planes are not of the same order. The inventory of the units of the expression considered (phemes, phonemes, syllables) is fixed, closed, and synchronic. The same does not hold true for the units homologous to the content.

Moreover, as a general rule the *scope* of the semantic relations exceeds that of the phonic relations. For example, the isophonies are isolated in a few dozen syllables: Hopkins defined the line as the greatest phonic unit, and even in poetry, regular isophonies do not go beyond two or three verses. Extending them is difficult because of lexical and syllabic constraints.

On the other hand, semantic isotopies are limited neither practically nor theoretically, no matter the length of the text. Finally, experiments in cognitive psychology (cf. Le Ny et al., 1982) confirm that sound is much more quickly forgotten than meaning (which persists in the form of simplified representations constructed along with interpretation).[15]

II. Dialectics and Dialogics

To describe the dialectic structure of a text, one can first of all construct its thematized graphs.

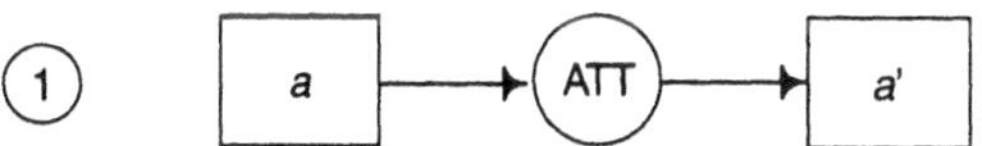

a: 'Diana'; *a'*: 'honour of the stars, forests, and Acheron'; ATT: attribution.[16]

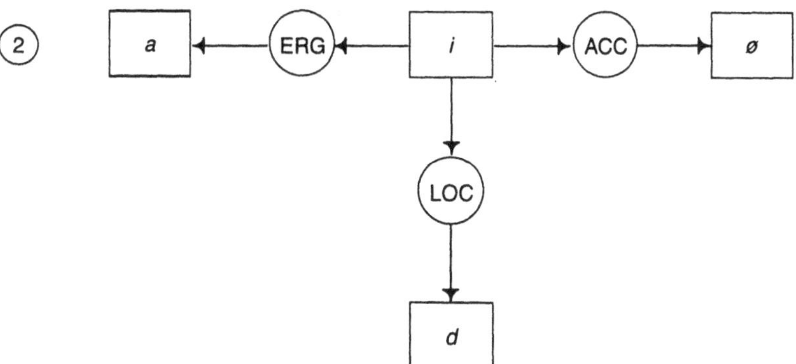

a: 'Diana'; ERG: ergative; *i*: 'presides'; ACC: accusative; LOC: locative; *d*: 'on high, middle, lower world'.

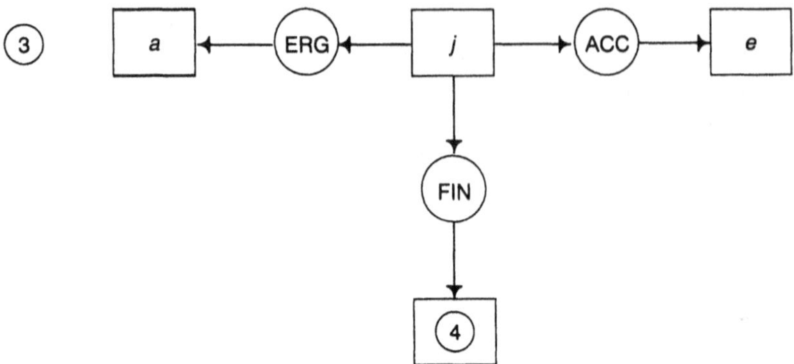

a: 'Diana'; *j*: 'guides'; *e*: 'horses', 'dogs', 'Eumenides'; FIN: final; 4: graph 4 (embedded).

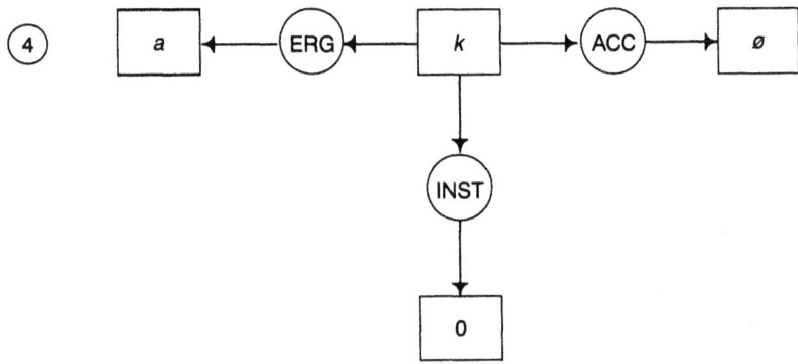

a: 'Diana'; *k*: 'enlighten', 'hunt', 'cast death and horror'.

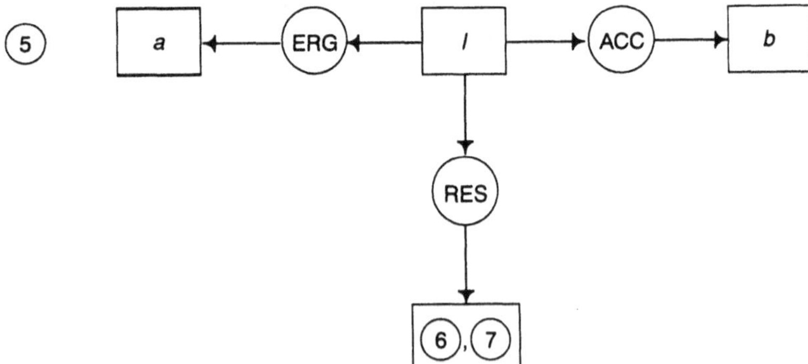

a: 'your' ---> |'you'|; *l*: |'make feel'| 'the brilliance, the hunt, the consternation'; *b*: 'one'; RES: resultative.

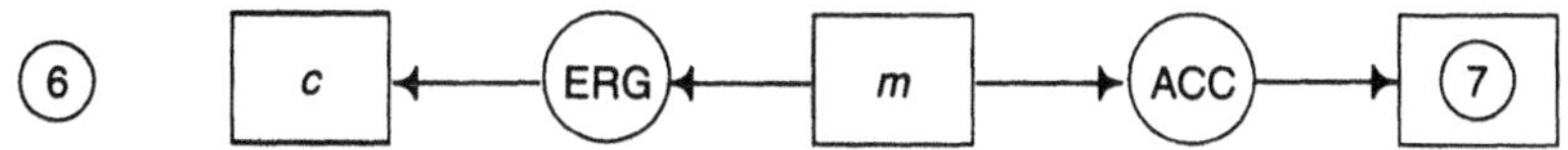

c: 'lofty Jupiter, Phoebus, Pluto'; *m*: 'deem'.

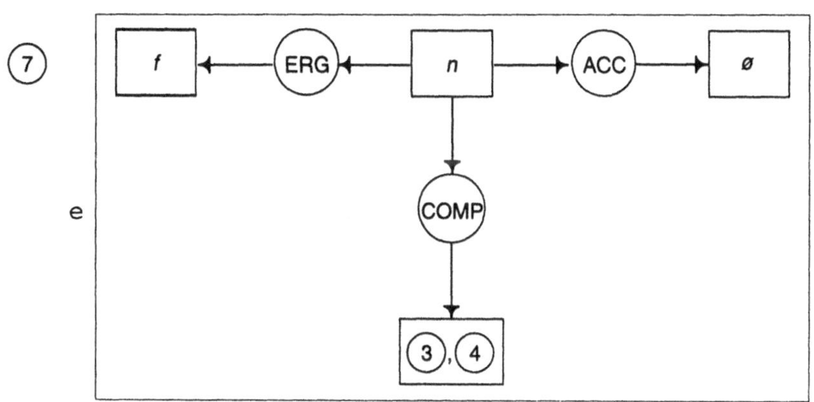

f: 'lightning, bow, and terror'; *n*: 'power'; COMP: comparison; ◇: possibility.

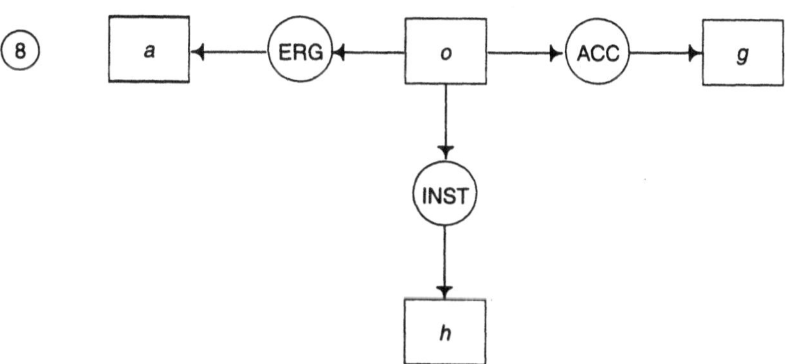

a: 'your beauty'; *o*: 'enchants, entrances, and torments'; *g*: 'the soul'; *h*: 'its rays, its snares, its frights'.

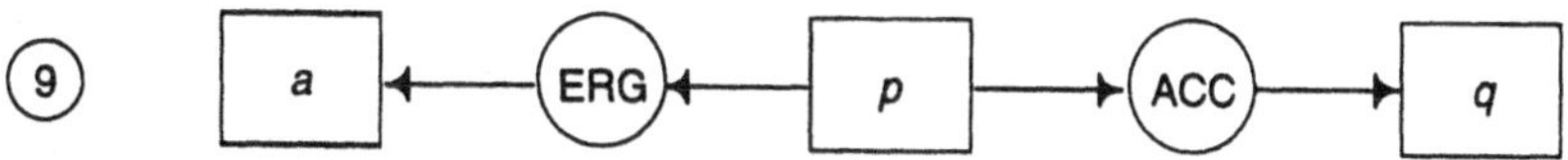

a: |'you'|; *p*: 'take, glow, do not lose'; *q*: 'me'.

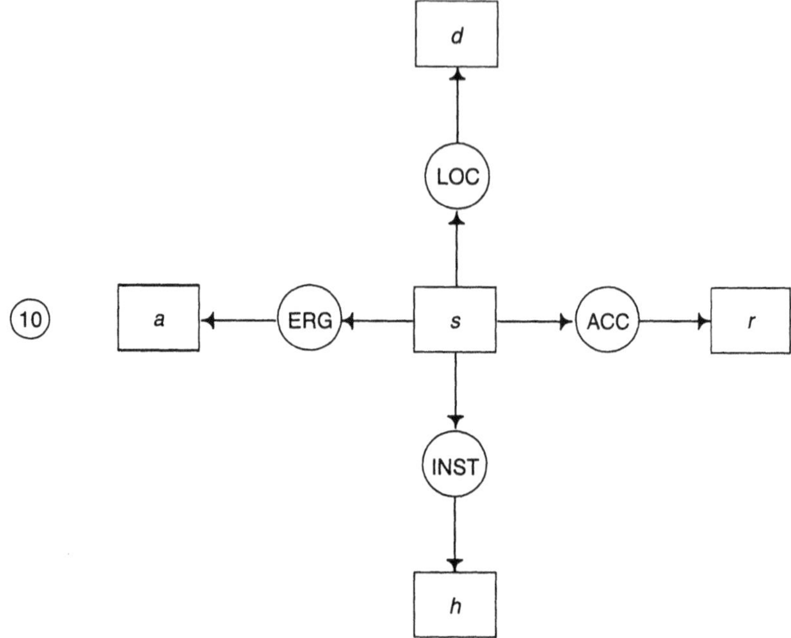

a: 'Moon, Diana, Hecate'; *s*: 'adorning, pursuing, tormenting'; *r*: 'our Gods, ourselves, and our shades'; *d*: 'in heaven, earth, and hell'; *h*: 'forceful harmful flares, fires, nets, and ambushes'.

1. Relations of a Temporal Order

Nothing in the text allows us to introduce such an order between graphs. One cannot say that the structure of the text is narrative in the strict sense of the term. If we compare the graphs, it seems that formulas 2, 4, 5, 8, 9, 10 are closely homologous. The processes and the primary cases (ERG, ACC), where they are instantiated, are so instantiated by the contents belonging to strong equivalent classes (A, B, and C). The same holds for the secondary cases (such as INST and/or LOC in 2, 4, 8, 10). The other graphs do not invalidate this remark. The first is attributive (in accordance with the rhetorical code: presentation of the principal actor, and with the genre: praise of the addressee). The third highlights an ordinary transformation: the ergative acts on the instrumental;[17] it can be reduced to a typical form. The sixth and seventh introduce a transformation of the typical form: if the ergative has the feature /male/ then the process has the feature /inferative/. This inversion of traditional doxa[18] founds an *a fortiori* type of reasoning: If the most powerful gods believe they are less powerful than Diana, then ... The text has only one dialectical sequence, which itself is composed on a single archi-process (and of one of its non-narrative transformations).

2. The Construction of the Actors and the Agonists

This will enable us to describe the dialogical sector. The following table defines the actors by their roles.

	Lexicalizations			
Roles	Q_1	Q_2	T_1	T_2
1 ERG_1	*Diana*	*your beauty*	*your beauty*	*Moon, Diana, Hecate*
2 ERG_2		*lofty Jupiter, Phoebus, Pluto*		
3 ACC	*ø*	*one*	*soul, me*	*our Gods, ourselves, our shades*
4 $INST_1$ (ERG_1)	*horses, dogs Eumenides*		*its rays its snares frights*	*forceful flares and grievances, fires, nets, and ambushes*
5 $INST_2$ (ERG_2)		*lightning bow terror*		
6 LOC	*high world, middle, low*			*in heaven, earth, and hell*

We can thus enumerate six different roles. They express the casual links between classes of contents: for example, when 'snares' and 'nets' are instrumental, 'Diana' or 'you' are in an ergative position in the same graph; when 'lightning' is in an ergative position, 'Jupiter' is in an ergative position in the hierarchically superior graph, which enables us by conversion to assign it an instrumental position. Here $INST_1$ means the instrumental role relative to 'Diana' or to a content of the same class, and $INST_2$ means the instrumental role relative to 'Jupiter' or to a content of the same class. The roles are thus typical cases, obtained if need be by conversion, linking a class of contents to another.[19]

Each of the six roles is associated with several homologous actors on the three generic isotopies. Thus, 'horses', 'dogs', 'Eumenides' have the same role ($INST_1$) on the isotopies corresponding to classes A, B, and C. Two contents can share the same role and be situated on the same isotopy, without necessarily converging: hence 'dogs', and 'nets'. We shall say that these two contents correspond to actors, defined by the same role, by identical generic features, and by different specific features (which oppose them within the taxeme //means of hunting//). An actor can be represented by various lexicalizations; hence *nets* and *snares* are considered as two actants of the same actor; the same holds for *flares*, *fires*, and *rays*. The set of actors with the same roles make up an agonist. The agonist DIANA'S HELPER thus subsumes seven actors, of which two are represented by more than one lexicalization.

We can thus enumerate six agonists: (i) DIANA; (ii) THE VICTIMS; (iii) THE MALE GODS; (iv) DIANA'S HELPERS; (v) THE MALE GODS' HELPERS; (vi) THE THREE WORLDS.

Note: Certain agonists are syncretically designated in the text (for example, DIANA in the first quatrain is associated simultaneously with three worlds);[20] others are not so designated and we create an expression to designate them. To simplify, I note the actors as sememes (between apostrophes), whereas they are in fact classes constructed from sememes. On the other hand, I note the agonists by small capitals.

We can now complete the nodes of the graphs presented above. For example, the right node of graph 3 becomes: [DIANA'S HELPERS: *e*], where *e* designates in simplified notation each of the three values assumed by the agonist.

3. Dialogics

Four universes co-exist in the text:

(i) The standard referential universe, presented in graphs 1, 2, 8, 10. It only includes one world, the world that is. It is not assumed by any of the actors of the utterance.

(ii) 'Diana's' universe (graph 3). It includes only one world, that of expectations.

(iii) The universe of the victims includes a world that is, where the expectations of 'Diana' are verified (cf. graph 5); and a world of expectations, where the verification of the expectations of 'Diana' is desired (graph 9). The identity of the expectations in 'Diana's' universe and the victims must be linked with the genre of the sonnet, which we know, since Dante, to be suited to love. Here Diana and the victims include respectively among their actors the represented addressee 'you' and the enunciator 'me'.[21] The identity of the expectations is all the more remarkable. Moreover, the expectations of 'me' are negatively evaluated in the world of the victims (cf. *alas*, line 11). Therefore, Albert-Marie Schmidt notes, and rightly so, the masochism and voluntary servitude in relation to these loves (1953, 709).

(iv) The universe of the male gods does not include a world of beliefs (graphs 6 and 7), that confirms the world of reference (especially graph 10).

In short, all of the universes coincide. The dialogical structure of the text is therefore absolutely veridictory. This is a factor of semantic intensity: one could say that there is no escape possible.

4. Represented Interlocution

Three actors refer back to represented interlocution: 'you', 'me', and 'ourselves'. Let us now examine the references of these anaphorics.

a) In the traditional lyric love sonnet, 'me' designates the suitor; here it designates in addition the author as person invested with this role: this poem was destined for the Maréchale de Retz's album (and Jodelle did not bother to publish it).
b) Does 'ourselves' thus designate all mortals as opposed to the gods and the shades? I prefer to restrict its usage. On the one hand the only gods cited are male, and by presupposing the isotopy we can infer that these mortals are also males. On the other hand, Diana, an inflexible virgin, kills men (Orion, Actaeon, for example) but spares women (Iphigenia, Chloris).[22] Of course, the 'me' presupposed by the inclusive 'ourselves' designates a man, for, in our love poetry, men are the victims. This use of *ourselves* therefore designates men as mortals *and* as males.
c) How can we confirm the biographical data that specify the reference to 'you'?

(i) Claude-Catherine de Retz had adopted the name *Dictynne* (Artemis, the patron of fishermen). And Jodelle names her *Diana* in most of the poems found in her album.

Of course, but the hazardous cult of Diana was widespread among the poets of this period (Scève, Jamyn, Desportes, Aubigné are among its most fervent). And Jodelle himself did not hesitate in comparing other women to Diana (a certain Françoise, cf. *E.B.*, 360; a mysterious Anne, 362).

(ii) None the less, the name of the addressee is literally inscribed in line 11: *rets*[23] (snares). This occurrence is underscored by the homophone that precedes it: *rais* (rays) and also by the parasynonym *filets* (nets) line 13.

One could also object that *rais* is found in a poem dedicated to Françoise (360), and *ret* in another dedicated to Anne (370).

(iii) Without yet concluding, here is a final presupposition. The maréchale had taken for her motto *Le Noeud, Le Feu* (The Knot, The Fire).[24] Here *fire* and *nets* are juxtaposed, line 13, and we could consider 'noeud' 'knot' as a viable synecdoche of 'net'.

But, one could object once more that another sonnet (369) makes *noeuds* rhyme with *ardents feux*; now the lady in question is called Anne.

In short, no matter what the devil's advocate says, we have a network of textual presuppositions related to the maréchale's name, adopted name, and motto. None in itself is sufficient to determine the reference to 'you': the counter-examples are proof of this. But their convergence and their coherence with respect to the surroundings of this sonnet give these presuppositions a high degree of plausibility. Without revelling in literary history, we must seek interpretants that help actualize the contents inherent to the text.[25] The stakes are important and do not only concern anaphorics: for example, all we have to do is to think about the two significations of the word *rets* (snares).

III. Tactics

We can now examine the interaction of tactics with the other semantic components.

1. Tactics and Dialogics

The universes follow one another in this order:

lines 1–3	Reference universe
line 4	Diana's universe
lines 5–6	Victims' universe
lines 7–8	Male gods' universe
lines 9–10	Reference universe
line 11	Victims' universe
lines 12–14	Reference universe

The text therefore finishes by reverting to the initial objectivity, but only after having confirmed it in all the other universes. This return can evoke an impression of fatality, and these confirmations an impression of intensification.

Note the arrangement of the universes by lines, and their perfectly symmetrical expanses in relation to the centre of the text.

2. Tactics and Dialectics

As a general rule, in the absence of explicit temporal variations, a reader applies a postulate of succession by default. One commonly infers from the succession of sentences the succession of events that they are supposed to represent:[26] this is the case notably with 'narratives' *narrated* in the present, the historical, or the past historic, or more infrequently, in the perfect tense (cf. *L'Étranger* by Camus), in short, in all the cases where the verbal aspects are perfective.[27]

This principle does not apply here – on the one hand because the present indicative, the only conjugated tense in the text, takes on a gnomic value, as confirmed by the isosemy of the present participles of the last line that are of necessity imperfective; and on the other hand because the thematized graphs that share mainly the same invested contents follow one another through reiteration.

Rather than being related to the temporal succession of graphs, the study of tactics can be linked to the substitution of variable contents, and notably to the succession of actors (and their lexicalizations) in the position of primary actants (see following table).[28]

	DIANA	VICTIMS
Q_1	'Diana'	ø
Q_2	'your beauty'	'one'
T_1	'your beauty'	'the soul'
	I'you'I	'me'
T_2	'Moon', 'Diana', 'Hecate'	'our Gods', 'ourselves', and 'our shades'

The two series of substitutions progress in the same way by:

(i) Linking the actant with represented interlocution:
'Diana' ---> 'your beauty' ---> I'you'I
'one' ---> 'me' ---> 'ourselves' [including all male readers]

(ii) Particularising the actant:
'Diana' ---> 'your beauty'
'one' ---> 'the soul' ---> 'me'

The progressions (i) and (ii) are *pathetic* factors.

(iii) Multiplying the actors:
'me' ---> 'our gods', 'ourselves', 'our shades'
'you' ---> 'Diana', 'Hecate'.

This multiplication must be linked to the final intensification (prescribed by the norms of the genre). I evoke in this connection the *complete* form of the last graph, where the process and all the cases, even the secondary ones, are triply instantiated.

In specifying further the relations between tactics and dialectics, could we not extend the postulate of succession by default not only to the graphs but also to the variables that instantiate their nodes? We could then reconstitute the successions as: 1) *Moon adorning our Gods*, 2) *Diana pursuing us*, 3) *Hecate tormenting our shades*. But would this amount to saying, for example, that Diana first of all guides her horses, then her dogs, then her Eumenides? In fact, the plausibility of such successions depend upon the structure of the processes described by means of *scripts*.[29] From *he bought nails, screws, and nuts and bolts*, we can infer that these purchases did not take place in that precise order; whereas, in *he dined with a dozen oysters, a tournedos Rossini, and a strawberry bavaroise*, anyone with the slightest idea of our gastronomical rituals would introduce a strict order. We shall therefore have to return to thematics in order to propose an answer.

Nevertheless, the question asked in this way remains rather simplistic. Indeed, the technique of the *sonnet rapporté* (patched sonnet)[30] – of which Jodelle remains a master in France – cannot be reduced to simple syntactic interlacing; or if so then this interlacing entails some rather remarkable semantic effects:

(i) *By parataxis*. Every enumeration induces a presupposition of isotopy: if the contents share the same syntactic function and occupy adjacent syntagmatic positions, they are in a context of assimilation, and one presumes that they share common semantic features. Hence, for example, the disconcerting (and thus comical) nature of heterogeneous enumerations.

(ii) *By the 'establishment of a common factor.'* If, for example, three processes such as 'enlighten', 'hunt', 'cast death and horror' originate in the same actor in the same utterance, without our being able to introduce validly temporal intervals between them, then through assimilation, we tend to propagate features from one to another in order to 'resolve' or to attenuate the contradictions opposing them; as though there existed a secret complicity (or, more precisely, common semes) between 'enlighten' and 'cast death and horror.' The technique of the 'patched sonnet' uses interpretative laws to constrain the reader to posit a *coincidentia oppositorum*; here it coincides very well with the properly metaphysical thematics of the text.

3. Tactics and Thematics

If we represent the syntagmatic succession of the indexed contents in the three classes A, B, and C, we notice a remarkable semantic rhythm:

Q_1: *ABC*
ABC
ABC
ABCC
Q_2: *AABC*
ABC
AAAC
AAC
T_1: *ABC*
ABCC
ABCC
T_2: *ABC/ABC*
ABC/ABC
ABC/ABC

Let us analyse these data:

a) The rhythmic base cell is the series ABC, reiterated fifteen times. Now, if we consider the constituent contents of the three classes, the series ABC takes on as a meaning effect:

- a devalorization (going from positive evaluations to negative evaluations);
- a fall, in the spatial sense of the term (for example: 'high', 'middle', 'lower'; 'heaven', 'earth', 'hell');[31]
- a succession, in the temporal sense of the term. We know that in the Graeco-Latin tradition, and more generally in the Indo-European one, the history of humanity is that of decadence: we are in the Iron Age (according to Hesiod), or the Brahmanic *Kali-yuga*.[32] This axiological norm enables us to organize temporally A, B, and C.[33]

Hence, on the three notional, spatial, and temporal axes, the series A B C corresponds to concordant hierarchies (in the cultural tradition of the text, that remains, in spite of all, our own).

b) The two lines (7 and 8) that include the succession A C confirm the previous remarks: the absence of contents B is justified by that of the male gods on earth.

c) Between the quatrains and the tercets, the quantitative dominance of A is inverted into the quantitative dominance of C: in the second quatrain, we note 8A, 4C, 2B; in the first tercet 7C, 3B, 3A. The second tercet brings quantitative transformations to an end by paralleling the semantic frequencies: the last three lines each have twice the occurrences of the series A B C compared to the first four.

Regarding thematic analysis, the examination of tactics makes it possible to establish that the text brings about a transformation of contents. This arch-dialectical transformation cannot be said to be narrative. It does not result from a mediation brought about by the agonists, but simply by the successive appearance, repeated fifteen times, of the indexed contents in three semantically hierarchically organized domains.

4. A Detour by Way of Expression

I shall not examine phonematical tactics since the structures of assonance and alliteration are too regional for our purposes. By limiting myself to prosodic tactics, I also do not want to get involved in the debate on the syllabic, accentual, or metric nature of French verse. The representation that follows on this page is the result of a simple compromise between the three theses: I note short syllables by means of a short dash, long syllables by a long dash, accentuated syllables by an apostrophe, and internal pauses by an oblique bar:

Q1: - —́ - / -̦- —́ / --- —́ / - —́
- —́ / --- —́ / - —́ / - —́ - —́
--- —́ / - —́ / --- —́ - —́
--- —̦́ / - —́ / -- —́ -- —́

Q2: ----- —́ / - —́ / --- —́
- —̦́ / --- —́ —́ - / —́ / -- —́
--̦--- —́ / - —́ / -- —́ —́
----- —́ / - —́ / --- —́

T1: --̦ —́ / -- —́ / -- —́ / -- —́
-̦-- —́ -̦ / —́ -̦ / -- —́ - —́
- — / -̦ — / - — / -- —́ -- —́

T2: -̦- —́ -- —́ / —́ / - —́ -- —́
-- / - —́ / - —́ / - —́ / —́ / -- —́
- —́ / - —́ / - —́ / - —́ / —́ / -- —́

For lack of a stable and absolute rule, we can, and indeed must, contest the representation of such and such a line. But let us concentrate on the essentials.

(i) The binary structure of the alexandrine is questioned. No line is organized around an axis of median symmetry, neither through its metre, nor its accents, nor its pauses. In addition, we have an odd number of accents and an odd number of pauses. Except perhaps in the last two lines, the pauses at the hemistich are no more extended than elsewhere; the only incontestably long pauses are found at the end of the verses.
(ii) Only line 11 forms a syntactic and semantic unity. Everywhere else the run-on lines and enjambments are numerous in spite of the rather excessive punctuation (cf. the comma after readily). The movements of the resulting major prosodic units, on the semantic level, can be related to the movement of the reiterated passage of A to B then C, and to the effects of its final fall.
(iii) The juxtapositions of the accented syllables are exceptionally numerous (for the period): two in the second quatrain, four in the second tercet. Except for the first one, they take place precisely where we find the distortion of the established order A B C (line 7), and where the semantic features are repeated (lines 12, 13, 14). In this way they induce an impression of break (relative to the norm of succession of the accentuated and non-accentuated syllables) and of intensification (by increasing the number of accentuated syllables).
(iv) Final intensification – in conformity to the rules of the genre already underscored at all the other levels of analysis – is indicated by an increase in the number of accents (six per line in the last tercet)[34] and by internal pauses (five per line, in the last two).

Dissymmetries, enjambments, juxtapositions of accentuated syllables, increase in the number of accents and pauses, all of which creates an impression of *derangement* that Albert-Marie Schmidt mentioned regarding this poem.

If we now relate prosodic tactics to the thematic structure of the poem, the following correlations come to the fore: of the 68 accentuated words, 56 contain a sememe indexed in one of the three classes A, B, C. As these classes are composed of 56 sememes, all of the signifiers associated with them are accentuated. The correlation is perfect, 'too perfect' perhaps, in the last tercet.

The twelve accentuated words whose sememes are not indexed are for the most part (10) in a peripheral position in the line.

In short, the emphasis of accentuation on the thematic structure is very dense, increases in each verse, and ends up reaching an absolute maximum in the last one.

Verse strophes	Number of accents	Signifiers of the classes A B C accentuated
Q_1	18	13 (≠5)
Q_2	18	14 (≠4)
T_1	14	11 (≠3)
T_2	18	18 (≠0)

IV. Epilogue in the Form of an Excursus

A ternary tactic structure corresponds to a ternary thematic structure. Why is this so? Previously I remarked on the succession of ages according to Hesiod, and Indo-European ideology. We shall now give reasons for having alluded[35] to this.

1. The Three Worlds

My text illustrates a ternary cosmology, banal in our cultural tradition, but that cannot be taken for the expression of universal 'common sense.' In Graeco-Latin antiquity, three worlds were commonly distinguished: the heavens, hell, and the earth in the middle.[36]

In my text, we saw:

(i) A nocturnal sky where the moon glistens (see 'so great is the brilliance, Moon ..., adorning our Gods, your beauty bright, stars ... honour'). Moreover, tradition credits it with a silvery-white glow (cf. the colour of its horses, according to Homer);
(ii) An earth where blood flows (see 'its dogs' [and the Actaeon myth], 'its hunt');
(iii) Finally, hell where Hecate reigns – sometimes presented as Hades' spouse.[37] It is the obscure world of the 'shades' (line 14).

The three colours – luminous white, red, and black – seem to correspond to the three worlds of the text (and of tradition). This triad of colours is also found in the Indo-European conception of the three spiritual principles or qualities (*guna)*: 'the *sattva* ("goodness") is a brilliant, white, luminous principle; the *rajas* ("ardour," "passion") is a red principle ...; the *tamas* ("spiritual inertia") is a black principle, "darkness"' (Haudry, 1986, 6).[38] Here the moon is presented as a benevolent force ('adorning ... our Gods'); and class A to which it belongs receives numerous positive evaluations.

'Ardour' and 'passion' suit Diana: cf. *prompt, capture, take me, torment, hunt*. We also know that Hecate is dark in every sense of the term. Finally, the succession of colours follows the cosmic cycle (in Hesiod as in the *Manu Laws*). The age of silver (white age, as in the Brahmanic *krta-yuga*) is followed by the copper age,[39] which in Hesiod corresponds to an age of heroes. This red age is followed by a black age, the iron age.[40]

The order of succession of semantic classes	A		B	C
localizations	heaven		earth	hell
gods associated	Phoebus	Moon Jupiter	Diana	Hecate Pluto
colours	gold	brilliant white	red	black
ages	gold	silver	copper	iron

Note: The colour gold attributed to Phoebus should not surprise us (cf. Jodelle, 371: 'That the sun gilded with its gold, gilds.') Jupiter is the god of the diurnal sky[41] (here, 'his great lustre' refers back to 'lofty Jupiter'), hence the colour brilliant white.

Thus, the worlds, the colours, the periods, and even the 'passions' converge in this text with what we know about trifunctional ideology. Certain links stand out, others are not excluded. For example, I established the qualitative and quantitative dominance of class C, which is, moreover, the *last* in the order of the tactic succession of the classes. The analysis of the dialectical structure accentuates the dominance of the feminine agonist. The narrative therefore ends with the harmful dominance of the feminine.[42] Men are only shadows tortured in hell by Hecate (see 'tormenting,' 14).

Of course, I do not claim that Jodelle articulated the trifunctional ideology of the Indo-Europeans in a coherent and complete fashion.[43] Certain links appeared interesting enough to highlight. The passion in the Renaissance for antiquity,[44] the coldness towards Judaeo-Christian tradition[45] – all of this could have favoured archaic reminiscences, to which this sonnet perhaps owes much of its attraction.

2. *Questions regarding 'Patched Verse'*

Another series of converging facts merit our attention. In this text, Diana (as agonist) is a trivalent (if not trifunctional) goddess: the qualifications, the attributes, the actions associated with her successively reflect each of the three values. This correlation between thematic structures and tactics is also found in a most noteworthy way in the titling of the trifunctional goddesses in Indo-European tradition. For example, Dumézil notes, 'in the mythology of Postgathic Avesta, a goddess emerges, whose complex titling clearly defines nature: Añahitā, her full name being Arədvi Sūrā Añahitā, that is to say the "Humid, the Strong, the Faultless"'[46] (1981, 104; see also 1945, 170–80; 1947, 56–64, on the trifunctional character of these names). In the Avesta again, the Fravasti are called 'good, heroic, saintly.'

Nearer to our times, we should cite Athena, who, during the minor Panathenees, was the object of three cults then called Hygieia, Polias, and Nikè. Finally, Juno of Lanuvium 'as triple with respect to her title as was the Avestic Anahita' (Dumézil, 1968, 123): *Juno Seispes Mater Regina.*

If this is the case with respect to the titles, why should this not be so afterwards? Three verbs, three complements, etc. would correspond to the three denominations. In other words, a ternary thematic structure can correspond to a tactic ternary structure.[47] And the establishment of this correspondence can be exclusive enough to weaken the ordinary syntactic constraints and enable setting up the technique of 'patched discourse.'

The manifestations of a trifunctional ideology naturally constitute a privileged domain of research. Jodelle's work offers many examples of this: we know that the Three Graces incarnate each of the three functions (cf. Dumézil, 1968, 580–6); now Jodelle's poem 'The Three Graces before Venus's Chariot' (M.-L. I, 300) is written in ternary 'patched verse' (in the first six stanzas). In his work we still find several such poems that present triads of gods: Neptune, Pan, Dictynne (M.-L. II, 333); Phoebus, Phoebe, Aurora (M.L. II, 184); Phoebus, Love, Cypris (336).

Du Bellay does the same with Pales, Ceres, Bacchus (*L'Olive*, 1549, sonnet XIX), Pallas, Lucine, and the Three Destinies (*Sonnet divers*, XXIX); so does Tamisier with Mars, Vulcan, Tisiphone (cf. Berger, 1930, 49); or Drummond with Love, Cypris, Phoebus (*English Poets*, ed. S. Johnson, 1810^5, 689). More generally, the link between the triadic thematic and ternary 'patched verse' is well established, even underscored.[48]

Let us leave thematics aside for the moment in order to investigate the technique of the poem in 'patched verse.' In theory, nothing permits the privileging of a ternary structure; and, in fact, Ronsard, Jodelle, d'Aubigné wrote poems in binary as well as quaternary 'patched verse.' Quinquinary or senary poems are rare in French (only Jodelle and Belleau dared attempt them), but we find them in Latin with Marbode, Mathieu de Vendôme, Hildebert.[49]

None the less, the poems in ternary 'patched verse' are more common. Bolte (1904, 271 ff) cites twenty-nine examples of German, English, or French poems in 'patched verse.' Is this due only to chance? All are ternary. The patient enumeration undertaken by Berger on sixteenth-century French poems enables me to give the following results: of 137 poems in 'patched verse,' 31 are binary, 21 quaternary, and 83 ternary.

This marked affinity for the ternary form is independent of any explicit norm, and is found in various poetic genres.

Let us try to find the cause in the history of the poem written in 'patched verse.' This form is not rare in the Latin poetry that has reached us. The most cited example remains Virgil's apocryphal epitaph. Pasquier presents it as follows:[50] 'In the case of ancient Latin Poetic games, our ancestors made much ado about this distich that some grammarian or poet wrote on the death of Virgil, linking it to his Bucolics, Georgics, or Æneiades: "Pastor, arator, eques, pavi, colui, superavi, / Capras, rus, hostes, fronde, ligone, manu."'

I shall not 'epilogue' on the great success of this verse.[51] I simply remark that it bears the trace of trifunctional ideology: 'eques' refers to military aristocracy (linked to the second function); 'pastor' and 'arator' refer to the third function, on which the productive classes depend.

Moreover – and this reinforces my hypothesis – the technique of 'patched verse' is noted in the poetics of ancient India (under the name of Yatha-Samkhya). Mammata Bhatta (*Kavyaprakasa*, 10, 22) defines it as a juxtaposition. Mahein Chandra Nyayaratna, in his edition of 1866, clarifies this definition,[52] and gives this example: 'Unique, Oh God, you inhabit nonetheless triply, wondrously$_1$, in the heart of the enemy, $_2$of the learned man and $_3$in the heart of she who has the eyes of a gazelle, increasing $_1$ardour, $_2$great joy and $_3$love, $_1$in the ardent courage of the hero, $_2$thought and $_3$pleasure.' [I have maintained his numbering for the exponents even though it does not correspond to today's conventional numbering.]

Here again, references to the three functions are clear: the learned man and thought belong to the first function; the hero and his courage, to the second; love and the eyes of the gazelle to the third.[53] I owe a debt to Bolte (1904) for linking the Yatha-Samkhya and European poetics. Nevertheless, at first glance, he refuses to see a historical link between ancient Sanskrit poetics and Latin poetry of the Middle Ages:[54] he lacks a series of mediations necessary to do so.

But the hypothesis regarding the existence of a relationship between them cannot be discarded. Decisive progress has been made since Bolte, with the discovery of comparative mythology, notably work undertaken on trifunctional ideology.

In any case, by studying on the one hand the triadic thematics of our sonnet, and on the other the ternary tactic structure, I arrived at converging results. Some of them were related to theoretical textual linguistics (that is, the interrelation between tactics and thematics); others, to historical and comparative textual linguistics, that is, the relationship between 'patched verse' and trifunctional ideology. As for this last point, I sketched only one direction of research.

The ideology governing the creation of poems in patched verse has become considerably obscured. Stripped of their raison d'être they appeared as sterile games, and many commentators condemned them over the years.[55] Sometimes however, as with Jodelle, such verse discloses the secret unity of the three worlds.

The notion of *text* that we have inherited from antiquity, and the image of the fabric that formed it, may originate in the formerly sacred technique of 'patched verse.' The syntactic and semantic interlacing that defines this verse takes on the image of a weft and a warp.

An indication of this is found in the lemma of a pleasant Byzantine[56] epigram that calls such lines of poetry *hyphantoi*, that is to say, cloth. D. Alonso (1971, 284) sees here, and rightly so, a Greek name for 'patched verse.' Let us go somewhat further: if dictionaries give *composing, writing* as the final meaning for *hyphaino*, is this not because 'patched verse,' instead of being an artful curiosity, was in Indo-European tradition the founding form of the very notion of *text*?

10

Goddamn! They Sure Made Short Work of the Blanquette of Veal!

No one took proper note of the fact that what I wanted was to carry out a purely philological piece of work, one that I believed was of great historical and social interest.

E. Zola, preface to *L'Assommoir* (1877)

I. Problematics

1. The 'Explication de texte'

Textual semantics can contribute something to didactics. In order to illustrate this I decided to study a short text and to test my thinking concerning 'lisibilité' in a school setting.[1]

As we know, the exercise known as 'explication de texte' is brought to us as part of a long tradition. Instructions from the French Ministry of Education put strict limits on the length of the text under study: 'an explicating reading applies a detailed scrutiny to a text that is necessarily short (at the most twenty lines of prose or verse).' The meaning discovered, these guidelines say, is the effect of a linear movement: 'It is in the course of the study that the force of this movement naturally appears. By resolving the text's difficulties as they present themselves one can progressively identify the directing idea and centres of interest' (Ministry of Education, 1980, *Programmes et Instructions*, 87).

These guidelines would seem to merit an extensive detailed study.[2] Here, however, I limit myself to enquiring into whether or not they are truly able to be applied, keeping in mind what we know about textuality.

2. The Extract Chosen for This Study

The passage chosen is found in chapter 7 of *L'Assommoir*. This chapter occupies a central position in that work, a novel that has thirteen chapters. It is given over to the description of a multi-course meal, a wedding feast given in honour of Gervaise. After a soup with Italian noodles and after the stew, a blanquette of veal is served. We find it being served on page 238 of the Livre de Poche edition (Paris: Fasquelle-Gallimard, 1974; cf. also *Les Rougon-Macquart*, Paris, Gallimard, Bibliothèque de la Pléiade, 1961, II, 574; for original see p. 238 of this volume). On the next page we witness the eating of the dish:

> Goddamn! They sure made short work of the blanquette of veal! There was hardly any talking, just hard chewing. People dug into the salad bowl containing the blanquette. A spoon stood in the thick gravy, a good yellowish gravy that shook like a jelly. They fished around, always successfully, for pieces of veal. The salad bowl was passed continuously from hand to hand while people bent their heads over it, looking for mushrooms. The great loaves of bread, which had been stood against the wall, behind the guests, seemed to melt away. Between mouthfuls you could hear glasses, their ass ends being banged down onto the table. The gravy was a little too salty, four litres of wine were needed to drown that mother of a blanquette, which one could swallow like cream but which put a fire in your stomach. There was no time to catch your breath, the pork loin, surrounded by a cloud, arrived right away, mounted on a hollowed-out dish and surrounded by big round potatoes.

Before focusing on this extract, I first isolated the group of paragraphs that begins with: '"Maman! Maman!" Nana cried out suddenly, "Augustine is dropping her bread into the roasting spit!"' and that ends with: '"Maman! Maman!" cried Nana of a sudden, "Augustine is putting her hands in my plate!"' Within this group, I chose the last paragraph, and then within that paragraph, I finally identified this extract, contained between the two prosodic demarcations 'Goddamn!' (*Ah! tonnerre!*) and 'God almighty!' (*sacré nom!*).

3. The Conditions under Which the Experiment Was Carried Out

This study was tested with two 'sixième' (grade 6, age 11–12) and one 'quatrième' (grade 8, age 13–14) classes in a school in the Val-de-Marne. The socio-professional categories of the heads of families concerned breaks down as follows: manual labourers, specialized workers, and service workers: 44 per cent; tradesmen 21 per cent; office and commercial staff 12 per cent; foremen 3 per cent; doctors, lawyers, etc., teachers, middle-level cadres 2 per cent; not working, including unemployed, 8 per cent; other: 10 per cent.

As for the nationalities of the pupils concerned, the figures are as follows (*nationality* is used in a cultural, not a legal, sense): French 35; North Africans 13; Portuguese 7; West Indians 5; Italians 3; other (Spain, Cape Verde, Central Africa, Congo, Pakistan, Yugoslavia) 7.

On a pedagogical level, the objective of the experiment essentially consisted of a semantic formulation of the difficulties encountered by the pupils when they were asked to read an apparently short and simple text. We inquired into whether or not these difficulties could be related to the nationalities and socio-cultural situations of the pupils.

Copies of *L'Assommoir* were distributed. The teacher (whom I thank for his friendly co-operation) gave the dates of the author, set the story in its time and place, explained the meaning of the title, and introduced the main characters found in chapter 7. Then we read the description of the first part of the meal, up to and including the peas with lardons. The teacher reminded the pupils as to the recipe for a blanquette of veal and then cleared up any unknown or misunderstood words. The French words in question were *guère*, *gelée*, *culs*, *convives*, *bougresse*, *épinée*, *flanquée* (hardly, jelly, ass ends, guests, mother of, loin, surrounded by).

The answers to the first question ('Have you ever eaten a blanquette of veal?')[3] led us to the conclusion that whether or not they had eaten a blanquette had no bearing on the nature of the answers given to subsequent questions. Since most of those who had never eaten a blanquette are foreigners, we can, in that matter, presume that nationality does not play a significant role, at least when the recipe has been explained.[4]

II. First Generic Isotopy

Without claiming to be exhaustively describing the content of the passage I limit myself to phenomena of isotopy relevant to part of its thematic makeup.

1. Taxemes and Semantic Domains

Certain taxemes are linked to particular sociocultural contexts: for instance the taxeme of place settings, or the taxeme of kitchen utensils.

These taxemes can in turn be included within certain semantic domains; Thus, the taxeme of place settings and that of kitchen utensils are part of the domain of //eating//. A sememe that is indicated by an equivocal morpheme can thus be identified according to the domain that is responsible for the generic isotopy of the text. For example, the sememes indicated by *cuiller* (spoon) are identified according to the domains of //eating// or //fishing around//. Sememes that are of the same semantic domain have a common generic seme.[5]

2. Analysis of the Passage

Sememes were sorted according to their relationship with the domain of //eating//. In order to make things simpler, each sememe is introduced by our naming the word that indicates it. Thus, I write 'mushrooms', when in fact it is the morpheme *mushroom* and not the morpheme *-s* that carries a sememe that belongs to the domain of //eating// (see following table).

//eating//		other domains	non-indexed sememes	
I	II	III	IV	
'blanquette'	'mushrooms'	'fished around'	a)	'melt away'
'loin'	'jelly'	'passed around'		'short way'
				'hand', etc.
	'spoon'	'fire'	b)	'they'
	'cream'	'wash down'		'hardly any'
	'pig'	'mother' (bougresse)		'always'
	'table'	'boy!'		
	'stomach'		c)	the imperfect ending -ait
	'potatoes'			the plural ending -s,
	'chewing'			etc.
	'swallowed'			
	'bowl'			
	'glasses'			
	'dish'			
	'loaves'			
	'gravy'			

Columns I and II include sememes that belong to the domain of //eating// (generally the rule in this context).

Column III includes sememes that have to do with other domains, and since we as yet have no satisfactory theory of figures, I do not speak of figurative meaning in connection with them.

Column IV includes sememes that do not belong to any domain, or that are compatible with many domains, indeed, as is the case with certain grammemes, with all possible domains. The subgroup *a* includes sememes that belong to lexemes; subgroups *b* and *c* group together sememes that belong to grammemes, free and bound respectively.[6]

3. One Stage in the Process of Interpretation

The first stage of the interpretative path concerns dealing with ambiguities because most of the signifiers can be relevant to several sememes. I thus try to identify a generic seme that is recurrent to several sememes and that is compatible with all the other sememes. Here, it is because the sememes of column I belong unequivocally (in terms of the signifiers that indicate them) to the domain of //eating// that we can determine that the sememes of column II belong to that same domain. As to the sememes of column III, a further operation is required for their reading: one has to suspend or neutralize the generic seme that connects them with a domain distinct from that of //eating//. For the sememes of column IV we can confirm only that they are compatible with the domain of //eating//.

These operations make up the generic isotopy that is identified by the recurrence of the generic seme of //eating//.

4. The Referential Impression

The generic isotopy that is thus identified defines what we used to call the 'subject' and what we now call the *topic* of the text described, that is, the part of the semantic universe that here is the locus of the referential impression. If I asked the pupils 'what is this text about?' invariably I obtained answers that referred in one way or another to the domain of //eating//.

The referential impression can be made multiple and, at the same time, it can be attenuated, indeed obliterated, in cases where the text refers us to several domains. This is so, for example, in 'metaphorical' texts where one can establish several generic isotopies.

Such is not, apparently, the case here. Although we note sememes that do not belong to the domain of //eating// (those of column III), their recurrence does not seem a priori to constitute another generic isotopy that might be superimposed upon the one I have just brought to light.[7]

5. The Carrying out of the Experiment

The 'sixième' pupils were asked to do this exercise: 'Draw up two lists: one for those words that have to do with eating, and one for those that do not' (the concept of *word* certainly has its problems but it is all the pupils know).

The first list posed no problem, but it was rarely complete. Some pupils included in it nominal groups such as 'pieces of veal' or 'the large loaves of bread'.[8] Most, however, broke those groups down, putting 'veal' and 'bread' in the first list, 'pieces' and 'large' in the second.

Showing her common sense, one girl included some words such as 'jelly' in both lists, arguing that they could produce two meanings according to context (see above the sememes of column II). One boy was the only pupil to include some grammemes in the second column, grammemes that in this case happened to be free ones. Many placed words such as 'spoon', 'dish', or 'bowl' in the second list of words. They had understood 'eating' in the sense of 'food' and had thus excluded from that domain those utensils that are used in eating (more precisely, sememes that include an applicative seme /for eating/).

Finally, two 'errors' warrant our attention. Three pupils put 'mother' (*bougresse*) in the first list. After carrying out the instructions given including a collective reading of the passage, they had read *bout (de) graisse* (piece of fat). This approximating and antigrammatical homophony reminds us to note this obvious truth: a reading of a text is possible only if it correctly identifies the text's morphemes. Let us thus leave to higher education the exercise of anagrammatic readings.

Further, several pupils put 'litres' in the first list. For them, as is true for this context, this word means 'bottles of red wine.'[9] This meaning was so obvious for one of them that, when the text was read out, he wrote 'litres of wine', so sure was he that was what he had heard. This is a problem of diastratic evaluation: for many French families, as for the characters in *L'Assommoir*, the word *litre*, unaccompanied by any other notation, always, by default, has that meaning.

III. An Initial Specific Isotopy

1. The Seme of /intensity/

If we examine the sememes of column III, we observe a surprising recurrence of the seme /intensity/. Now we will look to see if it is also recurrent in the other sememes and therefore whether or not it constitutes an isotopy. We know that this seme is grammaticalized in many languages, for example, in the case of relative or absolute comparatives. It can also structure parts of words, that is, be a component of the overall word.[10] Indeed, certain taxemes are characterized by relations of linearity or progressivity between their sememes, for example from 'glacial' to 'burning' or 'minuscule' to 'enormous'.

2. Establishment of the Isotopy

Here is the list of those sememes. A gloss has been supplied where it was necessary in order to clearly identify the chosen seme.

'Goddamn' ('Ah'):	An interjection that marks strong feeling.
'tonnerre':	Very loud, intense noise.
'quel':	Suggests a lot of blanquette (in this context).

'hole' ('trou'):	Making short work of the blanquette is how we translate making a 'hole' or *trou* in it. Presupposes an almost solid consistency.
'chewing' ('mastiquait'):	'Chewing' is more intensive than *mâcher*; see the Robert dictionary, which describes it in those intensive terms.
'hard' ('ferme'):	Energetically, intensely.
'bowl' ('saladier'):	The biggest such container in the household, 'The blanquette appeared, served in a salad bowl, there being no other big enough dish.'
'food' ('plantée'):	Suggests an almost solid consistency.
'thick' ('épaisse'):	Intensive along the axis of consistency.
'good' ('bonne'):	Intensive along the axis of value.
'yellowish' ('jaune'):	A very deep colour when we are talking about a white gravy. The Larousse dictionary speaks of a stew in a white gravy, for 'blanquette.'
'shook' ('tremblait'):	Suggests a maximum consistency for the gravy.
'jelly' ('gelée'):	Idem.
'around' ('dedans'):	Suggests great depth for the blanquette and its gravy (as opposed to *dans*, for example).
'fished' ('pêchait'):	Suggests a substantial body of liquid or semi-liquid, and not insignificant activity.
'continuously' ('toujours'):	In this context, suggests an inexhaustible supply.
'was handed from hand to hand' ('voyageait'):	Movement over significant distance.
'bent' ('penchaient'):	Suggests great depth.
'great loaves' ('grands pains'):	Earlier the story had spoken of 'large four-pound loaves, as large as ...'
'melt' ('fondre'):	Rapid disappearance.
'banged' ('retomber'):	Glasses are banged down onto the table (hence the noise).
'too' ('trop'):	Below I will comment upon the quantificational phrase 'un peu.'

'four' ('quatre'):	Here, a large quantity (cf. a gradation *vis à vis* the previous page, where mention is made of drinking a first glass, 'four fingers' of pure wine, to wash down the noodles.
'litres' ('litres'):	Intensive in relation to 'fingers.'
'drown' ('noyer'):	To drink a lot, washing down a food.
'mother of' ('bougresse'):	Emphatic, 'hypercoristic.'
'cream' ('crème'):	Suggests a lovely taste and something that goes down easily.
'fire' ('incendie'):	Extreme heat.
'catch your breath' ('souffler'):	Suggests almost a panting, therefore the putting out of a great effort.
'time' ('temps'):	In this context ('There was no time ...'), suggests things moving along very quickly.
'mounted' ('montée'):	Suggests considerable volume.
'hollow' ('creux'):	Idem.
'big' ('grosses'):	Idem.
'round' ('rondes'):	Suggests the greatest mass possible for the dimensions in question.
'cloud' ('nuage'):	Big vaporous cloud.

Thus the seme /intensity/ appears in a recurrent way in different taxemes: consistency, verticality, temperature, sound, taste, etc. We can see that thinking about synaesthesia should not be left only to symbolic poetry.

3. Grammemes, Prosodic and Tactical Features

The seme /intensity/ can also be constructed as a function of the content of certain fixed grammemes, and also, on the other hand, as a function of certain features of expression.

a) We note a remarkable redundancy of grammemes for the plural; cf. 'pieces' ('morceaux'), 'bent their heads over it,' ('les visages se penchaient'), 'glasses, their ass ends being banged down onto the table,' ('les culs de verres'), etc. One can attribute the seme /intensity/ to their corresponding sememes, and this is especially so because they are bound, linked to lexemes that already include that seme. Summing up, /intensity/ seems to be one of the virtual sememes of the

grammeme for the plural. One might actualize it in any context in which recurrence of that seme defines an isotopy. All this has to do with what traditionally has been left to stylistics.
b) Two prosodic signs (exclamation marks) can, in this context, also include in their content the seme /intensity/. This is also true for the repeated phrases: 'thick gravy' ('sauce épaisse'); 'a good gravy' (une bonne sauce'; 'from hand to hand' ('de main en main'); 'always successfully' ('il y en avait'); 'looking for' ('cherchaient'); 'put [fire in your stomach]' ('vous mettait un incendie dans le ventre'); 'there was no time' ('pas le temps').[11]

4. *Inherent and Afferent Semes*

The operations that made possible the construction of the seme /intensity/ are of two distinct types.

a) For most of the sememes, paradigmatic substitution with members of the same taxeme allows us to identify clearly this seme: thus, *dedans* (in) is an intensive of *dans* and this gradation belongs to the linguistic system. Likewise 'thick' (épaisse) would be an intensive of both 'smooth' (*onctueuse*) and of 'fluid' or 'light' in a context involving gravy.
b) In general use of the language also, 'yellow' is intensive relative to 'white' along a scale (or a taxeme that is organized according to a relation of progressivity) that goes from the clearest to the darkest colour. However, we have to resort to a norm that is not integrated within the functional system of language in order to infer, by syllogism, the following evaluation: the blanquette is by definition a 'dish served in a white gravy,' a gravy in which the normal proportions are one egg yolk to three quarters of a litre of bouillon (see Bernard, *Les Recettes faciles*, Hachette, 1965, 106). Now, in this text, the gravy is yellow and thus must include many egg yolks, even too many, if one pays attention to the most heeded cooks.

The case of the word 'salad bowl' (*saladier*) is even more instructive: to serve the blanquette in a salad bowl does not suggest that this salad bowl is the largest possible dish. But in this context *saladier* is the object of a further definition: the largest such dish that, in this household, might serve as a platter. Hence my proposed interpretation.[12]

5. *The Carrying out of the Experiment*

The pupils in the three classes, children who, of course, have no training in semantics, were invited to 'note and identify everything that marks intensity,' whether or not such marks were 'words.' Indeed, as far as words are concerned, the pupils were allowed to propose an equivalent that was affected by an operator of intensity. For example, *gobait* 'gobble' = intensive of *avaler* 'swallow', in 'they gobbled up the peas by the spoonful.'

None of the items in paragraph 3, on 108–9, was noted. On the other hand, the items of paragraph 2, on 106–8, were almost all identified. Correct answers were, however, much more frequent in the case of inherent semes than for afferent semes, the latter, as we have seen, being identified or constructed by much more complex operations because their actualization is accomplished only by default, although it requires specific instructions.

IV. A Second Specific Isotopy

1. The Seme of /vulgarity/

Our blanquette is served as part of a holiday feast. Most of the guests have never before been invited by the Coupeau family. It is thus an exceptional meal, which indeed will forever be unique. Good manners are therefore all the more observed: 'they were on their best behaviour, they showed each other courtesy' (239). This fictional situation makes the recurrence of the seme /vulgarity/ all the more remarkable.

In most dictionaries this seme is used to indicate an inferior category on the diastratic scale. The Larousse, for instance, distinguishes between *fam.* (familiar), *pop.* (popular), and *vulg.* (vulgar). I know that these judgments are relative and I discuss them later.

Here is an inventory of the recurrences of this seme, accompanied by justifying glosses.

'Goddamn'
('tonnerre!'): One should not swear.

'short work'
('quel trou dans la blanquette!'): An effect of suddenness, confirmed by the parataxis and by the contrast with the preceding paragraph. Now, one should never eat quickly.

'blanquette'
('blanquette'): One does not serve a stew as part of a holiday feast, especially not a gruel (see Lévi-Strauss, *Le cru et le cuit*, Paris, Plon, 1964).

'There was hardly any talking'

('on ne parlait guère'):	One is supposed to talk during a meal.[13]
'hard chewing' ('on mastiquait ferme'):	One should eat with apparent effortlessness.
'hard' ('ferme'):	Popular form for 'fermement,' 'avec énergie.'
'dug into the salad bowl' ('le saladier se creusait'):	One should use the appropriate serving dish.
'the spoon stood' ('une cuiller plantée'):	You do not stand eating utensils in the serving dish.
'in the thick gravy' ('dans la sauce épaisse'):	'The gravy should be quite light' (Bernard, 106).
'that shook like a jelly' ('qui tremblait comme une gelée'):	Idem. When you have guests, you obey accepted culinary norms, that is part of savoir-vivre.
'they fished around for pieces of veal' ('là-dedans, on pêchait les morceaux de veau'):	It is uncouth to pick and choose from the serving dish.
'the salad bowl was passed continuously' ('le saladier voyageait'):	You do not just keep on and on helping yourself.
'from hand to hand' ('de main en main'):	It is up to the hostess to serve the guests.
'people bent their heads over it, looking for mushrooms' ('les visages se	

penchaient et cherchaient des champignons'):	You do not hunt and pick from the serving dish.
'the great loaves of bread' ('les grands pains'):	Bread should be served presliced or, even better, as little rolls.
'that had been stood against the wall' ('posés contre le mur'):	You put out the rolls on small side plates. As Naima, fourteen years old, said, 'standing them against the wall is gross!'
'seemed to melt away' ('avaient l'air de fondre'):	You do not stuff yourself with bread.
'between mouthfuls you could hear' ('entre les bouchées, on entendait'):	You are supposed to chew quietly.
'the ass ends of the glasses' ('les culs de verres'):	One should use long-stemmed glasses.
'ass ends, of the glasses' ('culs'):	A vulgar way of saying 'base.'
'hearing the glasses, their ass ends being banged down' ('on entendait les culs de verres retomber'):	One should avoid banging eating utensils and china.
'the gravy was a bit too salty' ('la sauce était un peu trop salée'):	You do not over-season.
'four litres of wine' ('quatre	

litres'):	Wine should be served in bottles, (or carafes).[14]
'litres' ('litres'):	One should drink moderately.
'to drown' ('noyer'):	Vulgar way of talking about accompanying food with drink.
'mother of' ('bougresse'):	Vulgar.
'which put ... in your stomach' ('qui vous mettait'):	The dative 'vous' is a popular form.
'a fire in your stomach' ('un incendie dans le ventre'):	Result of over-seasoning. You do not talk of your belly or stomach, especially when at table.
'there was no time to catch your breath' ('on n'eut pas le temps de souffler'):	You do not serve dishes right on top of each other.
'catch your breath' ('souffler'):	Popular for 'resting up after putting out an great effort.' Eating should not require effort.
'loin' ('épinée'):	Popular form for 'échine.'
'pork' ('cochon'):	Popular form for 'porc.' 'The word *porc* ... is of a more sophisticated nature than the word *cochon*' (Robert dictionary).
'big potatoes' ('de grosses pommes de terre'):	You should serve small or medium potatoes.

2. The Heterogeneity of the Isotopy

This isotopy is manifested by units of differing magnitude. The phrases quoted above can be divided into two groups: morphemes; syntagmas or utterances.

To the morphemes there correspond inherent semes. Thus 'mother' (*bougresse*) will include the seme /vulgarity/ in all contexts, in positive as well as negative phrases. Thus it is proper to language itself.

To the syntagms or utterances there correspond afferent semes, constructed by logical syllogisms of the type: 'They were looking for mushrooms; now, one should not fish around in the serving dish; therefore they are vulgar.' Most of our glosses presented the topoi that are necessary in order to supply these enthymemes.

This isotopy can be of the order of several norms. In order to make those norms explicit, I have used certain referencing quotes. I could have chosen others. The isotopy so constructed would not have been fundamentally different for all that.

My reading can be criticized for its rather 'maximalist' nature; one can judge *Goddamn!* (tonnerre!) harmless, and one can say, in connection with the salad bowl, 'It's not that Gervaise lacks manners, it's that she has no money' (Emma, fourteen years old). The isotopy so constructed would exist just the same, but would include somewhat fewer items.

On the other hand, we certainly found 'bourgeois' readers for whom 'if you cannot afford it, don't receive guests.' Is the point of view of the implied narrator any different?

3. *The Experiment*

The pupils were asked to 'note everything that indicates vulgarity.' They easily found 'vulgar words.' In their enthusiasm they even invented some. The pork loin was surrounded (*flanquée*, flanked) by potatoes. This *flanquée de*, almost ambiguous in this context, was seen by some as vulgar, as was *convives* (guests) where the sound of the prefix *con* (silly bugger) may have been suggestive.

However, they had difficulty discerning vulgarity of behaviour in this fiction. The best results were obtained from young North African girls, who are likely better trained in manners and hospitality than the others. However, when I put together all of the occurrences of such vulgar behaviour that were identified it still came to only half the number found in my list above.

This isotopy was 'read' in an incomplete way by all of the pupils. But since there are more afferent semes here than others, the degree of legibility or 'readableness,' when expressed in terms of semes read, varies from pupil to pupil. This is a function of their ability to construct logical mediations that make the actualization of afferent semes possible, whatever those semes might be. It also varies according to how well they know their table manners and the degree to which they consider those manners important.

V. Problems of Evaluation

Now let us be precise about the relation between the two specific isotopies that we have just read in the text and that I have designated as i_2 (/intensity/) and i_3 (/vulgarity/).

1. Who Is Speaking?

Before going any further I have to ask this question, and I have to ask it of the pupils too. Because it is a difficult question, it will be optional, but only for the pupils. Here then is an expedition into the dialogical.

Here we have to turn to the concept of universe: the total package of propositions uttered in a given text by a given actor, in that text, who gives out signs, linguistic or otherwise, constitutes the universe of that actor, whatever the truth value of his propositions.

In a text whose style is semidirect, as is the case in point, signals such as quotation marks are not enough for delimiting the universe. We can, however, assign propositions to these universes through inferences whose personal deictics, both spatial and temporal, and whose diastratic deviations and evaluative norms, are privileged operations.[15]

A. Person and Speaker

In this text, the subject *on* seems to be inclusive. For the pupils there is no doubt on that score, because their competence includes only an inclusive *on*.[16] This presumption is supported by the *vous* (in 'vous mettait un incendie dans le ventre' – 'put [to you] a fire in the stomach' = 'put a fire in your stomach'). This 'ethical dative' suggests a first person, one who has experienced this fire. Finally, the exclamation marks suggest a speaker who figures among those eating.[17]

B. The Judgments Made

These evaluations, or judgments, allow us to corroborate our initial presumptions. In 'a thick gravy, a good, yellowish gravy,' ('la sauce épaisse, une bonne sauce jaune'): 'good' ('bonne') indicates a positive evaluation of the /intensity/ content (a content common to both 'yellow' ('jaune') and 'thick' ('épaisse') see above). This evaluation is directly related to the nature of the eating actors. We have here a truly anthropological phenomenon. To be able to evaluate taste requires, of course, contact with the food in question. Likewise, not only is 'mother of' ('bougresse') intensive in this context, it can also amount to a positive judgment. We also know that the gravy is salty and, if we were to go beyond the boundaries of our passage, we could also show that /salty/ receives a positive judgment in the universe of the assumptions of several of the actors here, especially Coupeau, and the inevitable Bec-Salé (Salty-mouth), called here Boit-sans-soif (Drink-without-thirst).

Although the eaters judge this food positively, the narrator, throughout the chapter, does not hesitate to judge it negatively (see 'lardons, stinking of horses' hooves' ['des lardons ... puant le sabot de cheval'] 240). He similarly judges the eaters: 'they were bursting at the seams, these goddamn slobs! Mouths open, chins dripping with grease, their faces looked like derrières, so red that one could say the derrières of rich people, bursting with prosperity' ('ils pétaient dans leur peau, les sacrés goinfres! La bouche ouverte, le menton barbouillé de graisse, ils avaient des faces pareilles à des derrières, et si rouges, qu'on aurait dit des derrières de gens riches, crevant de prospérité,' 245).[18]

C. Diastratic Deviations

Beyond the inclusive 'on,' 'bougresse,' 'culs,' 'noyer' are unanimously attributed to the eaters: 'that's how they talk,' say the pupils.

On the other hand, 'guests' ('convives') is unanimously attributed to the narrator: this word, unknown to most of the pupils, cannot belong to what they assume to be the lexicon of these eaters. Many of the pupils think the same in the case of *visage* (as opposed to *figure*). One can go even further in citing the expletive *l* in 'si l'on ne parlait guère' (if they scarcely talked).

D. Initial Conclusions

The passage I chose does not yield up any propositions of contradiction that, within one and the same period of narrative time, would be proof of the presence of several universes. However, the other extracts I have cited from the same passage, allow us to conclude that we do indeed have two universes here. There is the universe of the eaters and that of the implied narrator. In our passage, diastratic deviations signal this twofold nature. Thus:

Isotopies	i_2 (/intensity/)	i_3 (/vulgarity/)
Person	inclusive ('on')	exclusive ('ils')
Judgment	positive (e.g., 'bonne')	negative (e.g., 'puant', 'stinking')
Diastratic position	inferior (e.g., 'culs') = the 'ass ends' of the glasses	superior (e.g., 'convives', 'guests')
Universe	eaters	narrator

With the exception of some rare cases of direct discourse, the manifestations of the two universes are inextricably bound up with each other and, if I have separated them for reasons of my demonstration, that should not minimize the effect of complexity that thereby results.

Let us not forget the very important fact that two isotopies correspond to the two universes. The thematic and dialogic components are also clearly correlated. These two universes contain different evaluative norms that can produce two different readings.

2. Norms for Judgment and Thresholds of Acceptability

Along any quantitative or qualitative scale one can place one or more thresholds of acceptability,[19] which define on that scale those segments that are positively or negatively valorized. The scale can then be said to be evaluative. Of course a given term can be placed above a certain threshold in one universe and below that threshold in another.

For example, just after the blanquette: 'Le meilleur, dans les pois, c'étaient les lardons grillés à point, puant le sabot de cheval' ('What was best, in the peas, were the lardons, toasted just right, stinking of horse hooves'), we have:

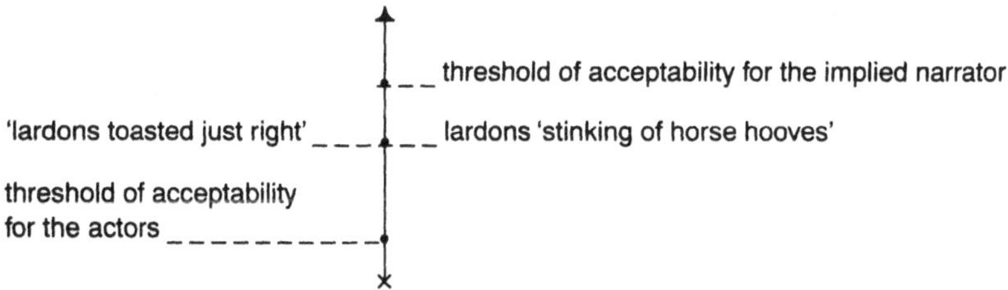

Note: We find the inverse configuration in an enlightening example, during the visit to the Louvre: 'Encore des tableaux, des saints, des hommes et des femmes avec des figures qu'on ne comprenait pas, des paysages tout noirs, des bêtes devenues jaunes, une débandade de gens et de choses dont le violent tapage de couleurs commençait à leur causer un gros mal de tête ... Des siècles d'art passaient devant leur ignorance ahurie, la sécheresse fine des primitifs, les splendeurs des Vénitiens, la vie grasse et belle des Hollandais' (More paintings, saints, men and women with faces that you couldn't understand, dark landscapes, yellowed animals, a whole confusion of people and things in overwhelming colours that began to give them a huge headache ... Centuries of art paraded before them and their stunned ignorance, the exquisite dryness of the primitive works, Venetian splendours, the sensuous and satisfying life of the Dutch), 90.

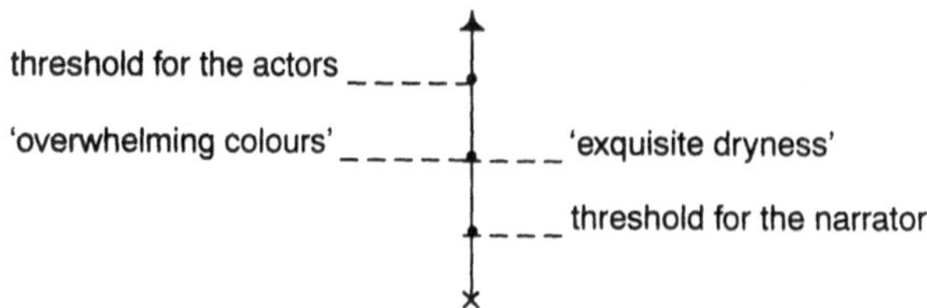

It should also be noted, at the end of the meal, that the actors remark, in connection with those who go *outside* to vomit: 'Quand on a été bien élevé, cela se voit toujours' (when you've been properly raised, it's always obvious), 263.

3. *Judgment Norms and the Hierarchy of Isotopies*

In the universe of the actors, intense terms, in the case of the meal, are valorized. The valorization of the quantity of food, notably, seems to be linked, for the host, to popular rules of hospitality (Pascal, fourteen years old: 'One's guests shouldn't want to go to a restaurant upon leaving'). For the guests, the valorization of the quantity of food seems linked to a fear of not getting enough (Karim, fourteen years old: 'They were happy, they had eaten enough for a week').[20]

In the universe of the narrator, the same intense terms are devalorized as a function of a code of table manners that must be adhered to when one eats. At the very least, certain limits must be respected. One must not drink too much, make too much noise, etc. More generally, perhaps, what is valued is a kind of humanism based on generally accepted virtues.

This contradiction between certain judgment norms does not mean that certain elements of i_2 cannot be interpreted in terms of i_3. They can indeed. Thus, many pupils classed the same elements as i_2 and i_3, saying about the guests, 'they're too much,' or, 'they're eating like pigs.' In other words, the /intensity/ content can be recast in terms of /vulgarity/, following an interpretive inference: if /intensity/ *then* /vulgarity/.

To sum up, according to this hypothesis, if the i_2 and i_3 isotopies both make an incomplete interpretation of the passage possible, we can none the less observe that i_3 makes possible a more cogent incomplete interpretation than i_2, because all of the elements of i_2 are interpretable according to i_3 whereas the inverse is not true.

4. Two Strategies for Reading

In general, universes of assumptions include an explicit enunciative focus (here, the eaters), or an implicit one (here, the narrator).[21] It is agreed that interpretative foci can correspond to given enunciative foci. The interpretative foci in question are in fact so many 'places' assigned to its potential readers by the text. As a function of their personal axiology, real readers will accept or not accept this invitation to occupy one or more of these interpretative foci.[22]

We can expect that to the two universes we have here there correspond two strategies for reading. Let us look at how the experiment confirmed that. The students were invited to answer the following optional questions: 'Can you put yourself in the place of these characters? Are you making a moral judgment about them?' Some pupils decided to put themselves in the place of the characters while at the same time refusing to judge them. They felt that in judging them, they might devalorize themselves. Most answered that they would not put themselves in the characters' place, even if they could, because they had judged them with such judgments as 'they're too gross.' One Portuguese girl tried to avoid this contradiction, expressing these revealing and nuanced phrases: 'I have no reason to get mixed up in their business, but I think it's nice to put on a wedding feast for someone, even if it is unsuccessful, or if you eat badly, or if you don't have much fun. But when I see this text, the guests, for their part, are happy, because you don't eat like that every day, so they're getting something out of it' (Emma, fourteen years old). To sum up, if he or she shares the assumptions of the actors, the 'naive' reader cannot escape the devalorization with which they are bound up, no matter the extent to which he or she had succeeded in at least partially establishing i_3, as was indeed the case with most of the students, even the semiliterate ones.

If, on the contrary, the reader shares the narrator's assumptions, he or she will thereby be obliged to devalorize characters with whom, under different circumstances, especially if he or she comes from the working class, he or she could easily identify. To avoid all that, one young Portuguese girl wrote: 'The author wants to demonstrate that in SOME [underlined twice by her] families, vulgarity is rather what reigns.' In this way she undoubtedly sought to avoid discrediting all working-class families.

Thus when 'putting himself in the place' of the actors, the reader is devalorized; 'in the place' of the narrator, he or she devalorizes others and devalorizes himself/herself at the same time (unless he or she espouses an 'anti-working-class' axiology, which was not the case with our sample). The reader thus is faced with two untenable reading strategies. Whence, perhaps, a kind of interpretative pathetic that doubly intensifies the narrative pathetic, something we see in the answers of the two Portuguese girls.

VI. Reading and Intratextual Relations

1. Two Types of Afferent Semes

Let me leave my pupils alone for a bit in order to make clear what the theoretical and practical limits assigned to the explication de texte exercise *make it impossible* to read.

In all the preceding, I have constructed two types of afferent semes. These can be identified as:

a) afferent semes that are constructed as a function of norms that are external to the text and expressed by such topoi as 'a stem glass is more chic than a mustard glass.'
b) afferent semes constructed as a function of norms that are internal to the text (for example: 'The salad bowl is, in that household, the biggest dish that can be used as a serving dish'). These norms can be socialized, as is so for those that are implicated in literary topics, or they can remain individual, thereby characterizing the semantic universe of a given speaker or scriptor.

Without claiming to have been exhaustive, I can now bring forward some intratextual associative networks of sememes that will then enable me to show how those networks allow the construction of afferent semes. Co-occurrences of morphemes permit me partially to note and identify these associative networks.

To do this I need a method different from the one used up to now. Indeed, in order to construct afferent semes as a function of norms that are internal to the text, I can no longer simply turn to knowledge of the linguistic system or of other social norms, and I have to quote much more extensively in order to bring out the recurring relations identified. I do this without regard to the linearity of the text because the intratextual semantic relations that are contracted by a given semantic unit – as long as it is not in a final or initial position – are both prospective and retrospective.

I first quote certain words and syntagms from the Zola passage in order to show how the relations between the sememes that they manifest reappear elsewhere in the same text.

2. 'The Thick Gravy, a Good Yellowish Gravy'

Because it is too salty, this gravy is part of putting '<u>a fire</u>' in your '<u>stomach</u>.'[23] A rudimentary semic analysis allows us to identify two qualitative semes (/viscous/, /yellow/) and a functional seme (/harmful/); because this harmful nature could be manifested by a burn, in some contexts we would find the seme /hot/.

The semic molecule so constituted can be represented as follows:

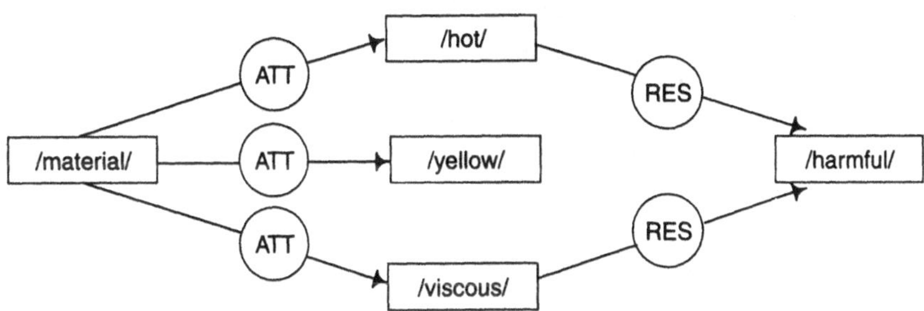

This graph can receive expansions (through transformation of the qualities that are in process: for example: /hot/ → /heating/; /viscous/ → /flowing/), and also as a result of transformations involving universes and dialectic intervals (for example /yellow/ can be rewritten as /gilded/ at the beginning of the story and in the universe of Gervaise).

Let us now examine the recurrences of this semic molecule. Gervaise, while eating a 'prune à l'eau-de-vie' (prune in brandy) at the Assommoir, during her first meeting with Coupeau, says to him, 'Seulement, je laisserai la sauce, parce que ça me ferait du mal' (But I won't touch the juice, because that would upset my stomach) 49. Now, we know that the brandy at the Assommoir is yellow: 'Give me the yellow one,' says Mes-Bottes (295). The semic grouping /viscous/, /yellow/, /harmful/ is thus reiterated. Likewise, when Gervaise begins to drink: 'Elle regarda ce que buvaient les hommes, du casse-gueule pareil à de l'or' (She looked at what the men were drinking, rot-gut like gold) 388.[24] Later, when she witnesses Coupeau's final convulsions: 'C'était le vitriol de l'Assommoir qui donnait là-bas des coups de pioche. Le corps entier en était saucé' (It was L'Assommoir's vitriol that was hammering him. His whole body was 'pickled' from it) 492.

Other substances are defined by the same semic grouping. Such is the case for the oil that Lantier consumes: 'Au bout d'un mois, il voulut mettre toute la cuisine à l'huile ... Son grand régal était un certain potage, du vermicelle très épais, où il versait la moitié d'une bouteille d'huile. Lui seul en mangeait avec Gervaise, parce que les autres, les Parisiens, pour s'être un jour risqués à y goûter, avaient failli rendre tripes et boyaux' (After a month, he wanted to cook everything with oil ... His great treat was a certain soup, with very thick vermicelli, in which he poured half a bottle of oil. He and Gervaise alone ate it, because the others, the Parisians, having accepted once the risk of tasting it, had almost barfed up their guts) 280.[25]

It is likewise for the goose grease, which, as is well known, is yellow, like oil. 'La blanchisseuse accourut et surprit le louchon en train de se brûler le gosier, pour avaler plus vite une tartine toute trempée de graisse d'oie bouillante' (The laundry girl ran up and caught the slob burning his throat by too quickly swallowing a tartine dipped in boiling goose grease)' 239.[26]

Finally, liquid gold was both the alcohol and the money of this household. 'Si la paie fondait dans le fil-en-quatre, on se la mettait sur le torse au moins, on la buvait limpide et luisante comme du bel or liquide' pensait Gervaise pendant qu'elle 'mijotait dans une bonne chaleur' (If one's pay melted away into fil-en-quatre, at least one was putting it onto one's torso, one drank it limpid and shining like liquid gold, thought Gervaise while she simmered in her comfortable warmth) 392. Also, 'Ah! ce n'était pas le zingueur qui ouatait ses frusques avec de l'or! Lui, il se le mettait sous la chair. Gervaise ne pouvait pourtant pas prendre ses ciseaux et lui découdre la peau du ventre' (Ah! It wasn't the roofer who packed gold away in his clothes! He tucked it away under his skin. Gervaise couldn't very well take her scissors and unstitch the skin of his belly) 367. And there is no need to remind ourselves that the household lives on Goutte-d'or (drop of gold) Street ...

Even the rain that falls on the day of Gervaise's wedding is linked with the semic grouping we have been studying: '"Ah bien!" s'écria Mme Lerat en entrant, "nous allons avoir une jolie saucée! ... On dirait qu'on vous jette du feu à la figure"' ('Ah well!' cried Mme Lerat upon entering, 'we're going to have a fine drenching' [using saucée]! ... It's like having fire thrown at your face') 82. After the drenching (saucée), 'toute la rive droite était dans l'ombre, sous un grand haillon rouge cuivré; et du bord de ce nuage, frangé d'or, un large rayon coulait' (the whole of the right bank was dark, under a big tattered, copper-coloured cloud. From the edges of this cloud, where it was streaked with gold, there flowed a fat ray) 95. Boche, during the downpour, says 'que Saint Pierre éternuait là-haut' (that Saint Peter was sneezing up there) 84; one can infer /viscous/ from 'saucée' here and from 'sneezing' also. Gervaise, for her part, 'était restée les yeux fixes ... voyant des choses graves, très loin, dans l'avenir' (had remained staring ... seeing grave things, very far in the future ...) 85; cf. /harmful/.

Without going into greater detail in the analysis of these quotes I note at least that the text, through an associative network, allows us to constitute an idiolectal paradigm that includes the sememes 'juice', 'oil', 'grease', 'drop', 'gold', 'rain', and the sememes of parasynonyms: 'vitriol', 'fil-en-quatre', etc.; the recurrence of the morpheme /*sauce* (gravy)/ was my clue in constructing this paradigm.

The locus of the harmful action of these substances can be designated by 'snout' (the slang gueule), 'face,' 'torso,' 'stomach,' 'guts,' 'belly,' 'paunch,' etc.

If we come back to the passage previously studied, we are now ready to take up once again the semic molecule.

'The great loaves of bread ... seemed to be melting away.' Now, these great loaves of bread are elsewhere compared to 'yellow dolls.' Furthermore, throughout the text, a process of liquefaction, or of deliquescence, is endlessly alluded to: 'Gervaise mollissait' (Gervaise was going limp) (351); 'l'argent s'évaporait' (money evaporated) 367, 'la paie fondait' (wages melted away) 392. The /viscous/ seme mentioned above in fact describes one stage in this process. This is so much so that, in the extract, interpretation can actualize, in 'melt', not only the seme /disappearance/, but also the seme /liquefaction/.

Several lines on, the pork loin is a butter. Now, we know that it arrives in a 'cloud of steam.' We thus can note here the recurrence of the semes /yellow/, /hot/, /viscous/ cf. 'quelque chose de doux et de solide qu'on sentait couler le long de son boyau ...' (something sweet and solid that you could feel running along inside one's gullet) 240.

3. What a Hole in the Blanquette!

A. Before her marriage, Gervaise speaks of 'avoir un trou un peu propre pour dormir' (having a clean 'trou' [literally a hole, but she means a 'spot' or 'place'] to sleep), 'un trou à soi' (a 'trou' all her own) 45. Already, before the meal, 'il se faisait des trous chez elle, l'argent avait l'air de fondre' ('Trous' [a matter of 'lacking' things] were appearing in her place, the money seemed to be melting away) 196. Afterwards, the household is going to go and live 'dans le trou le plus sale' (in the most dirty hole) 354. Gervaise, indeed, is destined to die in a 'trou': 'comme on venait de trouver le père Bru mort dans son trou, sous l'escalier, le propriétaire avait bien voulu lui laisser cette niche' (since old man Bru had been found dead in his trou, the owner was quite willing to let her have that little corner) 494. With real premonition, old man Bru, all through the wedding feast, had kept singing 'un "trou la la, trou la la"' entêté et lugubre' (a hole ho ho, a hole ho ho, obstinate and sinister) 263. Maman Coupeau will be left – another premonition – 'au fond du trou' (at the bottom of the hole) 352.

The meaning of trou is thus linked to death, as it is also to alcohol, which causes death: 'the sweat of alcohol' coming out of the still should 'inonder le trou immense de Paris' (inundate all the vast hole of Paris) 50. It is also linked to excrement: 'l'oie venait de laisser échapper un flot de jus par le trou béant de son derrière' (the goose had just let loose a flood of juice through the gaping hole [trou] of his derrière) 243.[27]

Of course, according to its particular use, trou manifests several different sememes: 'habitation', 'orifice', 'lacking things'. But to the extent that our text assigns the same afferent semes to these different sememes, the semic kernel of trou – that is, the grouping together of its stable semes (see Pottier, 1974, 328) – is all the more extended. For example, when trou manifests the sememe 'habitation', it includes, as do the other sememes, the afferent seme /death/. This is not only because Gervaise dies in a trou: when she wishes for a 'cleanish little place (trou) in which to sleep,' these words have to be read in terms of their context, that is this, text where elsewhere an undertaker invites her to 'faire dodo dans l'ombre' (go sleepy-byes in the shadows) 354, and says, finally, 'Fais dodo, ma belle' (Go sleepy-byes, my beauty) 495.

I should add – and it is something we have already seen with fondre (to melt away) – that the semic kernel can also be extended through the actualization of inherent semes that ordinarily are neutralized in certain contexts.

This twofold extension of semic kernels accounts for, at the level of morphemes, the 'overabundance of meaning' that modern criticism often finds in literary texts.

B. The blanquette is a stew made of white meat, as its name suggests. Gervaise sees Lantier, just before the meal: 'La blanchisseuse ne riait plus. Elle était très blanche' (The laundry girl was no longer laughing. She was very white) 235. The blanquette is served: 'les rideaux ... laissaient tomber une grande lumière blanche' (the curtains allowed in a bright, white light) 239. Once the goose has been carved, 'Gervaise, énorme, tassée sur ses coudes, mangeait de gros morceaux de "blanc"' (Gervaise, enormous, elbows on the table, ate huge pieces of white meat) 244. At dessert time, when she is asked to sing, 'elle se défendit, la figure blanche' (she demurred, white-faced) 253. When the undertaker mistakenly comes to carry her away, she has a 'figure blanche comme une assiette' (her face is as white as a china dish) 372. This whiteness, which is attributed to Gervaise in dozens of contexts, would be just a minor index if our main context here did not involve 'drowning that mother of a blanquette.' Now, 'bougr(esse) (mother) includes /human/, as an inherent generic seme, and that is what actualizes in '-esse' the seme of /femininity/. These two semes are thus afferent to 'blanquette.' For the same reason, 'noy(er)' (drown) brings up the seme of /death/, an afference that is the result of /immersion/.[28]

Further, in certain contexts, Gervaise is substituted for a stew. During the meal, Gervaise serves a stew, the blanquette, to Goujet. At the end of the book, she offers herself to him in exchange for a stew: 'un restant de ragoût ... fumait devant le cendrier. Gervaise, dégourdie par la grosse chaleur, se serait mise à quatre pattes pour manger dans le poêlon ... A la première pomme de terre qu'elle se fourra dans la bouche, elle éclata en sanglots. De grosses larmes roulaient le long de ses joues, tombaient sur son pain ... Elle avait fini. Elle demeura un instant la tête basse, gênée, ne sachant pas s'il voulait d'elle. Puis, croyant voir une flamme s'allumer dans ses yeux, elle porta sa main à sa camisole, elle ôta le premier bouton' (Some leftover stew lay steaming in front of the stove. Gervaise, warmed up from the great heat, would have gone down on all fours if that would have gotten her something to eat from the pot. With the first potato she stuffed into her mouth, she began to sob. Great tears rolled down her cheeks, spattered onto her bread. She was done. She kept still for a moment, her head lowered, embarrassed, not knowing whether or not he was going to take her up on her proposition. Then, believing she could see him beginning to light up, she reached for her top, she undid the first button) 471–2.

Summing up, the blanquette belongs to the same class of actors as Gervaise, the goose, and Maman Coupeau. It should not surprise us if Gervaise shares certain semantic features with actors that belong to the same actorial class as she. We have seen this in the case of the goose; we can confirm it with the blanquette.[29]

If one were to decide to give Gervaise special status among these actors, one could conclude, although it would be an over-simplification, that during the meal she offers herself up for consumption and devours herself in the form of the blanquette and the goose, whose gravy and juices are described in the same way – but which, however, are as different as bouilli (stewed) is from rôti (roasted). (For the importance and validity of this difference one can consult Lévi-Strauss, *Le cru et le cuit.*)

4. 'Culs' and 'Cochon' (Asses [Anatomical] and Pig)

A. Gervaise is threatened with the possibility of suffering 'une culbute dans la boisson' (a tumble into the drink) 390. After this culbute, when she attempts to prostitute herself, 'son ombre faisait la culbute à chaque pas' (her shadow tumbled with her every step – she did have a limp) 467. That day, 'le ciel était barbouillé comme le cul d'un poêle' (the sky was dark and greasy like the ass end of a stove) 441.[30] Coupeau pushes her onto the sidewalk, saying that 'une femme devait savoir se retourner' (a woman should know how to turn over) 457. In the street, 'ses savates éculées crachaient comme des pompes' (her worn-out shoes spat like pumps) 423. She dragged along 'sa paire de ripatons éculés' (her worn-out feet). When she thought of her landlord, 'elle l'avait où vous savez, et profondément encore' (she had him 'you know where' and in deep at that) 444. Then, 'a cette heure, son endroit devrait être bigrement large, car elle y envoyait

tout le monde ... dans le derrière, le quartier qui la méprisait! Tout Paris y entrait, et elle l'y enfonçait d'une tape' (Right then, 'her place' must have opened pretty goddamned wide because she consigned everybody there, in her derriere, the part of town that showed her such scorn! All of Paris was shoved up there and she stuffed it all in with a shove of her hand) 444.
B. The day of Gervaise's wedding, 'Boche et Bibi-la-Grillade, l'un après l'autre, injuriaient le vide, lui lançaient à toute volée: "Cochon!" et riaient beaucoup, quand l'écho leur renvoyait le mot' (Boche and Bibi-la-Grillade, one after the other, would curse into the emptiness, yelling 'Pig!' and then they would laugh uproariously when the word echoed back to them) 92. Cochon is linked to alcohol: 'elle aurait voulu ... goûter à la cochonnerie' (she would have liked a taste of the pig swill) 391. And cochon is linked to Coupeau as well: 'son cochon était en train de crever à Sainte-Anne' (her 'pig' was dying at Sainte-Anne) 477. He was 'à l'hopital et il venait y crever la couenne rapeuse' (in the hospital, bursting his rough hide) 381. Nana also calls him cochon (361).

5. *Associative Networks*

Without describing all of the associative networks that the sememes of the passage under study are part of, I can now clarify their status. An associative network is the whole group of relations that allows us to note the recurrence of a semic molecule, whether that molecule is linked to a specific morpheme or not.[31]

This recurrence bundles together specific isotopies. Sememes that belong to the most diverse taxemes and domains are recurrent in places other than the passage described. For example, when Bijard the drunk whips his daughter (337), his yellow eyes (cf. 'alcohol' etc.) were starting out of their black holes (trous) (cf. 'death', etc.; in fact, he ultimately does kill her). Or when Gervaise consigns everybody to where the sun never shines: 'dans le derrière, son cochon d'homme!' [cf. 'ass,' 'filth,' etc.] (in the derrière, her pig of a man).

This phenomenon, of which there are many examples, *excludes* the hypothesis according to which the recurrence is haphazard. It allows for the hypothesis that the associative networks described are linked in a unique network that covers the whole of the text.

The table at the top of 127 is a topological representation, with three zones and two limits.

These occurrences are classed according to actorial perspectivisms. The occurrences found in the passage under study are in Roman characters. The others are mentioned only by way of example.

Sites	Semes	Occurrences
Zone 1	/viscous/ /yellow/ or /gilded/	gravy, vitriol, oil ... bread, butter
Limit 1	/absorption/	a) drown, inundate b) abandon one's self, get drunk, go limp
Zone 2	a) /englobing/ /voluminous/ b) /hot/ /harmful/	a) belly, snout, guts, paunch ... b) fire, heat, agitation ...
Limit 2	/excretion/	a) ass, hole ... b) burst, empty one's self, let loose; flat broke, decrepitude ...
Zone 3	/viscous/ /yellow/, /filthy/	juice, pee, filth, pig, swill ...

The *sites* mentioned are linked by operations that are of the order of dialectics, more precisely of *molecular dialectics*: The whole group of these operations describes, according to judgments noted within the text, a process of degradation or deterioration.

a) Movement from zone 1 to zone 3 is often presented in terms of a descent: 'on entendait le liquide jeté d'un trait tomber dans la gorge, avec le bruit des eaux de pluie le long des tuyaux de descente, les jours d'orage' (you could hear the liquid, having been downed in a single shot, falling on down into the throat, making the noise of rain water tumbling down a down pipe, on stormy days) 245. Coupeau, 'versait de haut' (poured from high up) ibid.; and Poisson 'eut du succès, parce qu'en parlant du drapeau tricolore, il leva son verre très haut, le balança, et finit par le vider au fond de sa bouche grande ouverte' (was admired because while speaking of the tricolor flag, he raised his glass high, balanced it in his hand, and finally emptied it into his gaping mouth) 253. This is like the notable recurring seme of /depth/ in our passage: 'becoming empty,' 'leaning over,' 'they were fishing around.'

This descent is of course a fall: Gervaise agrees to give up her dump of a room in a wine shop, A la descente du cimetière (at the incline of the cemetery) 349. The Lorilleux take great pleasure in her tumble into degradation ('degringolade,' 85). She 'tombait au trottoir' (became a street walker) 481.

b) The process described here is not exclusively of the domain of //eating//. It is equally valid in the case of the moving crowds of workers in Paris: 'la cohue s'engouffrait dans Paris, où elle se noyait, continuellement' (the crowd was engulfed by Paris, it was drowned by the city, continuously) 11. 'Paris qui, un a un, les dévorait, par la rue béante du Faubourg-Poissonnière' (Paris that, one by one, devoured them, through the gaping street of the Faubourg-Poissonnière) 12. 'De tous les gargots, des bandes d'ouvriers sortaient ... C'était un envahissement du trottoir, de la chaussée, des ruisseaux, un flot paresseux coulant des portes ouvertes' (From all of the little eateries, bands of workers poured out. It was an invasion and takeover of the streets, streams of people, a steady flow pouring out of the open doors) 47. The slow movement of the workers is here one of the manifestations of /viscous/ (cf. 48 and 12).

c) The process can be recursive, probably because of analogies between the semic molecules of zones 1 and 3,

Mes-Bottes calls brandy 'pissat d'âne premier numéro' (donkey's piss, first rate) 295. Under the 'great copper belly' of the still, he 'aurait voulu qu'on lui soudât le serpentin entre les dents, pour sentir le vitriol encore chaud l'emplir, lui descendre jusqu'aux talons' (would have liked to have the coil welded between his teeth so that he could then feel the vitriol, still hot, filling him up, falling down into him, right to his heels) 50.

When juice flows out of the goose's derriere, Boche jokes: 'Moi, je m'abonne, murmura-t-il, pour qu'on me fasse pipi comme ça dans la bouche' (I'll sign up, he murmured, to have piss shot like that into my mouth) 243.

d) The model I have presented has two dialectical states. I have just demonstrated the first. In the second, limits 1 and 2 permutate, and the process is inverted. We see, for example, excretions coming out of the mouth: vomiting at the end of the meal, 263; vomiting from Coupeau, 305; and, around Gervaise, 'de belles fusées, des queues de renard élargies au beau milieu du pavé' (great spews, enlarged fox tails right out in the middle of the cobblestones) 467.

This allows us to understand why drunks 'ont des ordures de barbes raides et poisseuses comme des balais à pot de chambre' (have garbagy, stiff, and sticky beards like brushes for cleaning out potties) 389. And, retrospectively, we can understand why, during the meal, the eaters 'avaient des faces pareilles à des derrières' (had faces that looked like derrières) 245, and the ladies had 'une culotte encore légère, le vin pur aux joues' (rosy-coloured cheeks; culotte also means panties) 246. Complementing this, there is absorption up the (anatomical) bottom: 'Tout Paris y entrait' (All of Paris went up there) 444.

In the text, the movement from the first state to the second is significantly called a culbute (tumble; cul meaning bottom), 390.

e) As for the human actors, the cycle absorption/excretion is described as a purely passive phenomenon. For example, for Gervaise, 'le ruisseau d'eau-de-vie coulait maintenant au travers de son corps' (the stream of brandy now ran all through her body) 293.

Now, if we now move to the level of the sentence, we note, for our extract:

(i) The effacement of contents that contain the seme /animate/ in the ergative case in 'short work of the blanquette,' 'four litres were needed,' 'placed against the wall,' time to 'catch one's breath,' 'mounted upon a flat serving dish,' 'surrounded by great, round potatoes.'
(ii) The putting of the contents that in language contain the seme /inanimate/ into the nominative or ergative in 'the salad bowl was dug into,' 'that shook like jelly,' 'the bowl went around,' 'the great loaves of bread ... seemed to melt away,' 'the ass ends of the glasses being banged down onto the table,' 'that put a fire into your stomach', 'the loin arrived surrounded by a cloud of steam.'

The passivity of the eaters, emphasized by the 'activity' of the food itself, gives a lot of readers, including many pupils, an impression of dehumanization, both moral and physical. And this impression is an effect, especially, of the very semantic structure of the utterances. This passivity of the human actors can be linked to the deterministic thesis of hereditary predestination, one that Zola demonstrated throughout the whole of the Rougon-Macquart cycle.

6. *A Grouping of Specific Isotopies*

The associative network has brought to light the recurrences of a semic molecule. These recurrences show us a bundling together of specific isotopies for which I use the symbol i_4.

The interpretive capacity of i_4 is great because it allows us to re-interpret certain contents already classed under i_1. If we return to the table on 127, we find that i_4 classes sememes that belong to the domain of //eating// just as, for that matter, it classes sememes that belong to yet other domains: i_4 thus allows us to interpret the contents of i_1, whereas the inverse is not so. In that respect, the interpretative capacity of i_4 is greater than that of i_1.

At this point in my analysis it is appropriate temporarily to suspend description. Without claiming that it has been completed, it seems to me to be at the least illusory to try to find in that text other specific or generic isotopies that might have an extensive interpretative capacity. None the less it has been suggested to me that 'what a hole in the blanquette' and 'drown that mother (of a blanquette)' were of an erotic isotopy. It is true, however, that, seen in the context of the text as a whole, the interpretative capacity of an erotic isotopy seems limited. On the other hand, i_4 seems much more powerful in this respect. For example, it just as readily brings together contents that one can consider to be erotic (cf. 'Jamais elle n'aurait cru que le nom Lantier lui causerait une pareille chaleur au creux de l'estomac' [She would never have believed that the name Lantier would install such a hot spell in the pit of her stomach]) as it does others that one can consider to be economic (cf. 'Il se faisaient des trous chez elle, l'argent avait l'air de fondre' [certain lacks were developing around her, the money just seemed to melt away]). That is exactly the reason for its powerful interpretative capacity, as it is also for the impression of 'profound truth' that it can instil. In order to judge the interpretative capacity of isotopies it is useful to evaluate their importance *vis-à-vis* the cohesion of the text described. If one does not do this, one runs the risk of identifying isotopies a priori and therefore finding in it only some fantasms that are the somewhat monotonous product of an over-active intelligentsia.

VII. Typology

A. The table at the top of 131 allows me to be precise about the differences between the four isotopies we have been studying.

a) *Density and Rarity*: An isotopy is said to be *dense* or *rare* according to the number of its sememe-occurrences in a given block of text in relation to the total number of sememes that make up that block of text. A partial count shows that i_2 and i_3 have a recurrence of the order of 10 per cent throughout our text and i_4 shows a rate less than 1 per cent.
b) *Extents of validity*: i_1 is valid mainly throughout chapters 3 (96–107, the wedding), 7 (221–63, Gervaise's wedding feast), and 9 (350–2, the meal following Maman Coupeau's burial). For the whole of the book i_2, i_3, and i_4 are valid, with varying degrees of density. A narrative analysis would make it possible to show that i_4 becomes more dense where we find operations whereby contents are dialectically transformed. i_1, i_2, and i_3, because of their density on the passage chosen for study, could be demonstrated there without reference to the rest of the text. On the other hand i_4, because of its rarity and its idiolectal character, can be constructed only if the process concerns the whole of the text.
c) *Instances of codification*: describing the effects of the individual norm in the text pre-supposes describing the effects of the other instances. In that respect, i_4 can be seen as a fundamental, basic isotopy.

number	Semes making up isotopies	Types of isotopies	Presence of grammemes	Dominant type of semes	Extent of validity of the isotopy	Instance of principal codification
1	/eating/	generic	–	generic inherent	partial dense	linguistic system
2	/intensity/	specific	+	specific inherent	total dense	linguistic system
3	/vulgarity/	specific	+	specific afferent	total dense	social norms
4	/hot/ /yellow/ /viscous/ /harmful/	specific in a grouping	–	specific (inherent and afferent)	total rare	idiolectal norm

Because i_1 and i_3 are valid for the whole of the text, without however presupposing a knowledge of that text, they offer the most pedagogical possibilities and pupils will easily be able to find them elsewhere in the text.

We have seen that i_1 is the locus for referential impression. Therefore, establishing i_1, i_2, and i_3 makes it possible partially to re-define the naturalism usually credited to Zola, by making reference to the features of /reality/, /intensity/, /vulgarity/.

B. This chapter has presented three main aspects of different importance respectively:

a) The microsemantic description of a short extract, using isotopic analysis. This description rejected, in the event, the limits normally placed of on the 'explication de texte.' To the extent that it is scientific, or at least rational, it was able to predict interpretive paths proper to naïve readers and it was able to account for the unity and diversity of those readers.
b) The readings of those pupils gave rise to observations of sociological and psychological natures, which remain incidental, because we do not wish here to enter the domains of sociolinguistics or psycholinguistics.
c) The main thing in my view was, despite all, not specific to the text studied. It had to do: (i) with describing the elementary operations of interpretation represented by the actualization of inherent semes and by the construction of afferent semes; (ii) with formulating the conditions for these operations as a function of norms that are both linguistic and non-linguistic. If there remains much to be done, at least it is a step toward constituting a model for interpretative competence.

11

Daddy Hen

If your hen wants to be a cock, if your wife wants to be the master ...

Anonymous (17th century)

Toine[1]

I

Old man Toine was known for miles around, big Toine, Toine-ma-Fine, Antoine Mâcheblé, who was called Brûlot, the taverner of Tournevent.

He had made the little hamlet famous, the hamlet that was hidden away in a fold in the gully that went on down to the ocean, a poor peasant hamlet with ten Norman houses surrounded by ditches and trees.

They were there, those houses, huddled up against each other in that grass- and gorse-covered ravine, behind the curve in the small valley that was the source of its name, Tournevent (turn-the-wind). They looked as if they had sought shelter in that hole in the ground, like birds that hide in furrows on stormy days, a shelter against the strong ocean wind, the off-shore wind, hard and salt, which works at you and burns like fire, dries and destroys like a winter's freeze.

But the whole hamlet seemed to be the property of Antoine Mâcheblé, called also Brûlot, Antoine who was, indeed, as often called Toine and Toine-ma-Fine, because of a phrase that he constantly used:

'My Fine is the best in France.' His Fine was his cognac, of course.

For twenty years he had been showering the area with his Fine and his brûlots (burning brandy), for whenever he was asked: 'What am I going to drink, daddy Toine?' he would invariably answer: 'A brûlot, my son-in-law, it heats your guts and clears your head; there's nothing better for the body.'

He also had this habit of calling everyone 'son-in-law,' even though he had never had a married daughter, or, indeed, a daughter to marry off.

Ah! Yes, he was well-known, Toine Brûlot, the biggest man of the canton, and even of the arrondissement. His little house seemed absurdly too small and narrow and squat to hold him, and when you saw him standing erect in his doorway, where he spent whole days, you would wonder how he was able to enter his home. He went in every time a drinking client came there because he had, as he saw it, a rightful standing invitation to have a little glass of anything drunk in his place.

His café carried the sign *Au Rendez-vous des Amis* (The Friends' Meeting Place), and indeed he was, was old man Toine, the friend of all around. People came from Fécamp and from Montivilliers, to see him and laugh upon listening to him because he could have made a tombstone laugh, that big guy. He had a way of teasing people without angering them, of winking to express what he didn't say in words, of tapping his thigh when carried away with fun and every time he would drag laughter out of your belly in spite of yourself. And indeed it was a wonder just to watch him drink. He drank as much as was offered him, and he would drink anything, with happiness shining in his cunning eyes, a happiness born of his twofold pleasure, the pleasure of treating himself, and the fun of gathering up a whole lot of money.

The jokers of the area would ask him: 'Why don't you drink the ocean, old Toine?'

He would answer: 'Two reasons – first, it's salt water, and second, it would have to be bottled, because my belly isn't supple enough to be able to drink from *that* glass.'

And then, you really had to hear him quarrelling with his wife! It was such high drama that you'd willingly have paid to see it. They had been married thirty years, and they argued every day. Only Toine was having fun, but his wife would get mad. She was a tall peasant woman, with the long stride of a shore bird and carrying, atop her flat, scrawny body, the head of an angry screech owl. She spent her time raising chickens in a little yard behind the cabaret, and she was famous for the way she could fatten up her chickens.

When a meal for the 'higher ups' was given in Fécamp, for it to be really successful, one of old lady Toine's little charges had to be on the menu.

But she was born in a terrible mood and she just kept on being discontented with everything. Angry at the whole world, she particularly had it in for her husband. She resented his fun, his fame, his health, and his stoutness. She called him a good-for-nothing because he earned money without working for it. She called him a slob because he ate and drank like ten men, and never a day went by that she didn't say, with exasperation: 'He'd be better off in a pigsty, pig that he is! He is so fat, he is disgusting.' She'd shout into his face: 'Just you wait! You'll see! You'll burst like a seed bag, you bloated slob!'

Toine would laugh uproariously, patting his belly and answering: 'Hey there, Mother Chicken, my little board, try to fatten up your chickies like that, try and see what it's like.' And drawing a sleeve up his enormous arm: 'Now there's a wing, old lady, there's a wing.'

And his clients would bang on the tables and shake with laughter, stomp their feet and spit on the ground in their delirious fun. The furious old lady would start again: 'Just you wait, just you wait. You'll see, you'll burst like a seed bag.'

Toine, indeed, was wondrous to behold, he had become so thick and fat, red-faced and out of breath. He was one of those enormous people that death seems to toy with, with tricks, jokes, and sinister buffoonery so that its slow destruction is made to appear irresistibly funny. Instead of showing itself the way it does with others, in white hair, thin bodies, wrinkles, inexorable wasting away that leads one to say: 'Damn it all! Has he ever changed,' in Toine's case that bitch death seemed to take pleasure in fattening him up and making him funny and monstrous at the same time, colouring him in reds and blues, blowing him up, giving him the appearance of superhuman health. The deformities death visits upon all others were, in him, funny, a riot, entertaining, rather than being sinister and pitiful.

'Just you wait, just you wait,' old lady Toine would repeat, 'you'll see.'

II

Eventually Toine suffered an attack and was paralysed. They laid him out, this colossus, in a little room that was partitioned off from the café. This way he could hear what was being said out there and he could chat with his friends, 'cause his mind was clear, although his body, a huge body, which he couldn't move or raise up, was immobile. It was hoped, at first, that his great legs would again gain strength, but this hope soon evaporated and Toine-ma-Fine spent his days and nights in his bed. They made his bed up only once a week, thanks to the help of four neighbours who would raise him by his four limbs while someone turned his mattress over.

He remained in good spirits, however, but with a different kind of fun, more timid, more humble, with a childlike fear of his wife who squawked all day:

'Look at that big slob, look at that good-for-nothing, layabout, drunken sot. You asked for it, you asked for it!'

He no longer answered. He would only wink behind her back and then turn over, the only movement that he could still pull off. He called this exercise a 'flip-to-the-north' or a 'flip-to-the-south.'

His big entertainment now was to listen to the conversations going on in the café, and to talk through the wall when he recognized the voices of friends. He would cry out: 'Hey! my son-in-law, is that you, Célestin?'

And Célestin Maloisel would answer: 'It's me, old man Toine. Are you hopping about, big bunny?'

Toine-ma-Fine would say: 'No hopping yet. But I'm not thin yet, I'm sound.'

He soon began to have his closest friends in his room and they kept him company, even though he was sad to see them drinking without him. He would say: 'I really mourn not drinking with you, son-in-law, not sipping my Fine, damn it all. As for the rest, I'm okay, but not being able to drink, that I mourn.' At that point old lady Toine's screech-owl head would appear at the window and she'd screech: 'Just look, look at him, this big layabout that I have to feed, wash, and rub down like a big old pig.'

And then when she had gone, a red-plumed rooster would sometimes jump up to the window, look into the room with his round and curious eye, and then crow sonorously. Sometimes too, one or two hens would fly over to the foot of the bed, looking for crumbs on the floor.

Toine-ma-Fine's friends soon gave up sitting in the main room of the café and instead, every afternoon, gathered to chat around the big man's bed. Even laid out in bed like that, that jokester Toine entertained them well. That old fart could have made the devil laugh. Three friends especially came every day: Célestin Maloisel, a tall, thin man, twisted a little like the trunk of an apple tree, Prosper Horslaville, a wizened-up, ferret-nosed little man, full of malice and sly as a fox, and Césaire Paumelle, who never spoke, but who had fun anyway.

They would bring a board in from the yard, place it on the edge of the bed, and they would play dominoes, for God's sake, long games, from two in the afternoon to six.

But soon old lady Toine became unbearable. She couldn't stand to see her big old layabout of a man having fun, playing dominoes in his bed, and every time she saw a game starting up, she'd leap onto it in a fury, overturn the board, grab the pieces and board, take the game back into the café, declaring all along that it was all she could bear to have to feed that big do-nothing slob without having to watch him having fun, thumbing his nose at the poor people that had to work all day.

Célestin Maloisel and Césaire Paumelle would lower their heads, but Prosper Horslaville would annoy her further, finding fun in her anger.

Seeing her one day more exasperated than usual, he said: 'Hey, old lady, you know what I'd do, in your place?' She waited for his explanation, staring at him with her owl eyes. He started again: 'He's as hot as a stove, your old man, from being in bed so long. If it were me, I would have him cover eggs.' She stood stupefied, while he teased her, staring at the thin, tricky face of the peasant, who continued: 'I'd put five under one arm, another five under the other, while on the same day giving eggs to a hen to cover. Both sets would hatch. When they were hatched, I'd take your old man's to your hen for her to raise. That'd give you a lot of chickies, eh, old lady.' The dumbfounded old lady asked: 'Can this be?' 'Well, why not? Since we have hens sit on eggs in a warm little box, we can have them covered in a bed just as well.' She was quite struck by this logic and took off, calm and reflective.

Eight days later she came into Toine's room with an apron full of eggs and said: 'I've just set up the yellow hen to sit on ten eggs. Here are ten for you. Try not to break them.' Toine, bewildered, asked: 'What is it you want?' She answered: 'You're to cover them and hatch them, good-for-nothing.' First he laughed, but then, as she insisted, he absolutely refused to put this seed of future chickens under his arm, presumably so that they would hatch under his body heat. But the furious old lady shouted: 'You'll have nothing to eat until you take them. We'll see.' The worried Toine said nothing. When he heard noon being struck, he called out: 'Is my soup ready?' The old lady shouted from the kitchen: 'There's no soup for you, you fat do-nothing.' He believed she was joking and waited, then asked, begged, swore, tossed, and turned with desperate 'flips-to-the-north' and 'flips-to-the-south,' banged his fist on the wall, but he had to resign himself and allow five eggs into his bed, up against his left side. Then he got his soup.

Then the daily domino game began. But Toine seemed not really to have his heart in it and would reach out only slowly and tentatively.

'Is your arm tied down then?' asked Horslaville. Toine answered: 'I seem to have a heaviness in my left shoulder.' Suddenly, they heard people coming into the café. It was the mayor and his deputy. They asked for two glasses of Fine and began to chat about the affairs of the region. Because they were talking in a low voice, Toine Brûlot tried to put his ear up to the wall and, forgetting the eggs, he carried out a quick 'flip-to-the-north' that ended him up in an omelette.

Old lady Toine came running at the sound of his swearing, guessed at what disaster had befallen the eggs, and uncovered him with one swipe. She first stood utterly still, suffocating with fury and unable to talk in the face of the yellow cataplasia that plastered her husband's side.

Then shaking with fury, she leapt onto the poor paralysed man and began to hammer him on the belly, as she used to do to her laundry, by the pond. Her hands rose and fell with dull thuds. Her fists flashed like the paws of a rabbit drumming on a drum.

Toine's three friends laughed themselves breathless, coughing and sneezing, crying out, and the big guy, in his alarm, tried to parry his wife's attacks, but carefully, so that he wouldn't break the other five eggs on the other side.

III

Toine was defeated. He had to cover the eggs and hatch them, he had to give up his dominoes, keep quite still, because the ferocious old lady kept his food from him every time he broke an egg.

He kept on his back, eyes fixed on the ceiling, quite still, with his arms raised like wings, warming with his body heat these white-shelled seeds of chicken life.

He spoke only in a low voice as if he were as afraid of noise as he was of movement, and he was worried about the yellow hen, sitting on her eggs, carrying out the same assignment as he was.

He would ask his wife: 'Did the yellow hen eat last night?' and the old lady would go from her hens to her man and from her man to her hens, obsessed and preoccupied by the chicks that were growing in both bed and nest.

Those around who knew the story would come there in their grave curiosity, and would ask for news of Toine. They would silently enter his room as you do when entering a sick person's room, and they'd ask: 'So? How's it going?' Toine would answer: 'Not bad, but I hate the way this overheats me. It feels like ants crawling up and down my skin.'

Now, one morning, his wife came in, quite moved, and said: 'The yellow hen has hatched seven of her eggs. Three of the eggs were bad.' Toine felt his heart beating. He wondered how many chicks he would hatch. He asked: 'Will it be soon?' with the anguish of a woman about to give birth.

The old lady answered furiously, tormented as she was by the fear of possible failure: 'Probably.'

They waited. His friends, having been alerted that the time was near, soon arrived. They too were worried.

People around talked about nothing else. They'd go each next door, asking for news.

Around three o'clock, Toine got sleepy. He was now sleeping away half the day. He was suddenly awakened by something unfamiliar tickling him under his right arm. With his left hand he grabbed a little beast covered in yellow down, and it wriggled in his fingers.

He was so moved that he began to cry out, and he let go of the chick, which began to run round and round his chest. The café was full. The drinkers rushed in, filled the room, formed a circle around him as if he were a performing acrobat, and the old lady, having arrived on the scene, carefully grabbed up the little beast that had huddled up under her husband's beard.

Everyone was silent. It was a hot April day. Through the open window they could hear the yellow hen clucking, calling her newborns.

Toine, sweating with emotion, anguish, worry, murmured: 'I have another under my left arm now.'

His wife plunged her big skinny hand into the bed and brought out a second chick, with the careful movements of a midwife.

The neighbours wanted to see. The chick was handed around, receiving the attentive observations you'd expect for a real phenomenon.

For twenty minutes no more were born, then four emerged from their shells at the same time.

There was much excitement among the onlookers. And Toine smiled, content with his success, taking pride in this single-handed paternity. Not many like him had been seen before eh! Quite a man, after all.

He said: 'That's six. Goddamn, what a baptism!'

And a great roar of laughter rose from the crowd. Others were filling up the café. Yet more people were waiting outside the doors. They wanted to know: 'How many were there?' 'There are six.'

Old lady Toine brought this new family to the hen and the hen clucked in bewilderment, her feathers stood on end, and she spread her wings out to shelter her growing troop of chicks.

'There's another,' cried Toine.

He was wrong, there were three more. It was a triumph. The last broke open his shell at seven in the evening. All the eggs had hatched. And Toine, crazy with happiness, delivered of his task, glorying in it all, kissed the frail little animal on the back, almost smothering it with his lips. He wanted to keep it in his bed, until the next day, so seized was he by maternal tenderness for this little thing whom he had given to life. But the old lady took it away like the others with no ear for her husband's supplications.

The audience, utterly carried away, left, talking over the event, and Horslaville, who was the last to go, asked: 'So? Daddy Toine, I'll be the first you invite to your chicken fry, no?'

At this idea of chicken fricassée, Toine's face lit up and the fat guy answered: 'Of course I'll invite you, son-in-law.'

A study of this text makes it possible to illustrate the relationship between narrative analysis (which has to do with dialectics) and isotopic analysis (which has to do with thematics).

I. Dialectics

First of all I shall segment the text into three episodes that correspond more or less to the three parts of the short story. In no way do I claim to present an extensive narrative analysis, based on a complete inventory of its thematized graphics; that would require a whole book.

1. The First Episode

The Actors

For now, let us concentrate on the three main actors:[2] a) Toine (without yet distinguishing between the various names he has and the various descriptions of him); b) his wife ('the old lady,' 'his wife,' etc.); c) the peasants. This actor is sometimes designated collectively, sometimes partitively, sometimes distributively: *on*, *le pays*, *un consommateur*, *la contrée*, *les gens*, *les farceurs du pays*, *les consommateurs*, *des buveurs*, etc. (they, the area, a drinking client, the surrounding area, people, the jokers from around there, clients, drinkers, etc.).

The other actors, like the upper-crust people, the chickens, alcohol, will be mentioned only as needed.

Exchanges and Initial State of Lack

The exchange of alcohol is the rule between Toine and the peasants (lines 16–27):[3] 'He had been showering the area with his Fine and his brûlots.' In exchange Toine-ma-Fine 'had, as he saw it, a rightful standing invitation to have a little glass of anything drunk in his place.'

This exchange of alcohol is paralleled by an exchange of pleasures (lines 28–37): 'il vous tirait le rire du ventre ... une joie qui venait de son double plaisir' (he would drag laughter out of your belly ... a happiness born of his twofold pleasure). The valorization of this exchange is what creates Toine's fame (cf. lines 1–2).[4]

None the less, the sale of alcohol is an unequal exchange because, beyond making big money on it, Toine keeps back enough to drink all he can hold (see 'his twofold pleasure,' line 36). The word *rightful* (line 26) focuses attention on the illegitimate nature of the pretaste he would always take. According to practice that has always been observed in France, the owner of a drinking establishment has always been expected to stand his paying customers to a drink.

Toine thus receives more than he gives, and his great girth illustrates the advantage he secures for himself in this unequal exchange.[5]

Enough about drink, let us look now at food. Old lady Toine not only fattens her chickens, but her husband also ('he ate ... like ten men'): hence the comparison with a pig (line 54).[6] Now, Toine gives her nothing in exchange and, in particular, he has never given her a child (cf. lines 20–1).[7] His nickname for her, *ma planche* (my little board, line 57), suggests an obvious absence of bosom.

Note: The homonymy between *mé* for 'mer' (ocean) and *mé* for 'mère' (mother) allows us to think that Toine does not *consomme* (French write 'consummate' and 'consume' in the same way) his marriage. A propos of *mé* 'mer,' he concludes: 'my belly isn't supple enough to be able to drink from *that* glass' (line 40). 'And *then*, you really had to hear him quarrelling with his wife' (line 41).[8]

Toine is thus a debtor *vis-à-vis* his wife and the peasants. The names he uses on others demonstrate the nature of his debts: (i) he calls his wife *la mé* (Mom), even though he has never had a child with her; (ii) 'He also had this habit of calling everyone "son-in-law," even though he had never had a married daughter, or, indeed, a daughter to marry off.' Thus he owes daughters to men seen collectively.

The areas in which he is to be found wanting thus go from matrimony to parenthood. This imbalance we see in the case of matrimonial exchanges echoes the imbalance we see in his economic exchanges. Such is his initial state of lacking – relative to the system of social values – which the story eventually will redress.

Note: The almost Lévi-Straussian tone of this first part of my analysis should not surprise the reader. Only after a 'classic' narrative analysis of a text can we characterize its various internal versions.

Confrontation and Conflict
The old lady takes the initiative in laying down the challenge that begins the process by which the initial lack will be corrected. She does so by repeating an 'animalizing' threat ('He'd be better off in a pigsty ...' [line 54]), and a threat of death ('you'll burst ...' [line 55]).[9] Toine answers with a challenge that also is of an animal isotopy, 'try to fatten up your chickies like that,' 'now there's a wing' (lines 57–9).[10] The people from around there reinforce the provocational nature of this challenge with their laughter (in their delirious fun). The subsequent conflict pits Toine against death. We see only the attack carried out by death (lines 64–72). Nothing is said about Toine's resistance against this attack; or rather we can say that the *counterattack* function provided for by the narrative model alluded to above is 'replaced' by the empty space separating the first two parts of the story. The consequence of the conflict is manifested (line 75).[11] The test comes to an end, classically, through a displacement (lines 75–82).

One can thus think that the old lady and death are two actors of the same agonistic order:

(i) They carry out the same fattening-up process: the old lady 'was famous for the way she could fatten up her chickens' (line 46). Death, for its part, 'seemed to take pleasure in fattening him [Toine] up' (line 68). Furthermore, death generally manifests itself in 'thin bodies' (lines 67–8) and the old lady has a 'flat, scrawny body' (lines 44–5).[12] Correlative to that, Toine compares himself to a chicken (cf. 'a wing,' lines 58–9). Thus we have:

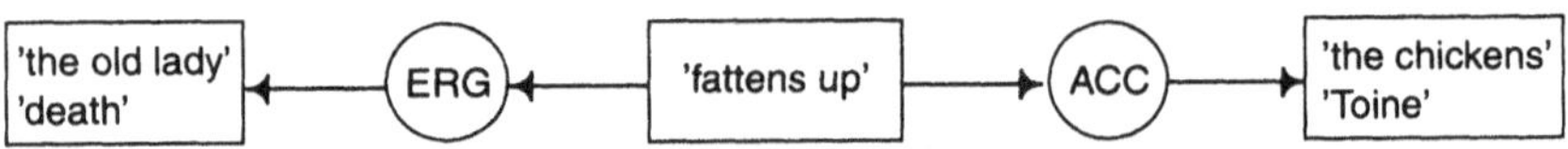

The connection between the old lady and death is, in this case, of a symbolic type, whereas that between Toine and the chickens is of a metaphorical nature. The second adds to the plausibility of the first.

(ii) Further, the narrative roles of the old lady and of death complement each other: within the context of the same test, one takes the initiative *vis-à-vis* confrontation, and the other *vis-à-vis* conflict.

The validity of the above is seen when death realizes the old lady's threats. The description of death's ravages is indeed set off between two instances of *just you wait* (lines 55 and 61–2).[13] The threat of being changed into a pig (line 54) is realized after Toine's attack (cf. 'this big layabout that I have to feed, wash, and rub down like a big old pig,' lines 100–1).

2. *The Second Episode*

The beginning of this episode (lines 83–114) repeats the beginning of the first episode, but on an iterative mode (cf. 'more timid, more humble,' lines 83–4).

The Taming of Toine

Deprived of all movement,[14] Toine continues his social exchanges with the peasants, but only three of them come to see him regularly: he talks, but he is laid out in bed and he has to talk 'through the wall' (line 91), no longer 'standing erect in his doorway' (line 24). He makes them laugh, but less so ('even laid out in bed like that [...] Toine entertained them' lines 107–8). They still all have fun, but playing dominoes, a harmless little game if ever there was one.[15] The unequal exchange of alcohol has come to an end, or rather, we now have the inverse: whereas in the first episode Toine drank more than the peasants, now he mourns the fact that he sees them drinking without him (line 97). This is one stage on the way to cancelling out the initial lack. But through his repeated old 'son-in-law' phrase (lines 92 and 98), Toine continues to present himself in terms of being one who owes daughters to men, seen as a group.

The confrontation between Toine and the old lady is also repeated, but on an inferative mode as far as Toine is concerned ('he would only wink behind her back,' line 87). This battle that opposes their respective strengths grows greater, and goes against him because the old lady does not lose her anger. Toine's debt to her in fact has grown greater: he no longer earns any money, he takes up her time, and he is more unable than ever to have a child with her.[16] Even though they are limited, his social exchanges with those from around there – and in particular the engrossing game of dominoes – are an obstacle to the cancelling out of his debt to the old lady. So, she moves into action and '*overturn[s]* the *board*' (line 117).[17] The egg-sitting she is going to make him take on is incompatible with this game. Toine 'would reach out only slowly and tentatively' (line 147). But this egg sitting is a way to make him productive (economically), and in a way offers a means for him to cancel out his matrimonial and fathering debts.

The Mission

Here the group of peasants splits and they have to choose between two narrative roles: gently giving in, in the manner of Toine now, ('Célestin Maloisel and Césaire Paumelle would lower their heads' [line 121]), or continuing to provoke the old *mé* ('Prosper Horslaville would annoy her further, finding fun in her anger' [line 122]). Prosper separates himself from the group of peasants and advises the old lady to make Toine's idleness productive and to transform his bed, the locus of laziness (enforced), into a locus of procreation.[18] In carrying out this typical helper (adjuvant) role, Prosper makes it possible for a new test to begin.

The confrontation now takes the form of an enforced contract. The old lady forces Toine to use his arms as wings and to bring the eggs to hatch. She thereby establishes a socially equitable exchange: work (performed by the husband) for food (cooked by the wife).[19] This forced contract becomes an obstacle between Toine and the peasants: we saw this in the case of the dominoes game. This is especially evident when Toine (one they had only recently been coming to *listen* to [line 30]), breaks the eggs when turning over in bed in order better to be able to listen to news of the area (line 151). The old lady's reaction marks the beginning of the conflict that follows the forced contract.[20] This conflict has analogies with the conflict of the first episode: Toine suffers *attacks* (line 162) and cannot defend himself.[21] The first lines of the third part of the story present the consequences of the conflict.

3. *The Third Episode*

It begins this way, with a slight gap between tactical and dialectical structures.[22]

Toine's Prowess (lines 167–207)
The animal actor 'the eggs,' introduced during the preceding episode, was in that episode the object of a forced, imposed transmission. Here it becomes Toine's receiver (sender – receiver) with Toine giving his warmth to it. This forced gift – the giving having been imposed by the old lady – appears as a correcting of the unequal exchange of the first episode. Alcohol and warmth are interchangeable in this text; the nickname Brûlot (burning brandy) (see lines 2, 13, 18) brings together both contents and it is again used to designate Toine when he begins to cover the eggs (line 151). But if we are going to be able legitimately to speak of correcting an imbalance of exchange, we would have to be able to show that the chicks and the peasants are two actors of the same agonistic order. Now, we cannot at this point so state (see pages 150ff).

Indeed, through her order ('[Toine] had to cover the eggs,' line 164), the old lady picks up and carries through on the challenge proffered by Toine in the first episode: 'Now there's a wing' (line 58) is countered now by 'arms raised like wings' (lines 167–8) and the 'like that' of 'try to fatten up your chickies like that' (line 57) can now receive a new reading, not just as a comparative ('like my arm') but instrumentally ('with my arm'). Finally, the insulting comparison 'like a seed bag' (lines 55 and 62) is somehow validated: Toine in a way holds 'this seed of future chickens' (line 138) or 'white-shelled seeds of chicken life' (line 168).[23]

The successful answering of the initial challenge allows us to anticipate a cancelling out of the initial lack, in conformity with the 'chiasmic' structure that we frequently see in folk-tales:[24]

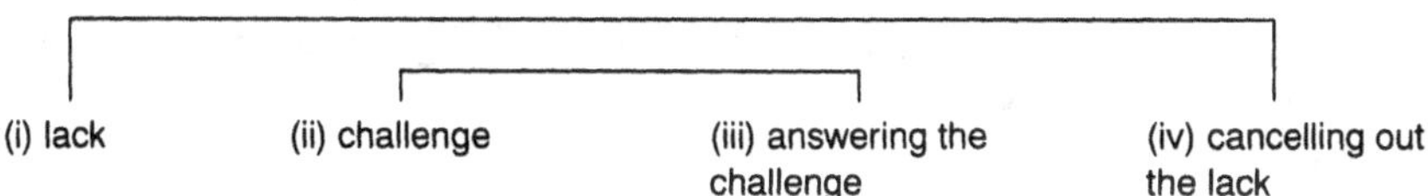

The story of the demonstration of prowess that cancels out the lack can be divided into two sections:

A. The competition with the yellow hen is a negative or derisory form of confrontation (cf. line 170, 'and he was worried about the yellow hen'). That competition, of course, includes a challenge (articulated by the old lady: 'The yellow hen has hatched seven of her eggs,' lines 180–1), and a threat (cf. 'anguish,' line 182).

At this point in the story, the antithetical characterizations that set Toine in opposition to his wife in the preceding episodes are suspended; the two are described in the same way to the extent that they share the same emotions: 'His wife came in, quite moved' (line 180) and 'Toine felt his heart beating' (line 181). To Toine's anguish (line 182), there corresponds the 'fear' that torments the old lady (line 184).

This parity that is finally established between Toine and his wife installs a paradoxical correction whose explanation we can see: Toine had never made his wife fruitful, but she makes him 'fruitful' by setting the eggs to hatch under his arms.

Another correction to imbalance takes place. The epistemic exchanges between Toine and the peasants that marked the beginning of the story (lines 1–5 and 22–5) are taken up again: people come now, not out of curiosity ('It was a wonder just to watch him drink' [line 34]), but rather 'in their grave curiosity' (line 175), to watch him keeping the eggs warm.[25]

Note: On the tactical level, the competition between Toine and the yellow hen, and then the visits by the peasants from around there, are described in short alternating paragraphs that follow the scheme *a b a b*. They present a progressive intensification (lines 169–74, 175–9, 180–5, 186–8).

B. The second section describes the conflict that follows the confrontation, that is, the act of prowess itself and its consequences. It is divided into five groups, graduated in intensity: (i) lines 189–97, (ii) lines 198–207, (iii) lines 208–11, (iv) lines 212–17, (v) lines 218–28. Typically their structure involves interactions of three kinds.

a) The exchange between Toine and the chicks can be schematized as follows: he gives them life (line 223); he thereby comes to feel great emotion (lines 193, 200, 220), being 'crazy with happiness.'
b) As for those from around there, Toine provides a spectacle for them ('the drinkers rushed in, filled the room, formed a circle around him as if he were a performing acrobat' [lines 194–5]; see also lines 196, 205); he is covered with glory by these events ('It was a triumph'; he is 'glorying in it' [lines 219, 221]). For him, it is a restoration of his initial popularity.

Note: If one could in a univocal way code these narrative exchanges as we can for a folk-tale, the first exchange would correspond to the main test, and the second to the glorifying test.

c) Interaction with the old lady is reduced to a case of a forced act of giving on his part: she gathers up the chicks and carries them away 'with no ear for her husband's supplications' (line 224). This sanction, a negative one for Toine, is positive for her – according to the system of social values: she receives her due from Toine, first in terms of work (covering the eggs), then in terms of offspring (the chicks). These reparations correct the initial lack, that is, in so far as she is concerned.
d) Following the reparations made to the old lady (along the axis of filiation), there are reparations or contract fulfilment concerning Horslaville (along the axis of alliance). These latter take the form of a contract: upon Prosper's mandating (line 226), Toine answers with a performative acceptance: 'Of course I'll invite you, son-in-law' (lines 228–9). He thus compensates for the inequity of the initial exchanges with the peasants: he wrongfully used to take of their drink; he now extends an invitation to eat, as is fit and proper.

This last answer of Toine's, to be admired in every respect, could, because of its ambiguities, be enough to cause us to reject all of the preliminary readings we have just been reporting:

(i) Toine is happy to offer to Prosper what he has just refused his wife. A superficial psychology of the 'characters' of the story might readily account for this inconsistency by referring to Toine's naïveté.[26] We shall see how that naïveté sets into play a change of generic isotopy.

(ii) He returns to just one man, and in the form of food, the drink he owes to all.
(iii) He is quite happy at the promise of eating the 'child' he had been protecting.[27]
(iv) His payment or reparation is made to Prosper, who is the one behind the old lady's order to cover and hatch the eggs.

4. *The Code for Narrative Loci*

In order to corroborate, however, the narrative segmentation that I have just proposed, we must now study the movements of the actors, and in this we must be ready to indulge in a digression.

In the first episode, two loci are in apparent opposition to each other: the café, an open locus where social exchanges take place (Toine spends his time 'in his doorway'); and 'a little yard behind the cabaret,' a closed locus where the old lady raises her chickens. Thus two antithetical spaces are linked to Toine and his 'old lady.'

An intermediary locus, the room, appears in the second episode: one of its walls separates it from the café (he could 'listen to the conversations going on in the café' [line 90]) and the other wall has a window that looks out into the yard (line 100). The two motions the paralysed man can make, the 'flip-to-the-north' and the 'flip-to-the-south,' mark oscillations between the above polar spaces. The dominoes game might have been a way to reconcile the two spaces, since the game itself comes from the café and the board from the yard,[28] but the old lady would 'overturn the board, grab the pieces and board' (lines 117–18). Thus the contradiction between the two spaces is maintained, because when turning his body towards the café Toine crushes the eggs (which come from the yard).

The third episode brings about a reconciliation. The drinkers, who have come in from the café, 'rushed in, filled the room' (line 194). The room's opening onto the yard is now validated: 'Through the open window they could hear the yellow hen clucking' (lines 198–9).

5. *Interpretations of the Narrative Structure and Internal Versions of the Story*

Albeit the digressions we have admitted to, the narrative structure whose articulations we have briefly presented describes the evenemential level of the story.[29] This structure has to do with the dialectic component of the text and, in theory, it could be described independently of the axiologies invested in this text (and which have to do with thematic component). The principle I have invoked is, however, in no way either a postulate or an axiom. Its inspiration is a methodological reductionism that is particularly useful for my exposé, but it must be only temporary.

Indeed, even at the evenemential level of the story, in order to be able to recognize and code its functions, we must refer (implicitly or not) to the thematic component.

Certainly, most of the theories of narrative that have been developed over the past thirty years militate in favour of the formalist illusion that a story is articulated by a formal structure that is independent of the contents invested therein. But the identification of narrative 'forms' (as is the case at a lower level where we can identify phrastic forms),[30] requires a knowledge of the thematic component of the text.

Thus, the coding of graphs that are thematized into functions cannot be presented strictly in terms of its being a preliminary stage of the narrative analysis itself: it is also in a way its end point. Indeed, interpretation has no absolute beginning point: the processes by which we assign meaning are neither sequential nor linear. You have first 'to have completed' your global description of the text before you can begin the coding (local) of its functions. That is one of the forms taken by the hermeneutic circle in the area of narrative analysis, and here that circle is in no way a vicious circle.

It will not be surprising, then, if the narrative analysis that starts off this study articulates an intrinsic interpretation: such an interpretation explores the interaction between all of the text's components. And like the others, the dialectic and thematic components can be separated only temporarily and artificially.

When we studied interactions between the actors of the text, and especially the exchanges that take place between them, I highlighted initial lacks and the mediating events that brought about their eventual correction: they are what fixes the dynamics of the story.[31]

But lacks and corrections thereto can be identified only in relation to a system of values; here, one of social values. Here are its principal topoi, seen in conjunction with the universes of the two actors:

> The old lady: You have to work if you want to live. You have to have children.
> The people from the region: Men should laugh and joke together. You have to take your turn picking up the tab. You're supposed to marry off your daughters.

In relation to these topoi, we can identify corresponding agonists for the actors, according to a classical narrative grammar. At the final stage of the story, we have:

agonistic level: agonists	hero receiver	helper receiver	traitor sender	object of value
evenemential level: actors	'the old lady' 'death'	'Prosper'	'Toine'	'the chicks'

According to the coding of the agonists, we can characterize the tests in the story as follows:

In the first episode, the hero's qualifying test (one that is disqualifying for the traitor) is successfully passed by the actor 'death': it is the attack that paralyses Toine.

In the second episode, the main test is passed by 'the old lady' when, through her 'attacks,' she forces Toine to lie still and hatch the eggs.

In the third episode, she receives her compensation, the object of value, but paradoxically it is Toine who is glorified in the eyes of those from around there.

Naturally, this internal version of the story raises many problems, of which these are the main ones. Those of that region should be the ultimate receivers of the object of value: in conformity with the canonical narrative structure, the initial lack will then be cancelled out. Here, aside from Prosper (about whom it will soon be seen that he is of an agonistic order different from those from around there), the ultimate beneficiaries in all likelihood are those of the upper crust (line 47) to whom the old lady sells her chickens. This significant deviation does not however cast doubt on our first internal version of the story. Instead it confirms it.

On the other hand, one must consider it in relative terms (without rejecting it, however) because it is in relation with only one sector of the thematic and dialogic components of the text: the universe of the old lady, for the most part. Now, the narration itself rejects this version of the story. It is known that traditionally the hero, the helper, and the object of value are of the domain of positive values. The traitor is of the order of negative values. Now, although the universe of the narrator is only implicitly presented, a simple inventory of judgments made shows:

(i) The chicks are not valorized.

(ii) The old lady is explicitly devalorized ('but she was born in a terrible mood' [line 49]; 'ferocious old lady kept his food from him' [line 165]). And death, an actor of the same agonistic order, is judged likewise ('that bitch death' [line 68]).

(iii) Prosper is scarcely treated better: 'a wizened-up, ferret-nosed little man' (lines 110–11), '[he] would annoy her further' (line 122). He is in the same class.

(iv) Finally, even if you grant that the people from the area make positive judgments of Toine such as 'that jokester' (line 108), 'old fart' (meant affectionately, line 108), other descriptions such as 'poor paralysed man' (line 158) or 'the big guy, in his alarm' (line 162) can be attributed only to the narrator. Although not positive, they are not unfavourable either.[32]

This would bring us to yet another coding:

agonists	hero	opposer	traitor	object
actors	'Toine'	'the old lady'	'Prosper'	'the chicks'

According to this coding, the initial lack would be caused by the attack. The old lady's blackmail would be the qualifying test. The covering of the eggs would be the main test and the successful hatching of them would be the glorifying test (that gives Toine back his celebrity status and reestablishes his euphoric exchanges with people from the area [lines 208–11]).

This other internal version fits well with the facts of the text. For example, the roles of 'traitor' are quite suited to Prosper (see his ruse, 'trickery' [line 127]) and his way of fooling the hero make him the final receiver.[33]

However, I have to emphasize the paradoxical nature of the tests:

(i) The qualifying test, which usually is deemed to have been successfully carried out when the subject acquires the appropriate competence, is here concluded when the subject is in fact deprived of a capability.

(ii) The main test is described in terms of a defeat ('Toine was defeated,' line 164). So now we have an unwilling hero ('un héros malgré lui').

(iii) The glorifying test is valid only within Toine's own universe and within that of the people from the area (but not in the universes of the old lady or of the narrator). It is deemed successful not because an appropriate compensation takes place, but rather because a dispossession takes place: the contrast between a subjective success ('content with his success,' lines 208–9) and an objective failure again disqualifies the 'hero.' His invitation to Prosper confirms his naïveté. Finally, this single glorification does not erase what common sense would see as the infamous nature of this transformation of a man into an egg-covering hen.[34]

Before comparing the two internal versions of the story, versions whose general outlines I have just sketched out, let us confirm that there are not indeed any others to be found at the level chosen for this analysis.

The universe of the people from the area does not allow us to produce an internal version that is distinct from the preceding because the values of that universe are not distinct from Toine's values: laughter, fun, and games (dominoes). These masculine collective values are in opposition to the old lady's, who sees only laziness and grossness in them. Her lousy mood stands in opposition to laughter; her skinniness to good fun; and her unending work to games and play (line 45).

As for the universe of the narrator's assumptions, to the extent that we can lay it out, it does not hold any explicit values. None the less, its enunciative focus is closer to the universes of Toine and his neighbours than to that of the old lady: indeed, the old lady's words are often reported in indirect style (cf. lines 53 and 115), whereas things spoken by the neighbours are often reported in semi-indirect style (cf. 'that old fart' [line 108] and 'for God's sake!' [line 114]).[35] Finally 'that bitch,' death, (line 68) is something we can attribute only to the narrator (the whole of the rest of the paragraph is in a style whose diastratic level cannot be linked to any of the actors). The tone of this intercalated 'bitch' shows us a narrator who is closer to Toine and his neighbours.[36] He shares their judgments, in fact, despite differences in tone (compare, for example, the popular turn of phrase 'he could have made a tombstone laugh' [line 31] and the literary tone of 'risibles, cocasses, divertissants,' 'funny, a riot, entertaining' [line 71]).

Despite the differences in tone, when the narrator, from the beginning of the first episode, adopts this enunciative position close to that of the peasants, he orients the interpretation in the direction of the internal version that is linked to them. Witness the inclusive use of *on* (translated as an inclusive 'you' in line 42), and even more the use of *vous* (translated as an inclusive 'you' in line 33). The reader so represented is induced to include himself among the people of that region.[37] In fact, as a rule, an implicit contract causes readers to adopt the enunciative position of the narrator.[38]

All of this makes the second internal version of the story more 'natural' and more easily constructed. However, on the evidence, the narrator does not stick to his initial enunciative position,[39] and this dissuades the reader from contenting himself with just one internal version.

If we now compare the two versions, the obvious disparities seen in the coding of agonists such as nature and the position of the initial lack cannot hide their profound unity. In both cases, an important lack seems to have been cancelled out through a derisory compensation: although he is happy with his success, Toine remains paralysed; the old lady receives ten more chicks, no more; and the neighbours content themselves with having been treated to a spectacle. The disparity between lack and reparation obviously has to do with the substitution of chicks for what were the initial objects of value. These little animals have only a very little economic value. Their value as offspring and their matrimonial value are assuredly minimal.

From what is an apparent success,[40] we can deduce an eventual real failure (in the text's referential universe, here that of the narrator).

II. Isotopic Analysis of the Story

An internal version of a text is the result of the interaction between one part of its dialectic component and a part of its thematic component. When its dialogic component includes more than one universe, each can be the site of an internal version.

If it conforms to textual interpretants, an internal version belongs to the intrinsic interpretation of the text. In and of itself, it is a *hypotext*.[41]

Hypotexts can differ, and indeed even to the point of been irreconcilable. That gives rise to an insoluble interpretative tension that can in turn be dialecticized. The fascination exerted by certain literary or religious texts, and the determined yet seemingly unsatisfactory readings they entail, are undoubtedly in large measure due to the fact that the reader goes round and round in circles as a result of the conflictual interaction between their hypotexts.[42]

The empirical unity of a text obviously does not ensure its semantic homogeneity. Besides the fact that it is the product of several kinds of systematicity at work in each of its components, the conflicts between its hypotexts can block all attempts at constructing a global, intrinsic interpretation of that text.

1. The Animal Isotopy

What are the other internal versions of this story? Several reasons can be given for undertaking their description. In the first place the versions constructed above do not explain certain parts of the text, especially its third paragraph. Then, the presence of non-human actors such as death and the chicks obliges us to explore thematic aspects of the text beyond just the //human// dimension.

In order to identify these paradigmatic parts of the text (which syntagmatically bring about isotopies), the simplest procedure consists in laying out the class of actors. Let us begin by identifying those actors that are of the //animal// dimension.

a) Toine obviously can be substituted for a chicken, not only because he is in competition with the yellow hen, but also because other actors act, with regard to him, as if he were: 'the old lady would go from her hens to her man and from her man to her hens' (lines 172–3). Or they speak of him in an equivocal way: 'I'd take your old man's to your hen for her to raise' (lines 129–30). He describes himself likewise: 'there's a wing' (line 58).[43] He takes on the same colour as the yellow hen ('the yellow cataplasia' [line 156]). Relations of contiguity are established between him and the hens: 'one or two hens would fly over to the foot of the bed, looking for crumbs on the floor' (lines 104–5).[44]

b) The old lady, on the other hand, and conversely, can be replaced by a rooster: 'And then when she had gone, a red-plumed rooster would sometimes jump up to the window, look into the room with his round and curious eye, and then crow sonorously' (lines 102–3). As a rule, she is described in terms of a male bird (as for her sex) or as a masculine one (as for her gender). She walked 'with the long stride of a shore bird' (line 44) and carried, 'atop her flat, scrawny body, the head of an angry screech owl' (lines 44–5). She squawked like a bird: '[she] squawked all day' (line 84), 'she'd screech' (line 100), and her look is the same, 'her owl eyes' (lines 124–5) – which could be compared with the 'round' eye of the rooster.

The 'mé Poule' (Mother Chicken, lines 55–6), who is so named in a deprecatory way is in fact a 'Mother Chicken' only in terms of the /human/ isotopy and in Toine's universe. On the /animal/ isotopy and in the narrator's universe she becomes a rooster, or a male bird.

The movement from one isotopy to the other is thus accompanied by a change in sex: the woman becomes male and the man female.

c) Prosper, for his part, 'becomes' a carnivorous animal. At least he is compared to a ferret and to a fox (lines 110–11).[45] He has their 'thin, tricky face' (line 127).[46]

The fox's taste for fowl is proverbial and 'vendre la poule au renard' (selling the hen to the fox) is said when one means 'to go against someone else's interests.' Thus Prosper's request for a chicken fricassee is remotivated along the animal isotopy. We should add that his name, Horslaville (lit: outside town), is not inconsonant with a wild animal.[47] In short, the fox and Prosper are actors of the same agonistic order. Even when they are indexed upon different isotopies, they of course share common semantic features.

d) In a correlated way the animal actors are described as humans.[48] Thus the old lady's chickens are called her 'little charges' (line 48). The newborn chicks are caught by her using 'the careful movements of a midwife' (line 203). Toine cries out 'what a baptism' (line 211) and compliments himself on his 'paternity.' Finally, they constitute a 'family' (line 215).

These children are more likely girls than boys, for anyone who knows French phraseology. The Littré dictionary notes that *ma poule* (my chicken) 'is said familiarly and with friendliness when speaking to a woman or a girl.'[49] And a proverb that applies to seducers claims that 'un bon renard ne mange jamais les poules de son voisin' (a good fox never eats his neighbour's chickens). If 'eat chickens' can mean 'seduce girls,' then the *son-in-law* at the end of the story takes on new meaning.[50] Alliance in terms of the /human/ isotopy becomes predation within the /animal/ isotopy.

Note: Such doublings up of isotopies are common with Maupassant: cf. 'cette mère poule ... avait pondu ses quatre filles depuis que je ne l'avais vue' (that mother hen ... had hatched her four daughters since I had last seen her) *Contes et Nouvelles* I, 1249; or 'sa femme toute jeune, maigre, petite, pareille à une poule cayenne avec une tête mince et plate que coiffe, comme une crête, un bonnet rose. Elle a un oeil rond, étonné et colère, qui regarde de côté comme celui des volailles' (his young wife, thin, small, like a Cayenne hen with a narrow, flat head topped off, like a chicken's comb, by a pink bonnet. She has a round eye that reflects surprise and testiness and it looks out sideways, as with fowl) ibid., II, 389.

We can thus construct a new internal 'version' of the story, one that is very simple and whose evenemential level can be summed up as follows: the fox convinces the rooster to force the hen to cover and hatch eggs, and this is so that he can eventually eat the chicks produced. Despite the fact that this version is so short, the tactical disposition of its constituents, the absence in it of any dialogic component, mean that this new 'version' presents itself as an internal variation of the first version we studied along the /human/ isotopy.[51] But whereas there Prosper was a helper (adjuvant) *vis-à-vis* the old lady, here the rooster becomes the helper for the fox.

At this point we should remind ourselves that a narrative text is not identical to itself along all of its isotopies. A story, essentially, is the result of the application of a thematic sector onto a dialectical sector. By varying the nature and extension of these sectors, reading and writing can cause very different internal variations to proliferate, ones that are impossible to homologate and that can be, indeed, irreconcilable.

Neither of these two variations, the one situated along the /human/ isotopy in the first version, or the one situated along the /animal/ isotopy, gives us a satisfactory reading.

The first is global but incoherent, at least if one tries to effect a reading that is uniform along the /human/ isotopy in order to make the claim that Toine gives birth, then promises himself a meal of his children, to be shared with his neighbour. The second version is coherent but incomplete.

Thus, neither of the two versions, considered alone, is plausible. Further, as we shall see when studying their connections, the interpretative path inscribed in the text refers indefinitely to one and the other.

Since the isotopies are separated only by a fiction that is necessary to my exposition, let us examine their interrelations in order to characterize the global interpretative path. First we should compare the actors, in order to make some preliminary clarifications:

<table>
<tr><td>/human/</td><td>'Toine'</td><td>'the old lady</td><td>'Prosper'</td><td>|'children'|</td></tr>
<tr><td>/animal/</td><td>'hen'</td><td>'rooster'</td><td>'fox'</td><td>'chicks'</td></tr>
</table>

(i) Toine and the yellow hen can be considered as two actors of the same agonistic order. Their juxtaposition in the text marks an interlacing of the two isotopies.
(ii) The names assigned to the animal actors are chosen because of their stereotypical nature. The label 'screech owl' is given to the old lady as is 'ferret' to Prosper. But too much emphasis on these names would mask certain semantic relations.[52]
(iii) |'children'| is obtained by rewriting 'chicks' along the /human/ isotopy.

Remarkable interrelations between the two isotopies present themselves as follows:

(i) Their *connections* are metaphorical (marked by equative contexts: syntactic parallelisms, isophonies, enclosings, contiguities in the fictive referent). The exception is the |'children'| <---> 'chicks' connection, which is of a symbolic nature.

Note: The fact that |'children'| is not lexicalized in the text might be a confirmation that the initial lack in this story has to do with the couple's sterility. None the less, along the /animal/ isotopy, the rooster certainly makes the hen fruitful by placing the 'seed of future chickens' under his arms.[53] The two thus reach the maximum fertility, so to speak, a score of ten out of ten, producing ten chicks from ten eggs.

(ii) The /human/ isotopy *dominates* the /animal/ isotopy. The first, which establishes the global referential impression, is a *comparing* one. The second is *compared*.[54]

(iii) As for the place on the evaluative hierarchy of these two isotopies, we see the inverse of dominance. Ordinarily, the //human// semantic dimension is judged positively in relation to the //animal// dimension.[55] Here, the inverse is in effect for Toine (who is proud of his production (line 209) as indeed it is also for his neighbours, who accord him a triumph (line 219). One might legitimately think that this inversion indicates the narrator's derision: such would be the case in a reading that a priori valorized the /human/ isotopy. But on the one hand we have seen that the enunciative focal point of the narrator was close to that of Toine and of his neighbours. And, on the other hand, very often in Maupassant animals have the good role and men the bad role. I cannot develop that point here, but novels such as *Coco* (I, 1038 ff) or *La peur* (I, 600–1) are convincing on that score. Evil animals such as the parrot in *Le noyé* (II, 1038–9) get their powers from humans.

More precisely, men have the negative characters that we attribute to animals (brutality, ferocity, etc.), whereas animals show 'human' values that we deem positive (love, fidelity, tolerance, etc.). That is why they are constantly compared with each other: these comparisons reveal their respective 'profound' truth.

For example, the 'maternal tenderness' (line 223) that Toine feels is in direct relation with the role of hen that corresponds to him along the /animal/ isotopy:

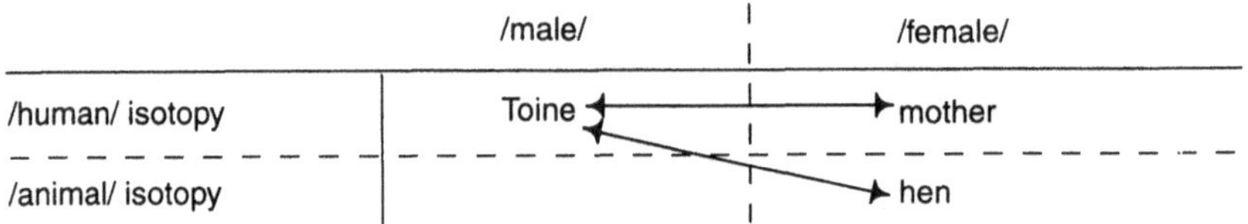

The 'Toine'/'mother' relation is a non-metaphorical comparison.[56] The 'Toine'/ 'hen' relation is a metaphorical connection (albeit implicit). But both bring about the same result: they inhibit the /male/ feature in the semantic description of 'Toine', that is, in less technical terms, they negate his virility.

Note: Here we can redefine the *être* vs *paraître* opposition, which is sometimes unwisely used in semiotics.[57] *Paraître*, in a given dialectical interval, is made up of all of the contents that, having already been actualized, are now inhibited (in particular when those contents belong neither to the universe of reference, nor to textual truth). *Etre* is thus made up of all of the inhibiting features at one given moment (in particular when they belong both to the universe of reference and to textual truth).

The main rewritings of one isotopy into another can thus be summed up as the following table shows.

/human/ isotopy *paraître*		/animal/ isotopy *être*
a) 'man'	⟶	/'female'/
b) 'father'	⟶	'mother'
b) 'woman'	⟶	/'male'/
c) /'sterility'/	⟶	/'fruitfulness'/
d) /'predation'/	⟶	'tenderness'
e) /'alliance'/	⟶	/'filiation'/
f) 'fun'	⟶	'serious'
g) 'nastiness'	⟶	'calm'
h) /'disqualification'/	⟶	/'qualification'/

These rewritings affect different actors. They require some further clarifications: d) Toine feels tenderness (line 223) and promises himself a chicken fry (line 228); e) to the alliance promised by the repeated 'son-in-law' phrase within the human isotopy there corresponds a filiation *vis-à-vis* the animal isotopy; f) the people from around there come to have fun (line 30) but they are serious (line 175); g) the old lady calms down (lines 132–3).; h) Toine's paralysis qualifies him for dispensing animal body heat. These rewritings, far from weakening the cohesion of each isotopy, in fact strengthen it. Indeed they show the hierarchical superiority of the /animal/ isotopy over the /human/ isotopy, such that the first of these seems to 'reveal the truth' about the second.[58]

Here I bring in tactical criteria to make clear the syntagmatic distribution of the two isotopies. Since the contents of the one and of the other are alternately manifested, they are interlaced. But it must be made clear that the beginning and the end of the text are both situated along the /human/ isotopy. And the /animal/ isotopy takes on increasing density,[59] to the point that the principal test (no matter which /animal/ isotopy version of the story) is strongly linked with it To simplify, one might say that the transformation of the contents takes place along the /animal/ isotopy, and this further confirms its hierarchical superiority.

2. *The Topographical Isotopy*

We can look at the second and third paragraphs of the text, which up to now have escaped analysis.

The description of Tournevent sets into place three actors whose lexicalizations are as follows:

(i) The site: 'a fold in the gully ... surrounded by ditches and trees ... that grass- and gorse-covered ravine ... the curve ... furrows';
(ii) The houses: 'the hamlet that was hidden away ... ten Norman houses ... huddled up against each other ... like birds that hide';
(iii) The ocean breeze: 'stormy days ... the strong ocean wind, the off-shore wind, hard and salt ...'

These actors are brought into relation with one another in two thematized graphs, which we can sum up thus, avoiding unnecessary notation: (i) the wind attacks the houses (cf. 'works at you and burns like fire ... dries and destroys'); (ii) the site protects them from the wind (see 'shelter,' a word used more than once).

The simple dialectical structure that makes up these two graphs does not warrant the label 'story,' to the extent that (and we have to recognize the variation that is articulated along the /animal/ isotopy) they manifest an antagonism for which there is no mediation. Nevertheless they indeed do represent a variation of the text, one that is articulated along a new generic isotopy and whose relations with the other versions we will have to study. First let us be clear as to the relations that exist between homologous actors.

A. The site of Tournevent has relations of contiguity with Toine. He is defined as the 'taverner of Tournevent.' Let us compare the descriptions of Toine and those of the site; that will bring to light several common features:

a) /convexity/: 'the curve ... that was the source of its name.' Now, Toine is 'the biggest man of the canton' (line 22); he is 'bloated' (line 55), 'blow[n] up' (line 70).
b) /folded/: the site is a 'fold in the gully,' a 'ravine,' a 'hole.' Now, against Toine's side (line 145), the 'fold' under his great arms (lines 138, 190, 201) is the part of the body that the text highlights.
c) /pubescent/: the ravine is 'grass- and gorse-covered' and the houses are 'huddled up against each other' there[60] (lines 6–7). Toine has a beard, and the first little chick is 'huddled under her husband's beard' (line 197).

These points in common are confirmed within the animal isotopy where the hen is substituted for Toine: the shared peculiarity in this case is the hen's 'underwing,' as in 'underarm' ('his arms raised like wings' [lines 167–8]); and pubescence, its feathers ('the hen clucked in bewilderment, her feathers stood on end, and she spread her wings out to shelter [see '*shelter*,' lines 8 and 9] her growing troop of chicks' (lines 216–17).

B. Correlatively, the houses have semantic features that allow us to homologate them with the chicks:

a) They number ten (line 4), as is the case with the chicks.
b) They are little in relation to the site ('poor peasant hamlet,' [line 4]) and, indeed, both are small *vis-à-vis* Toine ('His little house seemed absurdly too small and narrow and squat to hold him,' [lines 23–4]).
c) They are compared to 'birds that hide in furrows' (line 9). Thus the descriptions of both houses and chicks include the afferent generic features of /animal/ and /bird/. The chicks are 'hidden' under Toine's arms and beard.
d) Furthermore, 'the whole hamlet seemed to be the property of Antoine Mâcheblé,' (line 12). Toine takes one of the chicks in his fingers (lines 191–2) and wants to *keep* the last one in his bed (line 222),[61] which demonstrates a will to possess.

These points in common are multiplied or reinforced within the human isotopy where the people from the area are homologous with the chicks:

Just as Toine – and the hen – keep the chicks warm ('warming ... these ... seeds of chicken life,' line 168), so Toine keeps that country warm with his 'brûlots,' (line 18); we can also remember 'it heats your guts ...' (line 18). (For its part, the site shelters the houses from the cold because it protects them from the wind that 'destroys like a winter's freeze' [line 11].)

As is the case for the site and its houses, and for the hen and its chicks, Toine, too, in his relationships with other people, is in a relation of one to ten: 'he ate and drank like ten men ...' (lines 52–3).

Finally, the people of that area call him *père* (translated as 'old man,' 'daddy,' etc., lines 1, 17, 38, 93, 226) and we remember his unique 'paternity' *vis-à-vis* the chicks.

As for relations between those of that area and their houses, they go without saying.

Summing up, the relations between these couples of actors that are homologous *vis-à-vis* the three isotopies can be represented thus:

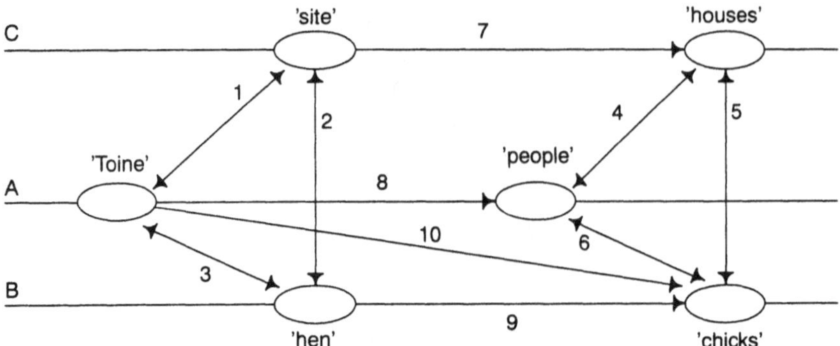

Legend: – The words between the apostrophes are constructed archsememes, designating actors.
– A, B, C: /human/, /animal/, /topographical/ generic isotopies.
– 1, 2, 3: relations of equivalence installed conjointly by the three specific semes /convex/, /folded/, /pubescent/.
– 4, 5, 6: relations of equivalence installed conjointly by the semes /ten/ and /small/[62] (for 5 and 6); to that is added /huddled/ for 5.
– 7, 8, 9, 10: the functional semes /warming/, /shelter/, and /filiation/ (by the giving of a name for 7, by the familiar name of 'old man' or 'father Toine' for 8).

> *Note*: The metaphorical connections[63] (relations 1 to 6) have among their interpretants only one explicit comparison (between birds and houses, line 9). It requires a re-enforcement provided by the inference *if* birds, *then* chicks). The other interpretants that are made explicit are recurrences of signs (such as 'ten,' 'huddled,' or 'shelter'). Beyond that, connections are set in place by analogical reasoning involving semes, independently of any constraints that might be imposed by locality.[64]

C. Finally, 'the ocean wind' belongs to the same class as 'the old lady', 'the rooster', and 'death'; here is why. We have noted the (dialectal) homonymy between *mère* (mother) and *mer* (ocean); it is the interpretant for our semic relations of identity:

a) /violent/: the defining violence of the storm should be likened to the old lady's physical violence (see 'began to hammer him on the belly' [lines 158–9]) and to her moral violence as well (cf. 'angry,' 'furious' [lines 50, 61]). Alas, the comparison between a woman and a storm remains banal.[65]
b) /drying/: the wind 'dries' (line 10). Now, death manifests itself in 'thinness' (lines 66–7), and the old lady is thin. One might object that there remains an aspectual difference between death and its desiccating process and the dried-out old lady, but both deprive Toine of fluids. Death does so by requiring him to 'go

dry' after his attack (and Toine laments, saying, 'not being able to drink, that I mourn,' [line 99] and earlier, 'I really mourn not drinking with you' [lines 97–8]). The old lady keeps his soup away until he accepts the eggs (line 142).
c) /noisy/: a storm is noisy (there is a French verb *tempêter* and expressions such as 'a storm of applause'). The old lady screeches (in Toine's face [line 100], and this shout is of course accompanied by her rushing breath). And the rooster is not to be left out (line 102).
d) /salty/: the old lady ('*Me*' for '*mère*'/mother) – or at least her homonym, the *mé* (for 'mer'/ocean) – is undrinkable: 'it's salt water' (line 39).[66] That can be linked to her maleness, indeed virility: according to our traditions, what is salty is for men and what is sweet is for women.[67] By contrast, Toine, who is a maternal figure, is linked with what is sweet: he is named Brûlot. This drink, regrettably no longer available, is made up of flambée brandy with some sugar added.
e) /destructive/: just as the ocean wind 'works at you ... and destroys' (lines 10–11), so death carries out its 'slow destruction' (line 65).

Note: Of course, the semes inventoried above are not without a relation between them and are especially linked by inferences such as: *if* /violent/ *then* /destructive/, or *if* /salty/ *then* /drying/.

D. The rapprochements between actors that we have just seen in detail can be completed by noting homologations between processes: for example, the site of Tournevent physically makes the ocean wind take a detour (as is indicated by its very name). Likewise, Toine laughingly dodges his wife's angry outbursts (line 56) and 'tries to parry' her attacks (line 162).[68]

It remains true that the analysis of the class of actors that makes up 'death,' 'the old lady,' 'the rooster,' and 'the ocean wind' reinforces the analysis of other classes ('the site' of 'Tournevent,' 'Toine,' 'the hen'; 'the houses,' 'those from around there,' 'the chicks').

The internal version of the story that is thus brought to light in terms of the topographical isotopy is undeniably a variant of the second version of the story along the human isotopy: it indeed reproduces its judgmental or evaluative structure; the ocean wind is negatively judged there, as is the old lady. On the other hand, the site of Tournevent and the houses are positively judged, as are Toine, the people from around there (and the chicks).

3. The Metaphysical Isotopy

It will have been noted that something is off here: 'death' does not have or does not yet have a correlative in the other classes of actors.

It deprives Toine of movement and, eventually, of drink.[69] On the other hand, Toine *gives* the chicks to *life*, ('this little thing whom he had given to life' [line 223]). And the chicks are very active: they 'wriggled' and 'began to run round and round' (lines 193–4). Schematically this gives us:

Episodes I and II		Episode III
I 'death' I	→	'life'
'to take'	→	'to give'
'immobility'	→	I 'movement' I

Note: *Give to life* is a lexia and, as such, its constituents are affected by semic neutralizations that could make our reading illegitimate.[70] In texts that are in general mythic (including literary or religious texts), we admit that any and every lexia can be, indeed must be re-semanticized. Our hermeneutic traditions have, of course, been important in convincing us that the letter kills: for allegorism, every word is virtually ('virtual' being used as linguists use it, in the sense of potential) metaphorical. My choice here is to go in the reverse direction by accepting everything 'to the letter.' Not only am I taking metaphors 'in their literal meaning' (which avoids having to propose a reductive reading for them), but I am also readily admitting that those 'literal' meanings are many. In general, in a given local context, only one is in effect. But at the level of the text, the global context gives rise to several different activations of meaning covering much territory, independently of the text's syntactic structures, which organize the lower level.

Can I, or should I go any further? The metaphysical isotopy thus constituted remains very limited because it includes only six sememes: 'being', 'life', 'death', 'devil', 'tomb', and 'mourning'.[71] To extend it, I should have to postulate symbolic connections that would make possible the introduction of new contents, thanks to a rewriting. Toine could thus become Man that fights death, or Maupassant fighting his illness, etc.

It is not necessary to do so, because elsewhere I have already demonstrated the weak points about allegorical readings, above all where Maupassant is concerned.[72]

As is, the metaphysical isotopy does not allow us to articulate strictly speaking a new version of the story. It is, however, articulated by a dialectic structure that is without mediation (therefore is not narrative) that can be formulated as follows: death deprives Toine; it gives living beings to life. Since death is judged negatively (in the narrator's universe) and life is judged positively (in Toine's universe), the reading of this isotopy conforms to the second version of the story along the human isotopy.

4. Towards a Global Interpretative Path

Let us synthetically put together the results we have obtained:

Isotopies	Number of versions	Actors			
human	2	'Toine'	'the old lady'	'those from around there'	'Prosper'
animal	1	'the hen'	'the rooster'	'the chicks'	'the fox'
topographic	1	'Tournevent'	'the ocean wind'	'the houses'	Ø
metaphysical	0	'life'	'death'	Ø	Ø

Here are the elements that make it possible to reconstitute a global interpretative path:

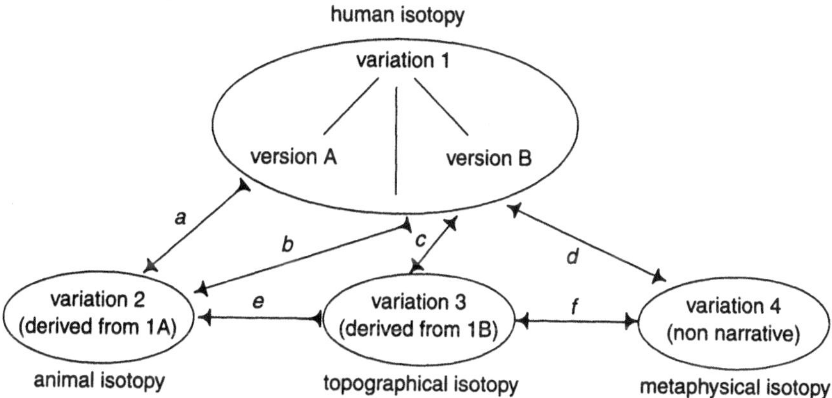

The one-way arrows represent metaphorical connections. Their orientation conforms to relations of metaphorical dominance; they go from the compared to the comparing. The two-way arrows link narrative variations.[73] This schema gives us interactions between the thematic (isotopies) and the dialectical (variations and versions).

The accessibility of a given isotopy is determined principally by the relations of compared/comparing.[74] This means that the animal isotopy is the most accessible (after the human isotopy, which is the most substantial, the most widely applicable, and which determines the referential impression). Third we have the topographical isotopy, which is connected with three others. Finally we have the metaphysical isotopy, connected with only two others. The global order of reading for these isotopies is thus the one I have adopted.

If the plausibility of a given variation depends – at least in one respect – on the number of its type connections, then variations 1 (version B), 2, and 3 enjoy equal plausibility (to the third degree); next comes variation 4 (to the second degree); finally we have variation 1 (version A) to the first degree. The global order of reading of the variations is the one I have adopted, with an exception in terms of importance, namely that the second version of the first variation must come last.[75]

Note: In the above I am dealing only with the global interpretative path (for a methodic reading), and I do not bring in the tactic component, which governs the relations between the global interpretative path and local interpretative paths. This is why I have not classed isotopies or internal versions according to distributional criteria.[76]

By way of a provisional conclusion concerning isotopies and variations of the story, two converging observations are inescapable.

a) The variations of the story do not allow for their homologation in such a way as to construct a type story of which they might be occurrences. For example, for a given class of actors we cannot say this is its corresponding one and only one agonist because the judgments involved are contradictory, not only of course between the various versions (articulated along the same isotopy), but indeed between variations (articulated along different isotopies). We thus cannot construct a type story that would enunciate the 'moral of the story' and whose different variations would be derivatives.

The dialectical structure of the text hence takes the form of a cycle of interconnected variations. This cyclical unfolding could go on indefinitely without ever arriving at a final, stable stage where the contradictions inherent to each variation as well as the contradictions between variations would be resolved. This contributes to the amorality of the text and most likely to its fascinating attraction.

b) The interpretative path described does not make it possible for us to choose an isotopy or variation or one where we might find the 'deep meaning' articulated. The dominant isotopy is not the fundamental deep one just because it is dominant. Certain variations seem plausible, but the implausible variations cannot be tossed aside. The interpretative paths of certain mythic texts show the form of a labyrinth, and that is why they indefinitely can attract and mislead their readers. For one who seeks to describe them, what is important is not 'what is the right way,' but rather the labyrinth itself. Here my only wish is to show its basic plan, that is, to show the unnoticed constraints that govern the lost wanderings of real readers.

III. Towards an Archthematics

The cohesion of the text remains assured thanks to the invariant contents of all of the versions and along all of the isotopies. I shall now detail how this is so by taking as an example, classes of actors, to be precise, those that have members in all of the isotopies. There are two of them: the actors with the greatest number of roles in these two classes of actors are on the one hand 'Toine' and, on the other, 'the old lady.' As we know, an actor is made up of generic features that index him as belonging to various isotopies.[77] Actors also have specific features that justify their inclusion in a given class of actors. When we study classes of actors we consider those specific features to be constants and we view generic features as variables. Indeed, the actors of a given class do not necessarily all possess the same features.[78] For example, 'the ocean wind,' 'the old lady,' and the 'rooster' are all noisy, but 'death' is not. It remains true that the specific features that are common to several actors account for the cohesion of the class: they constitute a semic molecule.

> *Note*: Since each semantic feature can be developed so that it becomes a dialectic role, the semic molecule that is specific to each actor of a class must be linked to the dialectic roles that are specific to that actor (in a given version or variant). The way that molecule develops into dialectic roles is a function of the constraints imposed by the domain and/or the semantic dimension manifested by the isotopy. For example, the people from around Tournevent, human actors, come into Toine's room via the café and leave by the same route; the café is the social locus par excellence. On the other hand, the chicks (who belong to the same class of actors) are brought in, still in their eggs, from the yard, and they are carried back there after hatching. The /human/ versus /animal/ opposition within the same class of actors thus corresponds to symmetrical and antithetical displacements within fictive space as it is articulated by a code of loci.

Let us now compare the most extensive classes of actors (see table on page 164).

Before we examine what this table gives us, here are some further supporting observations concerning some of its entries:

a) /masculine/ and /feminine/ are terms dealing with sex, along the human isotopy, and not gender.

categories	A			B				
	'Toine'	'hen'	'Tournevent'	'life'	'old lady'	'rooster'	'ocean wind'	'death'
a) /masculine/	+							
/feminine/					+			
b) /female/		+						
/male/						+		
c) /convex/	+	+	+					
/flat/					+			
d) /fat/	+							
/thin/					+			
e) /turned in/	+	+	+				+	
/turned out/					+			
f) /pubescent/	+	+	+					
/glabrous/					(+)			
g) /half-closed eye/	+							
/round, open eye/					+	+		
h) /soft/	+	+						
/strident/					+	+	+	
i) /cheerful/	+		(+)					
/angry/					+		(+)	
j) /hot/	+			(+)				
/cold/					(+)		+	
k) /sweet/	+							
/salty/					+		+	
l) /wet/	+							
/dry/							+	
m) /protector/	+	+	+	(+)				
/aggressor/					+	+	+	+
n) /before/	+		+					
/behind/					+	+		

c) Between a spheroid and a flat plane, there can be few points of contact: on the human isotopy, Toine and the old lady are not 'made for each other' (cf. 'my belly isn't supple enough' [line 40]).
d) Death manifests itself in thinness (cf. 'thin bodies' [lines 66–7]).
e) The old lady's body has dramatic, unique features: 'the head of an angry screech owl' (line 45); 'her big skinny hand' (line 202). This appears to be linked to her aggressiveness ('Her hands rose and fell' [line 159]).
f) The old lady is glabrous, by default.
g) Toine is in the habit of winking (and his eyes are mentioned only in the context of winking): see lines 32 and 87. This winking is of the euphoric (euphorisant) (line 32). On the contrary, the old lady fixes her owl-like stare (lines 124–5), and the rooster fixes his round eye in a stare (line 103). That also can be linked with their aggressions.[79]
h) Whereas the old lady screeches and shouts, Toine's voice is not strong (as you would expect with a colossus). On the contrary, at the end of the story, 'He spoke only in a low voice' (line 169). He seems to *fear* noise (line 169) as he *fears* his wife (line 84).
l) Toine is soggy with drink, red-faced, and out of breath (lines 63–4), sweaty (line 200). The ocean wind dries things (line 10), as does death.
n) What we have above are the habitual, typical localities of the actors. Toine 'stands erect in his doorway,' that is, in front of his café, and 'you would wonder how he was able to enter his home' (lines 24–5). The curve in the settlement of Tournevent, relative to the wind, is in front of the houses.

In order that this exposé not be too long, I leave the rest of these observations to the reader. Whether or not a reader wishes to contest a given semic identification (especially in the case of afferent semes, which I have placed in parentheses) is not important. The stability of the semic molecules that make up the two classes is remarkable.

It indeed goes beyond our text. For example, the parrot in *Le noyé* has features that are of class B (see *Contes et nouvelles*, II, 1042). It is a male bird or, at least, masculine, aggressive, with round eyes. It is linked both to death and to the ocean: the heroine buys it after the death of an old sea captain and it turns out to have been her husband, a sailor lost at sea, who taught him how to shout and hurl abuse. This quote needs no commentary: 'She felt herself weakening, as if touched by death ... And the parrot, in its cage, looked at her with its round eye, sneaky and evil ... She felt, she understood that it was indeed he, the dead man, who had returned, who had hidden in the feathers of this beast in order to take up tormenting her again, that he would swear, as before, all day, and would bite her, and shout insults ...' (translation of ibid., 1044).

In other texts, thinness, saltiness, and the ocean are linked to sexual abstinence. One can see this in the descriptions of old spinsters at seaside resorts, as is the case for *Miss Harriet* (ibid., I, 867). And above all, one can see it in *Épaves*, where the girls who are in need of being married off, after ten years of 'fishing for a husband,' risk becoming 'to a woman what a *salted fish* is to a fresh fish' (ibid., 327). Naturally, like old lady Toine, they are flat bodied, big, manly, and humourless ('they looked like telegraph poles ..., spoke loudly, with their manly, serious voices' [ibid., 328]).

Even beyond Maupassant's complete works, certain associations made between features are of the common axiological order we have seen in the phraseology of *Toine*. For example, there is nothing surprising about finding that /heat/ and /joviality/ are constitutive components of actors belonging to the same class: the French language has at its disposal the cliché *rire chaleureux*, and many other languages have this same link.[80]

I dare go even further in this direction. Can it not be said that these associations of features are widely generalized? In our cultural traditions, these associations are not rare. For example, Aristotle said about the Pythagoreans that they 'deemed good those things that were on the right, above, before, and deemed bad what was on the left, below, beyond' (translated from the French edition, *Fragment* 195, 1513 *a* 24 sq).[81] This kind of homologation can be consistent enough to cross language frontiers (cf. the word *sinister* in English, *sinistre* in French).

In other traditions, to my knowledge, it is Taoist thinkers who gave us the most extensive lists of categories.[82] For example, we find (cf. Pottier, 1987, 26–7):

X(A)	Y(B)
hot	cold
masculine	feminine
upright	prone
before	behind
joy	sadness
life	death
visible	hidden
expansion	contraction
yes	no

It is not important for us here whether these homologations are based upon synaesthesia or social conventions.[83]

Remarkably, these two lists, X and Y, in part take up again the features that are characteristic of the agonists A (of which 'Toine' is an actor) and B (of which the 'old lady' is an actor). Now, the X list corresponds to the essentially masculine set of principles (*yang*) the other to the essentially feminine principles (*yin*). This link can be further pursued: for example, on the /human/ isotopy, the feminization of 'Toine' is accompanied by rewrites: /upright/ becomes /prone/; /active/ becomes /passive/; /before/ becomes /behind/; /visible/ becomes /hidden/.

However, and this is no less remarkable, the two agonists, A and B, present inversions of yet other features characteristic of *yin* and *yang* (and these provisionally are revealing for us):

Y(A)	X(B)
passive	active
sunken	protrusive
wet	dry
soft	hard

We can agree – with no further demonstration – that certain of the homologations observed by Taoist philosophers have an anthropological scope (if only in terms of the physiological differences between the sexes). We might thus formulate this final hypothesis: the A and B agonists are both heterogeneous through their semic composition. Each juxtaposes contradictory features and the uncertainty as to the sex of certain of their actors in part conveys this heterogeneity.

The 'grotesque' nature of the text – emphasized by all its commentators – is in part due to this juxtaposition of features that are usually contradictory.

The 'dramatic' or 'jarring' nature of the text can also be explained by that juxtaposition: heterogeneous classes cannot be reconciled. Hence the failure or implausibility of all of the variations and internal versions of the story.

12

The White Care of Our [Sail-]Cloth

Strictly speaking, I envisage reading as a desperate practice, putting aside your folios of study, rubrics, parchments.

S. Mallarmé, *La Musique et les lettres*

Translators' note: On page 33 of Robert Greer Cohn's *Toward the Poems of Mallarmé* (Berkeley: University of California Press, 1980) we read: 'Mallarmé was asked, in 1893, to offer a toast at a gathering of young writers. The result was this "sonnet de circonstance," a miniature crystalline marvel, which Mallarmé placed at the head of his collection as a sort of introduction.'

The poem was entitled 'Salut.' The translation provided here is based on that of Cohn, and is presented in the side-by-side format he used on pages 33–5 of *Toward the Poems* ... The reader is referred to the detailed lexical analysis accompanying the translation.

SALUT

Rien, cette écume, vierge vers	Nothing, this foam, virgin verse
A ne désigner que la coupe;	To designate naught but the cup;
Telle loin se noie une troupe	Thus far-off drowns a troop
De sirènes mainte à l'envers.	Of sirens many upside down.
Nous naviguons, ô mes divers	We navigate, O my diverse
Amis, moi déjà sur la poupe	Friends, I already on the stern
Vous l'avant fastueux qui coupe	You the festive prow that cuts
Le flot de foudres et d'hivers;	The wave of lightnings and winters;

Une ivresse belle m'engage	A beautiful ecstasy incites me
Sans craindre même son tangage	Without fearing even its rocking
De porter debout ce salut	To carry erect this greeting [or toast, or health]
Solitude, récif, étoile	Solitude, reef, star
A n'importe ce qui valut	To whatever was worth [the effort of]
Le blanc souci de notre toile.	The white care of our [sail-]cloth.

My earlier analysis of the thematic component of this sonnet[1] was used to illustrate a study on isotopies (1972). Many authors have since done that study the honour of making it the object of their various criticisms and observations. If I propose this new, amended, and recast version of my earlier study, it is in part due to a concern to respond to and take into account those authors' observations.[2]

I. The First Generic Isotopy

This isotopy is defined by the recurrence of sememes belonging to the domain of //navigation//:

'Salut': safeguards (cf. 'safe harbour,' 'safety anchor')
'écume': 'foam' of the sea
'sirènes': 'sirens'
'se noie': 'drowns'
'nous': 'we', the sailors
'moi': 'I', the steersman (on the stern)[3]
'naviguons': 'navigate'
'poupe': 'stern'
'avant': 'prow'
'flot': 'wave'
'foudres', 'hivers': 'lightnings' and 'winters' are dangers faced at sea
'tangage': 'rocking'
'solitude': 'solitude' on the sea (which is a kind of desert)
'récif': 'reef'
'étoile': 'star' indicating direction[4]
'souci': 'care,' preoccupation of sailors, the object of sailing. (Cf. 'Au seul souci de voyager [Ce salut soit le messager / Du temps, cap que ta poupe double'] 72)
'toile': '(sail-) cloth', the sails set out to drive the ship
'blanc': 'white', colour of the sails

Indexing sememes along this isotopy is accomplished in four ways:

(i) The sememe includes the inherent mesogeneric feature /sailing/ (and would appear in the dictionary along with *mar.*): for example, 'poupe' (stern). Identifying this feature constitutes my indexing.[5]
(ii) The sememe includes the socially normed afferent feature /sailing/, which is actualized in context by a topos: for example, 'sirens'.
(iii) The sememe is compatible with the domain of //sailing// and the corresponding generic seme is afferent to it in this context: for example, 'solitude'.
(iv) The sememe is the content of an anaphora, and as such is saturated by the context.[6] The interpretative path that constitutes this isotopy is relatively simple.[7]

II. The Second Generic Isotopy

The construction of this isotopy requires external interpretants, in the first instance this note from the *Bibliographie* that was drawn up by Mallarmé for the Deman edition: 'This Sonnet, while raising my glass, recently, at a banquet of *La Plume*, with the honour of presiding over it' (77).[8] To make sense of this, it has to be pointed out that *La Plume* was of course a literary review, and for the more demanding readers, here are some ethnographic details: the banquet, still something that we practice, is a meal taken together, seated at a table covered with a white tablecloth. At the end of the meal, the person presiding, who has been chosen because of his eminence and often the most senior member of the assembled group, offers toasts from where he is seated, at the head of the table. Standing before the others, holding up a filled glass, he offers his best wishes for all present. The wine drunk at this time is champagne, as is always the case for French feasts, at dessert.

As a function of this socialized ritual of enunciation, we can proceed to a look at afferences, and saturate our anaphorical components. This gives us a second isotopy:

'Salut':	a toast (cf. 'standing before the others,'[9] which is a gesture of courtesy)
'Rien':	'Nothing', these lines (modesty is required of banquet speakers)
'écume':	'foam', the champagne froth (cf. 863: 'je tends ma coupe privée de mousse,' I extend my cup, lacking froth)

'vierge':	'virgin', a word that is never spoken. (It is good form when poems written for an occasion are as yet unpublished and, until the occasion, unheard.)
'vers':	'verse', that delivered by the speaker
'ne désigner que':	'To designate naught but', (the cup), as is common, the words of the toast refer to the situation of enunciation (an utterance of the type: 'I raise my glass').
'coupe':	'cup', champagne glass
'nous':	'We', the guests
'naviguons':	'navigate', dine
'moi':	'I', the person presiding
'déjà':	'already', has to do with the age of the person presiding. (The banquet was in 1893, when Mallarmé was 51 years old.)
'poupe':	'stern', end of the table (presiding speaker's place of honour)
'avant':	'prow', other end of the table if one's perspective is the presiding speaker's. (Reminds all of the youth of his audience, in contrast to 'I already on the stern.')
'fastueux':	'festive', attributes honorific importance to the listeners, who are thereby set in the place of honour (whereas the presiding speaker, who is in fact at the place of honour, describes himself as being at the lesser end of the table, again suggesting his modesty).
'foudres', 'hivers':	'lightnings', 'winters', refers to the situation. (The banquet took place in February.)
'ivresse':	'drunkenness', due to the champagne
'tangage':	'rocking', effect of the drunkenness
'porter (ce salut ...)':	'carry (... this toast)' an act performed by the presiding speaker
'ce salut':	'this greeting', (the phrase is *porter un toast* (offer a toast), rather than *porter un salut*).[10]
'debout':	'erect'; the presiding speaker is erect.
'souci':	'care', the guests' preoccupation[11] (celebrating literature)
'toile':	'[sail-]cloth', tablecloth
'blanc':	'white', colour of the tablecloth

This second isotopy shows a class of contents that is structured by the ritual of the banquet (and that has to do with the domain of //food and drink//).[12]

III. The Relations between Isotopies 1 and 2

A. The Interpretative Paths

The first isotopy included five sememes that had the inherent feature /sailing/ ('reef', 'rocking', 'stern', 'foam', 'wave'). The second isotopy contains only one sememe that might include the inherent feature /food and drink/: 'cup'. Further, the signifiers of *reef*, *rocking*, *stern*, and *navigate* have only one accepted meaning in language, whereas *cup* is polysemic.[13] That is why the interpretative path that permits us to establish i_2 is more complex than that for i_1 and requires an interpretant that is external to the text under study. Thus, i_1 seems naively but quite legitimately to be more 'obvious' than i_2.

B. The Connections

a) The metaphorical connections identify the specific semes that are common to two sememes or series of sememes.[14] Here, such a connection is established by the word *telle* (line 2 – 'thus'), between *écume* ('foam') and 'se noie une troupe de sirènes mainte à l'envers' (drowns a troop of sirens many upside down).[15]

Specific common semes	Sememes of i_1	Sememes of i_2
/multiplicity/	'troupe' (inherent) '-s' (inherent) 'mainte' 'many' (inherent)	'mousse', 'champagne foam' (afferent: cf. sparkling) 'mousse' 'champagne foam'
/descent/	'se noie' 'drowns' (inherent) 'à l'envers' 'upside down' (afferent: cf. 'plongée')	(afferent)

Note: This connection is not established in the case of inherent semes, hence a first reading of *loin* ('far-off'), which needs a long ('far-fetched') interpretative path. Indeed the disproportion between the objects compared in the fictive referent allows us to find a second reading (which complements the first): it is from afar that a troop of sirens can be compared to foam. Further, this disproportion has a humorous effect.[16] Presiding speakers at banquets, after all, should demonstrate humour.

b) As for symbolic connections, I see two sorts. One installs a generic seme within the source sememe: for example, 'toile' (['sail-]cloth') + /banquet/ → | 'tablecloth' |. The other symbolic connection combines the deletion of a generic seme (and eventually of specific semes) with the insertion of another generic seme (and eventually of other specific semes). For example 'prow' → | 'head of table' | ; (the specific semes that are kept here are: /hoıizontality/, /extremity/, /anteriority/); 'stern' → | 'opposite end of table' | (/horizontality/, /extremity/, /posteriority/); 'rocking' → | 'titubation' | (/movement/, /iterativity/).[17]

So, to sum up, we have three types of connections. To these are added three types of indexation of anisotopic sememes (like those of the anaphoricals), according to whether they are indexed along one isotopy, along the other, or along both.

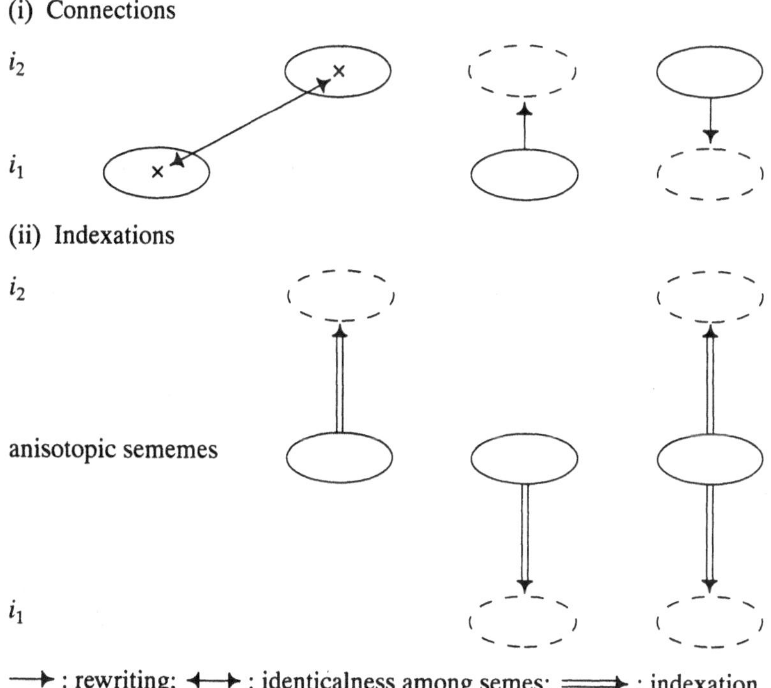

C. Dominance and Hierarchy

Traditionally, relations between two generic isotopies are summed up as follows:

Complexity of the path	Dominance	Hierarchy
i_2 complex ('latent')	comparing	judgment of being superior
i_1 simple ('apparent')	compared	judgment of being inferior

Now, we have this:

i_2 complex	compared	judgment of being inferior
i_1 simple	comparing	judgment of being superior[18]

The relation between dominance and hierarchy remains what it is in the traditions of poetry, and the movement from compared isotopy to comparing isotopy is thus accompanied by that gain *vis-à-vis* judgment that Ricoeur calls the *promotion* of meaning. None the less, the relation between the couple dominance/hierarchy and the complexity of the trajectories is inverted: the compared isotopy is 'latent,' because it is produced by a complex trajectory. So it is that the comparing isotopy brings about the referential impression (see the Groupe Mu: 'A sailor's story'). In other terms, which are inadequate but useful to sum up, where the poetic tradition would seek to mythify the practical (this banquet is a kind of sailing), this text 'practicalizes' the mythical (this sailing is a banquet).

Note: Let us keep in mind – as one should systematically always do – tactical criteria in the description of interpretative paths. The second isotopy is manifested in line 2 by the only one of our sememes that includes the inherent feature /food and drink/ ('cup'). After the enclosing word *thus* (line 3) we see the setting out of sememes that include the inherent feature /sailing/. Although i_2 is manifested in the first two lines, we can construct it only by a retro-reading: we identify the comparing isotopy (i_1) *before* the compared isotopy (i_2).[19]

IV. The Third Generic Isotopy

Why go further?
a) We know from the bibliographical entry that the text is of a toast offered to some writers.

b) *Verse* contains the generic feature /literature/.[20] *Verse* is not read on the i_1 isotopy.

c) The way i_1 and i_2 are constituted leaves other remnants:

(i) 'Rien' ('nothing') is not read on isotopy i_1.

(ii) Likewise 'vierge' ('virgin').

(iii) 'Solitude' is not read on isotopy i_2, where it would appear to be quite incompatible with 'diverse friends.'

These three sememes count the feature /negation/ among their constituent parts,[21] and this feature is recurrent in all of those texts of Mallarmé's that manifest the domain //writing//.[22] Because this domain is very idiolectal, in order to confirm the hypothesis of a third generic isotopy, I must turn to quotations from other texts. This procedure is to be used with caution.[23] That does not make it any less indispensable in our attempt to show the idiolectal relations at work in the text. Thus:

'Salut': salvation (cf. *Oeuvres complètes*, 856, 'La théologie des Lettres').

'Rien': This text (literature being defined by negativity; see, above all, Richard, 1961).

'écume': pen. 'Choit / la plume / rythmique suspens du sinistre / s'ensevelir / aux écumes originelles' (It falls / the pen / rhythmic suspense of the sinister / burying itself in the original foam) 473; 'Une ruine parmi mille écumes bénie / ... Si ce très blanc ébat au ras du sol dénie' (A ruin among a thousand foams blessed / ... If this frolicking so white denies the ground below it) 76; 'Tout son col secouera cette blanche agonie / ... Mais non l'horreur du sol où le plumage est pris' (His entire neck will shake off this white agony / ... But not the horror of the ground where his plumage is caught) 68; '... écumait en ébats / Un oiseau' (... foamed in a frolic / A bird) 104. The semes common to all of these are /whiteness/, /movement/, /iterativity/, /contact with a horizontal surface/.

'vierge': ideal (no contact with matter); cf. 'La virginité de la feuille de papier' (The virginity of the sheet of paper) 400; 'Les vêpres magnifiques du Rêve et leur or vierge' (The magnificent Vespers of Dream and their virgin gold) 1491; in connection with the whiteness of paper: 'Virginité qui solitairement ... elle-même s'est comme divisée en ses fragments de candeur, preuves nuptiales de l'idée' (Virginity that in solitude ... has divided itself into

	its fragments of candour, nuptial proof of the Idea) 387; 'La Fable, vierge de tout ...' (The Fable, virgin of everything ...) 544.
'vers':	literature; cf. 'La forme appelée vers est simplement elle-même la littérature' (The form we call verse is quite simply itself literature) 361.
'ne désigner que':	('to designate naught but') reference to an absence (cf. 'nothing' line 1; and literature as a reflexive designation, auto-referential: that of the empty inkwell – or inkwell full of nothingness).
'coupe':	('cup') inkwell (defined as an empty container); cf. 'l'hommage à Gautier': 'J'offre ma coupe vide' (I offer my empty cup) 54. In the same paradigm: 'Le pur vase d'aucun breuvage' (The pure vase of no drink), which does not consent to 'rien expirer' (to expire anything) 74; 'au salon vide, nul ptyx ... Car le Maître est allé puiser des pleurs au Styx / Avec ce seul objet dont le Néant s'honore' (in the empty room, no ptyx ... Because the master has gone to draw tears from the Styx / With this the only object with which Nothing honours itself) 68; 'cette fiole de verre, pureté qui renferme la substance du Néant'; 'L'encrier, cristal comme une conscience, avec sa goutte, au fond, de ténèbre,'[24] (This glass vial, a purity that encloses the substance of Nothingness; the crystal inkwell like a consciousness, with its drop, in the depths, of darkness) 370. Now, darkness, in the taxeme of light, and negation in the taxeme of modality, are homologous in Mallarmé. Hence the substitution that is possible between 'darkness,' 'ink,' 'nothingness' or 'nothing' (cf. the inkwell that contains a drop of darkness); and also the vial of Igitur that contains 'the drop of water that is missing from the sea' (both negated – it is missing, and black – it is midnight; see also 469).[25] The semes common to all of the above: /receiving container/, /crystalline/, /englobed/, /negation/.
'sirènes':	chimera, or negated ideality; cf. 'Chimère ... au reflet de ses squames' (Chimera ... in the reflection of her squama) 367; 'une stature mignonne ténébreuse debout / en sa torsion de sirène / le temps / de souffleter / par d'impatientes squames ultimes ...' (A pretty dark statue

	standing erect / in its siren's torsion / time / to give a slap / by impatient ultimate squama) 471–2.
'naviguons':	'we navigate,' we write. Cf. 'Voile, un des aspects du livre yacht' (Sail, one of the aspects of the yacht book) (*Le 'Livre' de Mallarmé*, ed. J. Schérer, Paris, Gallimard, 1977, 53A). Common semes: /movement/, /linearity/. As with the other linear motions, sailing is often compared to writing.[26]
'moi':	the writer.
'amis':	'writers'
'fastueux':	'festive,' linked to poetry; cf. 'Je crois que la poésie est faite pour le faste' (I believe poetry is made for festive splendour) 869.
'coupe le flot':	'cuts the wave,' denies matter. Cf. 'déchirer ... ce lac dur' (67).
'foudres':	'lightnings,' illumination of the genius (cf. 'Quel génie pour être un poète! quelle foudre d'instinct renfermer, simplement la vie, vierge, en sa synthèse et loin illuminant tout' (What genius is required for one to be a poet! what a flash of inspiration is needed to enclose, simply life, virgin, in its synthesis and far away illuminating everything) 869; cf. also, in connection with the book where everything ultimately ends up: 'l'hymne, harmonie et joie, comme pur ensemble groupé dans quelque circonstance fulgurante, des relations entre tout. L'homme chargé de voir divinement ...' (the hymn, harmony and joy, like a pure ensemble brought together in some lightning situation, relations between everything. Man who is charged with seeing divinely).
'hivers':	'winters,' sterility; cf. 'Quand du stérile hiver a resplendi l'ennui' (When the ennui of sterile winter has shone) 67.
'ivresse':	'ecstasy,' jubilation; cf. 'avec un coup d'aile ivre' → 'plume' (With a drunken flap of a wing – pen), 67. This jubilation is linked to surrection toward the Idea, cf. 'ainsi qu'aile l'esprit' (as the spirit soars) 60. We should also note, in *Toast funèbre*, that after Gautier there is 'Une agitation solennelle par l'air / De paroles pourpre ivre et grand calice clair' (A solemn agitation by the air / Of words drunk and purple and great clear chalice) 55.
'belle':	'beautiful,' artistic

'tangage':	'rocking,' movement of writing, cf. 'la plume / rythmique suspens du sinistre' (the pen / rhythmic suspense of the sinister) 473. Semes shared: /movement/, /iterativity/, /contact with a horizontal surface/.[27]
'debout':	'erect,' facing the Idea. All surrection is a movement toward that Idea, especially the writer's Idea and that of the pen: cf. 'une impatience de plumes vers l'Idée' (an impatience of pens (or feathers) toward the Idea) 305; 'Hieroglyphes dont s'exalte le millier / A propager de l'aile un frisson familier' (Hieroglyphs over which the thousand exult / In propagating with the flap of the familiar wing) 71.[28]
'salut':	'greeting,' or 'toast,' these verses dedicated to the enterprise of writing; in connection with this reflexive designation see above: the pen (← 'foam') designates only the inkwell (← 'cup').
'Solitude':	the writer's situation; cf. 'plume solitaire éperdue' (distraught solitary pen) 468; 'je suis un solitaire' (I am a solitary one) 869.
'récif':	'reef,' failure (of writing). Cf. 'prince amer de l'écueil' (bitter prince of the reef) 468; coiffed with the pen (feather) 'cette blancheur rigide / dérisoire / en opposition au ciel' (this rigid whiteness / derisory / in opposition to the heavens) ibid; all meaning 'not attaining the Idea.'
'étoile':	'star,' success (of writing as a production of thought: cf. 'UNE CONSTELLATION' 477).[29]
'souci':	'care' (the enterprise of writing)
'toile':	'vellum' (cf. the author who 'gréerait demain la voilure autrement qu'en vélin de quelque remarquable yacht' (who would tomorrow rig the sails, otherwise than in paper, of some remarkable yacht) 324; 'voile' ([sail-] cloth) along i_1 → 'velin' ('vellum') along i_3.
'blanc':	colour of paper (cf. 'l'homme poursuit noir sur blanc' (man pursues black on white) 370.

Here is how we can characterize the isotopy I have just produced:
a) As is the case for the preceding one, it has only one sememe that includes, in language, the isotope-creating feature: 'vers' (verse) includes the generic feature /literature/. Indeed 'vers' here receives an idiolectal application that equates it with 'literature.'[30] Thus, setting aside the contents of the anaphoricals, almost all of the sememes indexed along this isotopy have a semic content different from

their semic content within the linguistic system: this isotopy is thus essentially idiolectal.

This also explains why its interpretative path is much more complex than those of i_1 and i_2. This is evidenced by the frequent cases of recourse to interpretants that are external to 'Salut,' albeit that none of those interpretants is of the explicitly linguistic nature of the bibliographical note that allowed us to construct i_2.

Does this mean that i_3 is an extrinsic isotopy, one that is proper to this study but not to the text described? Let us immediately set aside the facile objection according to which the lexicalizations that enunciate it are of my own devising (even though for the most part I found them in Mallarmé himself). Here is the question: do they or do they not formulate semic molecules whose constitution is prescribed by the text?[31]

Certainly I might have settled for the first two isotopies, since none of the internal interpretants prescribes, using features that are inherent to the linguistic system, the constituting of a third isotopy. 'Rien' is not socially codified within the domain //literature//; 'vers,' on the other hand, is, but it would be sufficient to index it within i_2 (as I did for 'vierge' or 'désigner' ['virgin' and 'designate']).

If nothing 'explicitly' requires me to construct this isotopy, nothing forbids that either. Even better, the constructing of i_3, through having recourse to other texts, presumes there to be a global cohesion in the overall 'oeuvre' of Mallarmé, while at the same time demonstrating that cohesion within a specific text. This is so because constructing i_3 allows us precisely to describe relations of a systematic order.[32]

In the case in point, i_3 is quite consistent with what we know about Mallarmé's idiolect, and this is especially true since i_3 is constructed principally by means of symbolic connections, given the explicit wish to avoid lexicalizing semic molecules.[33] Of course we can contest such and such a connection or such and such a lexicalization, but that in no way vitiates the plausibility of the whole of i_3.

Is there not a little circularity there? One is explaining the isotopy by the idiolect and vice versa. No, because they do not both have the same theoretical status. Between them there is an indissoluble duality and separation that we know as competence versus performance. In short, I can characterize i_3 as an *intrinsic* isotopy with symbolic connections.

b) The connections with i_1 and i_2 are an important factor *vis-à-vis* plausibility. There is no metaphorical connection between i_3 and the first two isotopies but, on the other hand, there are indeed several symbolic connections (see following Tables I and II).

I see eight connections between i_1 and i_3 as opposed to just two between i_2

I

i_1		i_2
'écume' (foam)	→	| 'plume' | (pen)[34]
'naviguons' (we navigate)	→	| 'écrivons' | (we write)
'couper' (cut)	→	| 'mer' | (ocean)
'flot' (wave)	→	| 'matière' | (matter)
'hivers' (winters)	→	| 'stérilité' | (sterility)
'récif' (reef)	→	| 'échec' | (failure)
'étoile' (star)	→	| 'succès' | (success)
'tangage' (rocking)	→	| 'mouvement de | l'écriture' | (movement of writing)

II

i_2		i_3
'coupe' (cup)	→	| 'encrier' | (inkwell)
'nappe' (sheet)	→	| 'papier' | (paper)

and i_3. This is not simply because of the strongly symbolic nature of i_2, as we have already agreed that connections could be established between different rewrites. We shall soon see the importance of this disparity in connection with the interpretative path of the whole.

V. From the Interrelation between Isotopies to the Interpretative Path

Here we must ask the naïve question, what is the meaning of 'Salut' (or, as the Barthesians of the sixties used to say, what is its message)? None of the isotopies can sum up the meaning of the text, whatever its hierarchical position. If you accept this hypostasis of an isotopy, this inevitably brings you back to the unscientific theories of double meanings. These theories claim that interpretation must glean the apparent, literal meaning from a text, in order then to be able to reveal its hidden meaning, the 'true' meaning (see Rastier, 1987a, chapter 8). First let us remind ourselves that the three isotopies are separated only by means of a fiction that is necessary to our study; and the meaning of the text, as described here, cannot be found in any one of them, nor indeed in all three, but rather in the interrelation between the three.

A. The formalization proposed by Vaina (1974) supports *a contrario* these positions. Using Spanier's algebraic topology, it would have it that the topological invariants of simplicial complexes 'offer indications as to the repetitive structure of the text at a linguistic level that has been established *a priori*' (317, my translation). Based on my analysis of i_1 and i_2, it comes to the conclusion that 'the navigation isotopy is hierarchically below the banquet isotopy,' because in its representation 'there are no simplexes above 1-simplexes, a fact that implies only a little cohesion between the elements of the text;' (ii) 'there are more 0-simplexes that are not linked in simplexes of a higher level'; (iii) it has two cycles; and (iv) it has several linked components (cf. 322–3). A discussion of these formal criteria would lead us into an analysis that is out of place here, because in fact I contest the very principle of this formalization: it proceeds exactly as if the two isotopies were two distinct texts. Aside from the fact that it eliminates, with no justification, the third isotopy, it privileges certain intra-isotopic relations, while totally excluding inter-isotopic relations.[35] It is true that we often prefer to discuss the 'how' of formalization. The basic questions remain: What is being formalized? What are the conditions? What is to be done with what is left out or left over?

B. The refusal to carry out 'dull' readings naturally leads to the offering of a 'volumic' representation,[36] each isotopy being represented in terms of a figure involving the edge of a regular polyhedron, here a prism. Thus, for the first line, we have:

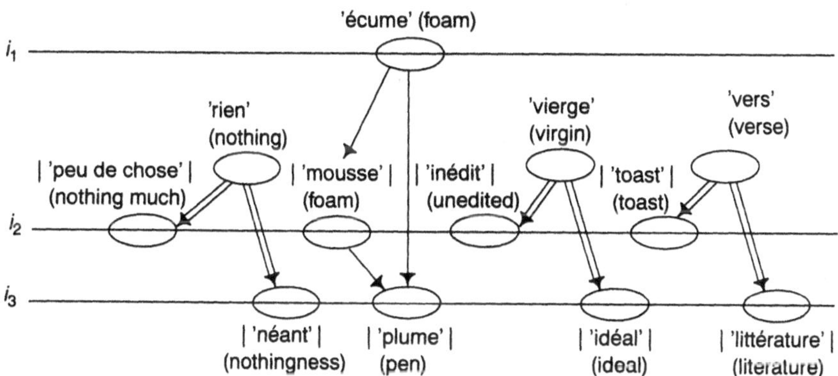

Here: → :rewriting; ⇒ indexation

When applied to the thirteen lines that follow, the same principle of representation brings out several remarkable features:

(i) The first and the last line are those showing the most relations (nine each), relations that are distributed along four and three sememes respectively.
(ii) The penultimate line is the only one that does not exhibit any of the relations we have noted. Hence its contrast with the last line, which is something that conforms to the traditional aesthetic of the 'pointe' (maximum effect). This opens up another line of inquiry: by using a tactic

criterion we can identify variations in density that bring about complex semantic rhythms.

(iii) Five signifiers, alone, are able to express fifteen sememes: *écume*, *tangage*, *naviguons*, *toile*, and *salut*.

C. Let us now bring together what we have learned in order to make a synthesis of the relations between isotopies.

a) The connections are numbered as follows:[37]

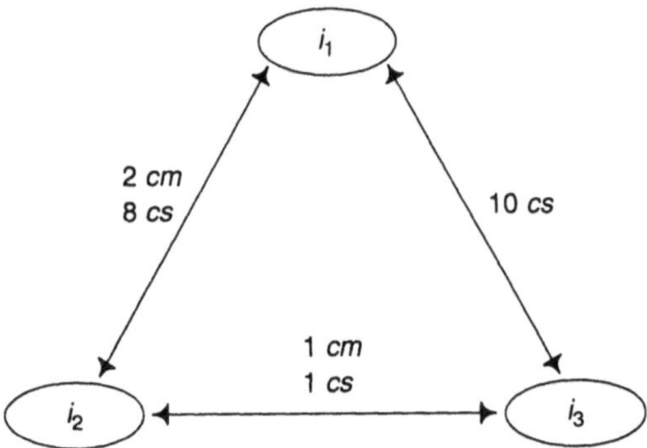

where: *c* represents *connection*; *m*, *metaphorical*; *s*, *symbolic*. If we agree that the metaphorical connections are greater than the symbolic ones (because their relata are both lexicalized in the text), we get the following classification:

$$i_1 = 18\ cs + 2\ cm; \quad i_2 = 9\ cs + 3\ cm; \quad i_3 = 11\ cs + 1\ cm.$$

Of course, the preponderance of i_1 in this matter will have an effect on the interpretative pathway.

b) The density specific to each isotopy can be evaluated by the number of its sememes:

$$i_1 = 20 < i_2 = 22 < i_3 = 28.$$

c) Its productivity can be evaluated by the number of rewritings it includes:

$$i_1 = 15 < i_2 = 21 < i_3 = 28.$$

d) We have seen that i_1 was the comparing isotopy, relative to i_2 (compared). Indeed, i_1 and i_2 are both linked to i_3 by symbolic connections oriented towards

i_3: if we call the relation of the symbolized to the symbolizing symbolic dominance,[38] i_3 is dominated by i_2 and i_1. Thus:

$$i_1 > i_2 > i_3.$$

e) The hierarchy of the generic isotopies is determined by their relative valorization. We have seen that i_2 was more valorized than i_1, but less so than i_3 because, in the idiolect under study, the domain //literature// takes on a maximal value (cf. ‘tout, au monde, existe pour aboutir à un livre’ (Everything in the world exists in order ultimately to end up as a book) 378.

To sum up:

	i_1		i_2		i_3
connectivity		>		>	
density		<		<	
productivity		<		<	
dominance		>		>	
hierarchy		<		<	

The order of relation between the three isotopies is thus conserved, whatever the discriminating criterion; this regularity is remarkable. We could agree that i_1 is a ‘mythic’ isotopy, codified by the literary topic (cf. ’sirènes’); i_2 is a practical isotopy (representing the situation of enunciation); i_3 is a ‘mystical’ isotopy, strongly idiolectal and articulating truth. As the study of connections shows, myth (i_1) would then be a mediation between the real (i_2) and the true (i_3).[39]

D. The interpretative path that I have followed here is of course not the last word in reading because it is limited to one part of the thematic component.[40]

It was in conformity with two rules that I should now make precise: (i) The first constructed isotopy is the one that has the most sememes that include in the linguistic system the isotoping seme. It is thereby the most ‘apparent’ isotopy. (ii) The second is the one whose connections with the first are the most numerous and the strongest.

That is why the path followed is divided into four stages: (i) the establishing of i_1; (ii) starting with i_1 and keeping in mind the bibliographical note, the establishing of i_2; (iii) starting with i_1, keeping in mind the bibliographical note and other texts from the period 1866–98, the establishing of i_3; (iv) the identification of the connections between i_3 and i_2.

E. A question now, by way of an epilogue. What signification does the text acquire from its place in the collected works?[41] More precisely: I constructed i_2 while keeping in mind the bibliographical note; especially by saturating the anaphoricals (cf. 'vous' → 'écrivains'); but the publication as an exergue of a collection surely has a modifying effect upon that reading.

a) Mallarmé limited the first edition of his *Poésies*, the only edition during his lifetime, to forty-seven copies. Urged by his friends, he first envisages in 1891 the publication of a 'grande édition' with supplements, to the tune of one hundred copies. 'Salut' is to be in that edition. He spends seven years choosing, at his leisure, the edition's format and basic character, but the Deman edition appears only in 1899, one year after his death. This amounts to saying that he cared little about the public's opportunity to become acquainted with his work.

One might claim that 'Salut' continues, in that collection, to be addressed to 'mes divers amis,' writers and artists; and not to the public in general. This presumption is corroborated by what we know about the *Livre*. It *was not supposed* to be published, but rather presented, privately, by the author, to his invited guests (paying or not). This is obvious in *Quant au livre*: 'A given era perforce recognizes the existence of the Poet. In order to count, according to their faces, his guests, he would present the manuscript only intimately, he is famous!' (377). I thus do not have to modify my reading.

b) The bibliography in the Deman edition further indicates: 'these poems, or studies engaged in with the intention of doing even better, just as you wipe off the tip of your pen before setting down to work' (77).

The oeuvre is the *Livre*. Now, 'Salut' has close connections with fragments we know to be or suppose to be from the *Livre*. On the one hand, *Un coup de dés*[42] develops two isotopies that are identical to i_1 and i_3. That appears in all of the references given above in connection with the constructing of i_3.[43] On the other hand, in the rough drafts for the *Livre*, we see connections between //navigation// and //literature// (for example, 'voile un des aspects du livre yacht' (sail, one of the aspects of the book yacht) 53 A. We also see connections between //navigation// and //banquet// (cf. 72 B, 80 B, 103 A, the juxtapositions of *banquet* and *yacht*). Thus, 'Salut' would be an exergue to the *Poésies* in the way of a prefiguration of the *Livre*, which is still to come.[44]

13

Referential Impression or the Sun and the Shepherdess

Or, figliuol mio, non il gustar del legno
Fu per sè la cagion di tanto essilio,
Ma solamente il trapassar del segno[1]

Dante, *Paradiso,* XXVI, 115–17

Thematics, more particularly the theory of isotopies, allows us to handle the problem of referential impression.[2] To illustrate this I have chosen Apollinaire's 'Zone,' from which I take all my examples, with no claim to describe it.[3]

The translation that follows is based on William Meredith's, in *Alcools: Poems 1898–1913,* New York, Doubleday, 1964. [Translator's note: The original text has been reestablished without punctuation; see 252–6 for French original.]

Zone

In the end you are weary of this ancient world

Shepherdess o Eiffel tower the flock of bridges is bleating this morning

You've had enough of living in Greek and Roman antiquity

Even the automobiles have an air of antiquity here
Only religion remains perfectly new religion
Has kept as simple as the hangars at the airport

Alone in Europe you are not antique, o Christian faith
You are the most modern European Pope Pius X –

And you whom the windows watch shame restrains you
From going into a church and confessing there this morning
You read the handbills catalogues posters that sing out loud and clear
That's the morning's poetry and for prose there are the newspapers
There are tabloids lurid with police stories
Portraits of the great and a thousand assorted titles
This morning I saw a pretty street whose name I forget
New and fresh it was a fanfare for the sun
Executives workers pretty stenographers
Pass through it four times a day from Monday to Saturday
Three times a morning a siren howls there
A surly bell barks toward noon
The inscriptions on the signboards and the walls
The plaques the notices bawl like parrots
I love the grace of this industrial street
Situated in Paris between the rue Aumont-Thiéville and the avenue des Ternes

Here is the young street and you are still a little child
Your mother dresses you only in blue and white
You are very religious and together with your oldest friend René Dalize
You like nothing so much as the ceremonies of the church
It is nine o'clock the gas is turned down and blue you steal out of the dormitory
You pray all night in the school chapel
While eternal and lovely an amethyst mystery
The flamelike glory of Christ wheels forever
It is the fair lily that we all tend
The red-haired torch that no wind can blow out
It is the pale and rosy son of the mother of sorrow
The tree thick-leaved with all the prayers there are
It is the double gibbet of honor and eternity
The star with six branches
The God who dies on Friday and rises from the dead on Sunday
This is the Christ who climbs the sky better than airmen
He holds the world record for altitude

Pupil Christ of the eye
Twentieth pupil of the centuries he knows how to do it
And changed to a bird this century rises like Jesus in the air
The devils in their abysses raise their heads to look at him
They say he is imitating Simon Magus in Judaea

They shout He takes to flight like a common thief
Angels hover around the pretty aerobat
Icarus Enoch Elijah Apollonius of Tyana
Float around the first airplane
They break ranks at times to pass those transported by the Holy Eucharist
Those priests who mount continually elevating the Host
The aircraft lands at last without folding its wings
Then the sky is filled with millions of swallows
At full wing come the crows the falcons the owls
From Africa come ibises flamingos marabou storks
The Roc bird celebrated in prose and verse glides down
Carrying in his talons the skull of Adam the first head
Hurling a shrill cry the eagle stoops from the edge of the sky
And from America comes the tiny hummingbird
The long and supple pihis arrive from China
Flying in pairs since each has a single wing
Then here is the dove herself immaculate spirit
Escorted by the lyre bird and the many-eyed peacock
The phoenix that funeral pyre who engenders himself
For an instant veils the scene with his glowing ashes
The sirens quitting their perilous straits
Arrive all three singing exquisitely
And all of them eagle phoenix pihis from China
Fraternize with the flying machine

Now you are walking in Paris alone in the crowd
Herds of buses roll along bellowing near you
The anguish of love claws at your throat
As if you would never no longer be loved
If you lived in ancient times you would enter a monastery
You're ashamed to catch yourself saying a prayer
You scoff at yourself and your laugh crackles like hellfire
The sparks of your laugh gild the background of your life
The painting is hung in a gloomy museum
And sometimes you go there and inspect it closely

Today you are walking in Paris the women are covered with blood
It was and I would prefer not to remember it it was at the time of the wane of beauty

Wrapped in her fervent flames Our Lady looked at me in Chartres

The blood of your Sacred Heart deluged me at Montmartre
I'm sick of hearing blessed words
The love I suffer from is a shameful sickness
And the image that possesses you keeps you in sleeplessness and anguish
It is never far from you, that shifting image

Now you are on the coast of the Mediterranean
Under the lemon trees that bloom the year round
You have gone for a sail with some friends
One is from Nice one from Menton the other two from La Turbie
Fearfully we watch octopus in the depths
And among the seaweed swim fish metaphors of the Saviour

You're in the garden of an inn near Prague
You feel altogether happy there's a rose on the table
And instead of writing your story you stare intently
At the rose beetle asleep in the heart of the rose

Appalled you find a picture of yourself in the veined agates at St. Vitus
You were mortally sad the day you saw yourself there
Looking like Lazarus unwitted by the daylight
The hands of the public clock in the ghetto move withershins
And you too move slowly backward into your life
Climbing up to the Hradcany in the evening
And hearing Czech songs sung in the taverns

Here you are in Marseilles surrounded by watermelons

Here you are in Coblenz at the Hotel du Géant

Here you are in Rome sitting under a Japanese medlar tree

Here you are in Amsterdam with a girl you think pretty but who is ugly
She is engaged to marry a student at Leyden
They rent rooms in Latin there *cubicula locanda*
I recall spending three days there and as many at Gouda

You are in Paris before the examining magistrate
Arrested like a common criminal

You made sad journeys and happy ones
Before you reckoned with falsehood and age
You suffered from love at twenty and at thirty
I've lived like a crazy man and I've wasted my time
You don't dare look at your hands anymore and I would like to weep
About you about her I love about all that has scared you

With tears in your eyes you watch these unhappy emigrants
They believe in God they pray their women nurse their babies
They fill the halls of the Gare Saint-Lazare with their reek
They trust in their star the way the wise men did
Hoping to get rich in the Argentine
And go back to their countries with a fortune
One family carries a red eiderdown with them the way you carry your heart
That quilt and our dreams are equally unreal
Some of these emigrants stay here living in slums
In the rue des Rosiers or the rue des Écouffes
I have often seen them in the evening taking the air in the street
They move only now and then like pieces in a chess game
They are mostly Jews their wives wear wigs
And sit anaemic at the rear of their shops

You are standing at the counter in a low bar
You order a cheap cup of coffee among the derelicts

You are in a great restaurant at night

These are not bad women but they have their troubles
And even the ugliest one of them has made her lover suffer

She is the daughter of a policeman on the Isle of Jersey

Her hands which I hadn't seen are hard and raw

I feel an immense pity for the scars on her stomach

I humble my mouth now to a poor girl with a horrible laugh

You are alone it is about to be morning
The milkmen clink their cans in the streets

The night withdraws like a beautiful half-caste
It is the false Ferdine or the solicitous Lea

And you drink this alcohol burning like your life
Your life that you drink like *eau de vie*

You walk toward Auteuil you want to go home on foot
And sleep among your fetishes from Oceania and Guinea
They are Christs of another shape and another creed
Inferior Christs of darker hopes

Farewell farewell

Sun severed neck

I. Problematics

Problems having to do with reference can be and probably should be posed in different ways according to the various planes of semantic description to which they are relevant: (i) identification of sememes and of their components (in microsemantics); (ii) interpretation of utterances; (iii) interpretation of the text. Under the term *reference* several relations that are in fact quite different from one another are often assimilated or juxtaposed.

a) The relation between sememes that are found within one and the same semantic universe can be called *intralinguistic reference*. Among such I include relations between hyponyms and hyperonyms, between antonyms, between sememes that belong to the same domain, but to different taxemes.
b) The relation between a sememe and non-linguistic objects, be they empirical or not, called *referents*. This relation corresponds to the relation that Frege calls *Bedeutung* and Russell *denotation*. Of course one might specify this type of relation according to the ontological status of the referents. However, one would want to avoid that because such a typology has been discussed for millennia, with very little result.

Note: Strictly speaking, however, it is not the sememe but rather the word that can be endowed with a reference. For example, we can agree that the sememe 'jou-' (the first syllable of 'jouer,' to play) has no reference, whereas the contents 'jouet' (toy) or 'joueur' (player) can receive a reference. Thus the content of a word is composed of one or more sememes (because the word, as we know, is a syntagm). The problematics of reference comes into play thus only at the level of the syntagm: hence it cannot be the basis of a fundamental semantics. The linguistics of the sign is already much too limited, but the linguistics of the word offers even fewer possibilities.

c) The relation of an utterance with a given semantic universe. It defines the validity of the utterance in question in relation to that universe. When relevant, it allows us to clarify its analytical truth a priori, or its truth in the weak sense (see Kalinowski, 1982, 13).

d) The relation of an utterance with non-linguistic objects or phenomena that its content is supposed to represent. It defines the truth values of that utterance: a synthetic truth (Quine) or an a posteriori analytical one (Kalinowski, 14). The utterances for which one cannot establish this type of relation can be called *fictive*, to the extent that they create a referential impression without any empirical truth effect.

If, within the framework of a logical semantics, I were to restrict myself here to an 'intensional' semantics, I should adopt definitions *a* and *c*.

This brief outline is inspired by our logical tradition. It is not of great use to me here because it deals with propositions (whether or not they correspond to linguistic utterances) in order to attribute to them a truth value, which is not easily decided upon in the case of texts of fiction.[4] But it cannot treat texts in any other way but as a succession of propositions that are linked by arguments. So true is this that the problem of the reference of texts has hardly at all been treated by logicians. Rather, it has been treated by specialists in poetics, for whom it is particularly relevant.

The hypothesis that I want briefly to illustrate here has to do with quite another order: the linguistic sign in and of itself (the morpheme) does not have any immediate and unconditional reference. Thus, the question of reference and the analysis of its conditions are not a matter for linguistics in the narrow sense,[5] even though that discipline should set itself the task (if it succeeds in enlarging its field of investigation) of modifying the way we have been asking this question for millennia.

In the first place, let us set aside the thesis according to which the signifier has in and of itself a reference. This thesis, illustrated by Morris – and which I have argued against elsewhere – simply ignores the signified and, through its simplifications, it makes much too quick work of all of our thought on semiotics since the Stoics.

Signifieds do not refer either, at least not directly and without conditions: the triadic model of the sign, popularized by Ogden and Richards, draws a straight line from signified to referent. Now, the conditions under which one can assign a referent to a signified are so complex that enlightened logicians such as Quine have seen fit to speak of indiscernibility (*inscrutability*) in this respect.[6]

Our western logical traditions, which since antiquity have dealt with meaning, have not systematically distinguished between signified and concept, and the term *concept*, in the milieu of cognitive research, continues to be used to designate the signifier (among other things). None the less this term would be well served to retain the technical meaning it has in philosophy, although there it is much too limited in scope to be able to fit the polymorphic nature of linguistic signifiers.

Without contesting its great suitability for all that has to do with formal languages, I want to set aside the logic of the problem of linguistic reference: the 'missing link' that will allow us correctly to inquire into the problem of reference is not the concept, but the mental image. And, as we know, mental images rightfully are the object of study for cognitive psychology.[7]

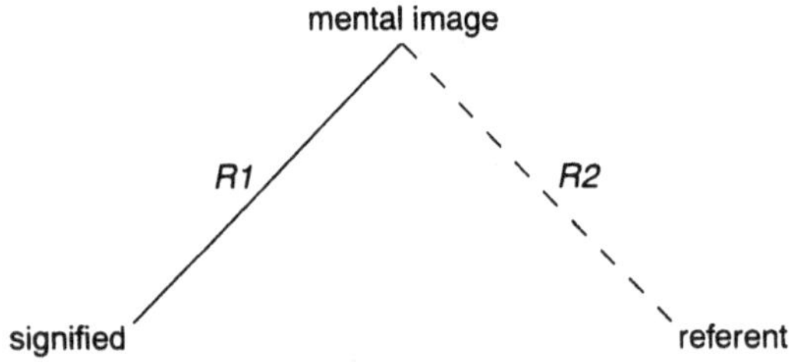

The problem of reference as posed in these terms now concerns linguistics only in terms of that discipline's relation to cognitive psychology.

The relation of mental images with phenomenal areas has to do with cognitive psychology: in this area questions such as typicality, recognition, and identification of objects, etc., are asked.[8]

Thus the two relations *R1* and *R2*, although my schema might lead one to think so, are in no way simple or commensurable.

(i) *R1*: The signified *determines* the mental images that are associated with it. It does not, however, constrain them, since an image-creating subject can spontaneously bring forth images that are not determined by linguistic context or situation of communication.[9] None the less the context subtly determines signifieds, which define each other by their interaction.[10] For example, in 'Bergère ô tour Eiffel' (Shepherdess o Eiffel Tower), the equative context of the parataxis allows for propagating, by presuming from isotopy, the feature

/verticality/ that is inherent to 'tower', and that thus becomes afferent to 'bergère' (shepherdess).[11] This use of 'bergère' has a correlative on the level of mental imagery: several listeners have assured me, with few abstentions and in a large majority, that they 'saw' a standing shepherdess; whereas real shepherdesses, who often are old and worn-out, are usually seated.

Our research can take two directions.

(i) Signs that in the logical tradition are reputed not to refer at all are generally free grammemes ('empty words'). But linked or bound grammemes do not refer either, to the extent that we associate no mental image with them. Finally, lexemes strictly speaking also do not refer: who can identify, for example, the reference made by *curs-* (which we find in *cursor* and *cursive*)?

To sum up, no linguistic sign 'refers,' because the property of giving rise to mental images is one that is proper to syntagms (which include the word) but not to each and every sign that constitutes those syntagms.[12] Thus contextual conditions must be met if a morpheme is to be able to be part of the formation of a mental image.

(ii) Textual semantics has to deal with, beyond the word and beyond the syntagms, the composition of referential impressions: it requires the four semantic components. None the less, the cohesiveness of referential impressions determines only one of the aspects of textuality.

II. For a Typology of Utterances

Utterances produce different types of referential impressions as a function of their type of generic isotopy (precisely: mesogeneric).

1. Reference to Only One Domain

In the simplest case, one (or several) sememe(s) of the utterance under consideration belongs univocally to one and only one domain, and all of the other sememes are compatible with that domain. The utterance in its totality then refers to that domain. Thus, in 'Toutes même la plus laide a fait souffrir son amant' (And even the ugliest one of them has made her lover suffer) 139, the sememe 'amant' (lover) belongs univocally to the domain //love//. In this context, other sememes are indexed within that domain. They are manifested by *laide* (ugly), by *souffrir* (to suffer), and by morphemes of gender. We can thus identify their classes as specified by their polar terms: respectively *physical evaluation* (beauty/ugliness), *phoria* (pleasure/suffering), *sex* (masculinity/femininity); without forgetting, for 'lover', *legal evaluation* (husband/lover). This not very feminist utterance thus brings together in juxtaposition all of the socially devalorized terms of these classes.

The generic isotopy of the utterance is assured by the recurrence of the generic seme /love/, which is inherent or afferent to all of the sememes cited. All of the sememes I have not cited, corresponding for the most part to grammemes, are compatible with the domain //love//, and none belongs to any other socially codified domain. This is why what we have here is a simple generic isotopy, which creates the univocal referential impression. Were we to ask the naïve question: 'What is this utterance about?' we would always obtain answers that, directly or indirectly, allude to 'love stories.'

2. *Reference to Several Domains*

In 'Bergère ô tour Eiffel le troupeau des ponts bêle ce matin' (Shepherdess o Eiffel Tower the flock of bridges is bleating this morning), the sememes 'bergère' (shepherdess), 'troupeau' (flock), and 'bêle' (bleat) belong to the domain //country//. On the other hand, 'tour Eiffel' is of the domain //city//. This is also so for 'ponts' (bridges) in this context where Paris is obviously the locus of enunciation that is represented (see also line 24). To this we can add here, 'matin' (morning), which indicates the time of the represented enunciation: 'Tu lis les prospectus les catalogues les affiches ... / Voilà la poésie ce matin' (You read the handbills catalogues posters ... / That's the morning poetry) 11–12. The content of the utterance is thus characterized by two interconnected generic isotopies that are formed by the recurrence of the semes /city/ or /country/ in the classeme made up by the sememes cited.[13] All the other sememes of the utterance are compatible with those two domains, but none belongs to any third domain.

These two isotopies create a plurivocal referential impression: the utterance cannot be completely interpreted as a function of just one or other of the two domains. Neither can it be interpreted as a function of the two domains conjointly, because they are in opposition to each other.

They are opposed in the linguistic system, and this opposition is overdetermined in the context. The opposition /city/ versus /country/ is in homologation *vis-à-vis* the opposition /modern/ versus /ancient/, whose terms are respectively evaluated as positive and negative. Compare on the one hand 'J'aime la grâce de cette rue industrielle' (I love the grace of this industrial street) 23 and lines 7–23 passim, and on the other hand, 'A la fin tu es las de ce monde ancien' (In the end you are weary of this ancient world) 1 and 'Tu en as assez de vivre dans l'antiquité grecque et romaine' (You've had enough of living in Greek and Roman antiquity) 3.[14]

Since pastoral themes are linked to our ancient tradition and urban themes were still recent in contemporary poetry, we can agree that the first lines of the poem set modern poetry in opposition to bucolic poetry. In line 2, the vocative *ô*, which is hellenizing and obsolete, signals the bucolic genre (it already has been seen at frequent intervals in the Virgilian *Bucolics* themselves); further, shepherdesses and flocks belong by etymological definition to the topic of the genre.

The contradictory evaluations of which their members are the object lead us to seek out the relations of dominance that exist between the two isotopies. The isotopy /city/ seems dominant: on it we see placed the fundamental deictics of the represented enunciation ('je' [I], see 15, 23; 'ici' [here], 4; 'maintenant' [now], see 'ce matin' [this morning], 2, 10). Further, it extends, almost without interruption, to the end of the poem (whose very title designates an urban or suburban space). On the other hand, the isotopy /country/ is much less dense and in addition is disengaged in relation to the represented enunciation. In brief, the isotopy /city/ might be compared to the isotopy /country/, which is the comparing factor.

3. No Reference to Any Domain Whatsoever

In 'Soleil cou coupé' (Sun severed neck) 155, we cannot identify a priori any socially codified semantic domain that would include the three sememes that correspond to lexemes. The context also does not allow us to index them by inference within different domains. This utterance, which many would call asemantic, seems therefore not to have a generic isotopy, simple or complex. As a result, it does not produce a referential impression. Whence its 'non-figurative' or 'surrealist' nature, one that is rare in our poetic tradition but that is in conformity with the wish for a new poetry that we see expressed at the beginning of this text.

III. Microsemantic Analysis

To go beyond this set of problematics, I shall now analyse more finely the second and the last lines, studying their specific isotopies.

1. Line 2

A. Let me first make clear which recurrences of specific semes (and no longer generic as above) allow for the juxtaposition of the two generic isotopies of line 2, despite the contradictory referential impressions they give rise to.

a) 'bergère' and 'tour Eiffel' (shepherdess and Eiffel tower)
These two sememes[15] can be set in opposition respectively by the semic categories: /small/ versus /large/ (*vis-à-vis* dimensions); /ancient/ versus

/modern/ (including here the aspectual opposition /terminative/ versus /inchoative/).

On the other hand, they are equivalent in terms of the recurrence of the seme /unicity/, which is inferred from the zero morphemes of the singular; and by the recurrence of the seme /verticality/, which is inherent to 'tower' but afferent to 'shepherdess' in the context of 'tower' within an equative parataxis. If, on the part of listeners to whom I submitted this analysis, all of them imagined the fictive 'shepherdess' to be standing erect, but nobody objected that the Eiffel tower stands on four legs, and the 'shepherdess' on two ... We see how presuming from a given isotopy, by defining a case of semantic relevance or pertinence, determines the cognitive representations that are associated with an utterance.

b) The 'troupeau des ponts' (flock of bridges)
I am not trying to erase the ambiguity of this syntagm by choosing between the two paraphrases: a flock made up of bridges and a flock on bridges. If we read the second of these, we can rewrite 'flock of bridges' as 'group of automobiles,' the seme /animality/ thus being suspended as will be the case with 'bleating.' This reading is confirmed by 'les automobiles' (4) and 'Des troupeaux d'autobus mugissants près de toi roulent' (herds of buses roll along bellowing near you') 72; we then would have:

'automobiles' : 'buses' :: 'bleat' : 'moo' :: | 'sheep' | : | 'cows' |

If we read the first paraphrase, and if we know that the Eiffel tower is on the Seine, and between the Louvre and the Saint-Cloud gate there are twelve bridges, of which several can be seen, from certain vantage points, to be in a row, we can establish the following proportion: 'shepherdess': 'flock of sheep' :: 'Eiffel tower' : | 'all of the bridges together' |. In the fictive referent, the order of size expressed by a unit of measure is a metre for the shepherdess or for a sheep, and a hundred metres for the Eiffel tower or a Paris bridge.

The first reading is compatible with the seme /sonority/; the second allows us to actualize the seme /big/ (*vis-à-vis* dimensions).

The semic categories that allow us to set 'bridges' or 'automobiles' in opposition to 'sheep' are the same as those that set 'Eiffel tower' in opposition with 'shepherdess,' respectively. Their common seme is /horizontality/, the 'stretched out' position being common to bridges, cars, and quadrupeds.

c) 'bêle' (bleat)
As a function of the preceding, 'bleat' can be rewritten | 'honks' | (as with a car) within the isotopy /city/. The categories that set these two sememes in opposition are the same as for 'shepherdess' and 'Eiffel tower', 'flock' and 'automo-

biles', respectively. We have to remember, however, that the relative opposition /small/ versus /big/ is situated now on the scale of sonorous intensity, and no longer on a scale of physical dimension.

B. If we put it all together, this is what we have:

Oppositive categories (allotopies)	a, b, c	/artificial/ vs /natural /big/ vs /small/ /inanimate/ vs /animate/ /inchoative/ vs /terminative/ /modern/ vs /ancient/	a', b', c'
Generic isotopy /city/	a : 'Eiffel tower'	a: 'bridges' 'automobiles'	c: l'honks'l
Generic isotopy /country/	a': 'shepherdess'	b': 'flock'	c': 'bleats'
Specific isotopies	aa': /unicity/ /verticality/	bb': /multiplicity/ /horizontality/	cc': /sonority/

Note: The oppositive categories make clear the content of the opposition /city/ versus /country/ in the text. The specific isotopies make clear what semes allow for the explicit metaphorical relations between *a* and *a'*, implicit relations between *b* and *b'*, *c* and *c'*, etc. We should note that the semes that are common to *a* and *a'* are opposed term by term to the semes that are common to *b* and *b'*, hence the effect of antithesis.

If the constitutive semes of the generic isotopies have a role in the creation of a referential impression, those of the specific isotopies are independent of it to the extent that they are actualized within one or other of the generic isotopies.

The actualization of semes is a complex process, above all for afferent semes. It brings into play norms the knowledge of which is indispensable for the establishing of an interpretative path. They are independent of the functional system of language. They can be independent or not of the context. Among these norms, those that we usually call knowledge of the universe are indispensable for arriving at an interpretative validity: for example, we should keep in mind here that in 1912 the Eiffel tower still was seen to be a universal symbol of modernism. We should also keep in mind that automobiles in the numbers involved in city traffic were a novelty (on the matter of encyclopaedic knowledge, cf. Rastier 1987a, chapter 9). I shall set out in detail below the role of these norms in the actualization of certain semes.

2. *'Soleil cou coupé' (Sun severed neck)*

This line has been a problem for commentators; one of them, to solve his problem, settles for seeing here a 'burp of a drunken man.'

A. We must now make clear which semic recurrences establish specific isotopies between the contents of the two syntagms ‘soleil’ (sun) and ‘cou coupé’ (severed neck).

a) /circularity/ is one of the semes that are afferent to ’sun’ (cf. locution such as *solar disc*).[16] This seme is also afferent to ’neck’ (cf. a lexia such as *tour de cou* [round collar]). However, its actualization requires an inference: a cylindrical form, cut perpendicularly and seen face on, appears as a circular form. Here, the actualization of the seme /circularity/ presupposes a representation of certain properties of space, as they would be perceived by an observer, especially if he is familiar with the *fin de siècle* Salomés à la Moreau and more generally with Catholic iconography (where there are many instances of beheading), or even familiar with republican iconography (a Chinese friend drew to my attention the extent to which the French readily bring to mind the picture of a neck upon the guillotine).

b) /redness/ also is a seme that is afferent to ’sun’ (cf. ‘piquer un soleil: rougir’ [to blush]). Hence, in our poetic tradition, we have frequent associations between ‘sun’ and ‘blood’; cf., for example, ‘le soleil s’est noyé dans son sang qui se fige’ (the sun has drowned in its blood which is curdling). In the text we have a morning sun: ‘Tu es seul le matin va venir’ (you are alone it is about to be morning) 144, and the reader must know that the sun appears to be red in the morning. Indeed here we need to have knowledge both of the context and of the universe if we are to actualize a seme.

In ’cou coupé’ (severed neck), also, we can infer /redness/, with a simple deduction: if the neck of a living person is cut, blood flows; blood is red (I point this out only in order to emphasize the multiplicity of operations needed for interpretation).

c) /effusion/ : compare on the one hand the rays pouring out of the sun, and on the other hand the haemorrhage we infer *vis-à-vis* the ’severed neck.’[17]

> *Note:* The three semes /redness/, /circularity/, /effusion/ are not related to ’neck’, but to ’severed neck’. The problem of semic neutralizations in context arises here: if the ’neck’ is defined in dictionaries as the part of the body that unites the head to the trunk, the severed head loses one of its essential properties – albeit vital. In short, any seme can be neutralized in context.

d) We have also, added to these three semes and through the analysis of our bound grammemes, the seme /unicity/ (corresponding to the zero number morpheme). And /masculinity/ corresponds to the zero gender morpheme: in order to justify the inference of gender to sex, we might show that 'sun' belongs to a class of masculine actors (including 'Christ', see 32) and 'severed neck' belongs to another class of masculine actors (including the 'tu' [you] of the represented enunciation).

B. Let us identify now the oppositive categories that define allotopies between 'sun' and 'severed neck'.

a) /big/ versus /small/ (in terms of dimensions): the context does not make it clear, as in 'Les Doukhobors': 'le cou tranché d'une tête immense' (the severed neck of a huge head). With common sense, we can readily accept a representation of the fictive referent such that the dimensions attributed to 'severed neck' will be much smaller than those attributed to 'sun'.[18]
b) /inchoative/ versus /cessative/: we can attribute the seme /inchoative/ to the morning 'sun', and this is confirmed by the first edition of 'Zone' (*Les soirées de Paris*, 1912, no. 11) where we read 'Soleil levant cou tranché' (Rising sun severed neck) 153. On the other hand, from beheading we can infer death and thus the seme /cessative/.
c) As a function of the above we can attribute the seme /rising/ to 'sun' and /falling/ to 'severed neck' (death is often presented as a fall or descent; cf. the phrase: 'fallen for your country,' and especially the context: 'sleep' [151], 'inferior' [153]).
d) Finally, we must note the opposition /luminous/ ('sun') versus /non luminous/ ('severed neck').

C. Now we have this:

Specific isotopies (common semes)	/circularity/ /redness/ /effusion/ /unicity/ /masculinity/	
Sememe	*'sun'*	*'severed neck'*
Oppositive categories (allotopies)	/big/ /inchoative/ /rising/ /luminous/	/small/ /cessative/ /falling/ /non-luminous/

Although apparently it is inadmissible and has no referential impression, the utterance 'Soleil cou coupé' (Sun severed neck) does not thus lack semantic cohesion.

Let us agree, with all other commentators, that it contains an 'image.' Now, the syntactic structure of that utterance is an equative parataxis in which 'sun' is in the nominative and 'severed neck' can be described as an attribute predicate; 'sun' is thus the compared content and 'severed neck' is the comparing one. Traditional metaphorical orientation is thus reversed because the comparing factor now can be evaluated as being dysphoric and the compared one as euphoric. Hence the pessimistic nature of what commentators have seen in this line.

To go even further, I shall have to describe other parts of the text, bring to light its dialectics of death and resurrection, punishment and redemption, of which this line is a remarkable synthesis.

The problem of referential impression is not posed only *vis-à-vis* the instant of interpretation of utterances: we have just shown that the problem is posed already at the instant of the identification of sememes, in order to actualize certain semes. It is thus necessary to resort to representations of the fictive referent, as a function of social norms (among which is included what we usually call knowledge of the universe). This has to do with a semantics that deals with the very conditions of interpretation.

IV. Referential Impressions and Textuality

Is the referential impression produced by a text the result of referential impressions produced by its utterances? Is it enough, for example, to conclude that the referential impression produced by 'Zone' is heterogeneous? I propose the following hypothesis: for macrosemantic analysis the cohesion of a text is in the first instance the effect of a network of semic categories whose elements are recurrent in different utterances, independently of the referential impressions produced by those utterances.

1. From Molecules to the Semic Bundle

A. Let us first note that the elementary semic molecule /big/ + /inchoative/ that characterizes 'Eiffel tower' and 'bridges' also characterizes 'sun'; correlatively, the grouping /small/ + /terminative/ characterizes not only 'shepherdess' and 'flock', but also 'severed neck'.

B. This recurrence is not isolated, nor probably is it fortuitous. We read these lines: 'C'est le Christ qui monte au ciel mieux que les aviateurs / Il détient le record du monde pour la hauteur / Pupille Christ de l'oeil / Vingtième pupille des siècles il sait y faire / Et changé en oiseau ce siècle comme Jésus monte dans l'air' (This is the Christ who climbs the sky better than airmen / He holds the world record for altitude / Pupil Christ of the eye / Twentieth pupil of the centuries he knows how to do it) 40–4. Then: 'L'avion se pose enfin sans refermer les ailes / Le ciel s'emplit alors de millions d'hirondelles' (The aircraft lands at last without folding its wings / Then the sky is filled with millions of swallows) 53–4. There follows the arrival of fifteen kinds of birds, some of which are mythical, coming from Graeco-Roman or oriental antiquity, 55–70. We thus have:

'airplane' : /big/, /modern/ (including /inchoative/), /unicity/
'birds' : /small/, /ancient/ (including /cessative/), /multiplicity/

This gives the following proportional relation: (cf. the table on 196):

'shepherdess' : 'flock :: 'Eiffel tower' : 'bridges' :: 'airplane : 'birds'

The recurrences thus shown bring to light, by the contrast they set up, several transformations in relation to line 2.

a) The opposition /verticality/ versus /horizontality/ is affected by the seme /movement/ and is formulated in this way: /movement/ + /verticality/ versus /movement/ + /horizontality/. On the one hand, the airplane's mouvements are described in terms of a vertical axis, notably in terms of a climbing bird. On the other hand, the birds arrive, flying horizontally, to fraternize with the plane when it has landed: The Roc 'glides' (58), the eagle 'stoops from the edge of the sky' (59), the phoenix 'an instant veils the scene with his glowing ashes' (66).

The valorization of ascensional movement, linked to the resurrection (It is 'God who dies on Friday and rises from the dead on Sunday / ... Christ who climbs the sky' 39–40]), begins as early as lines 4–6: 'Ici même les automobiles ont l'air d'être anciennes / La religion seule est restée toute neuve la religion / Est restée simple comme les hangars de Port-Aviation' (Even the automobiles have an air of antiquity here / Only religion remains perfectly new religion / Has kept as simple as the hangars at the airport). The opposition /ancient/ versus /modern/ is thus hierarchically lower than the opposition /horizontal movement/ versus /vertical movement/: and this is why the cars, although in fact ultramodern for that time, are devalorised when compared to the airplane.

b) The opposition /natural/ versus /artificial/ that we find in the first table is more relevant here: indeed, 'airplane', 'Jesus', and 'bird' (in the singular) can be substituted for one another (see 'Et changé en oiseau ce siècle comme Jésus monte dans l'air' (And changed to a bird this century rises like Jesus in the air) 44. We could show that, on the contrary, the real surreal and the untrue real are in opposition to each other and, for example, this is why we see the juxtaposition of real birds such as swallows with mythical ones such as the Roc, or winged and treacherous sirens.

C. Let us now study the class of contents – which is assuredly idiolectal – to which 'airplane', 'Christ', 'pupil', and also 'torch', and other references to Christ belong (31–5). In the components of this class we see all of the descriptive semes of 'sun':

/circularity/:	cf. 'pupil,' 'glory' (luminous circle), 'turns.'
/redness/:	cf. 'flaming,' 'red,' 'blood.'
/effusion/:	cf. 'torch,' 'flaming,' and 'The blood of your Sacred Heart deluged me at Montmartre.'
/climbing/:	cf. 'airplane,' 'He holds the world record for altitude,' 'this century rises like Jesus.'
/inchoative/:	cf. 'this century' (the text dates from 1913); 'airplanes' (aviation had only just begun: its modernity is emphasized).
/luminous/:	cf. 'glory,' 'flaming,' 'torch.'
/big/:	in relation to birds (see above).
/unicity/:	all of the sememes of this class are linked to grammemes of the singular.
/masculinity/:	cf. 'Jesus.'

The recurrence of the elements of just one semic molecule that is composed of nine semes and is lexicalized in the final *sun*, confirms the permanent presence throughout the text of a bundle of specific isotopies.

It allows for the readability of sememes that belong to the most diverse semantic domains. A priori 'pupil', 'Christ', and 'airplane', for example, do not have a common constituent. However, we have just seen that the combination of the elements of just one semic molecule[19] justifies anaphoras and substitutions between sememes, and indeed between all the sememes of their class. The semantic domains to which they belong then appear as variables.

2. The Cohesion of the Classes of Actors

Let us make sure of what has just been said. I have shown a relation between three sections of the text and have noted recurrences of semes that allow us to homologate the actors that make up the same semic molecules and, on the other hand, allow us to identify dialectic transformations that are based upon those molecules.

Classes of actors	A	B
line 2	'Eiffel tower'	'flock'
	↓	↓
lines 40–70[20]	'airplane' 'Christ'	'birds' ... 'skull of Adam'
	↓	↓
line 155	'sun'	'severed neck'

The semic groupings that constitute these classes are, for the first, /inchoative/ and /modern/, /European/, /artificial/, and/or /supernatural/. For the second, /terminative/ and/or /archaic/, /exotic/, /natural/.

Initially I shall extend these classes of actors in order to set out in detail the way in which they have been constituted and to reinforce their plausibility. For that, I shall have to resort to encyclopaedic interpretants.[21]

A. The First Class

I have eliminated 'shepherdess' from the first class despite Couffignal (1966), who bases himself on the known fact that Christ is traditionally compared to a shepherd. Here the comparison can be ignored because 'shepherdess' is evoked within the context of Graeco-Roman antiquity (as opposed to Christianity, which alone 'is not ancient'; cf. 7).

Because there is no direct accessibility between 'shepherdess' and 'Christ,' the complex metaphorical chain 'shepherdess' → 'Eiffel tower' → 'airplane' 'Christ' alone links these two actors.[22]

Let us look at 'Christ' and 'sun'.

The nine common semes listed on 202 proceed from a rich metaphorical tradition. Based mainly upon Malachi ('Et orietur vobis timentibus nomen meum Sol Iusticiae'), the identification of Christ with the sun was pushed far enough that Saint Augustine found in it the danger of a return to paganism. After having inspired innumerable sermons, canticles, and hymns, that identification still, until recently, maintained an important place in the liturgy.[23]

I have already referred to the other relations found within class A. They could be confirmed by making comparisons with other poems by Apollinaire: for instance, we read in 'Les collines': 'Tandis qu'au zénith flamboyant l'éternel avion solaire ...' (Whereas at the flaming zenith the eternal solar plane ...)

B. Class B

(i) 'severed neck' and 'bird'

The *amadina fasciata*, a kind of waxbill known by the name 'cou coupé' (severed neck), has a bright red band across its throat. This domestic bird is originally from Central Africa and its habitat covers the area from Senegal to Somalia.[24] The airplane is surrounded by other birds from Africa (57).

(ii) 'severed neck' and 'skull of Adam'

In the next lines, the Roc bird glides down, 'carrying in his talons the skull of Adam.' Now, from 'severed neck' we can easily infer 'head' and 'death', hence 'skull'.

C. The Relations between Classes A and B

(i) 'Christ' and the 'skull of Adam'

In crucifixions one often sees a skull at the foot of the cross. One enduring apocryphal tradition says it is Adam's. Not only did the tree from which the cross came grow out of Adam's skull, because Seth had planted its seeds in Adam's mouth at the time of his death,[25] but also many believe that Calvary was precisely on the spot where the first man was buried. This tradition, of course, appears in literature (for example, Hugo, 'L'âme immense d'Adam couché sous le Calvaire ...' [The immense soul of Adam, lying beneath Calvary'], *La fin de Satan*, II, 2, 21). Indeed *Golgotha* can be translated as 'the place of the skull' (Hebrew root *glg*).

Christ is sometimes called 'the new Adam.' Saint Paul indeed describes Adam as a 'figure of he who is to come' (Romans 2:14), although all the while opposing Adam and Christ: 'Just as all die in Adam, all will live again in Christ' (I Corinthians 3:22).

The movement in the fictive space of the Roc (carrying Adam's skull) towards the airplane (a substitute for Christ) thus initiates the closure of the cycle of prophecy. This will be further confirmed later on.

(ii) The airplane and the birds

The birds that fraternize with the plane come from everywhere (Africa, America, China are mentioned) and belong to various eras. Several are mythical (Roc, sirens, phoenix) or symbolic (dove, peacock). Four at least appear frequently in the Christian tradition, first and foremost 'la colombe esprit immaculé' (the dove herself immaculate spirit) 63. The peacock, in iconography, often drinks from the holy chalice. The eagle, king of the birds, is an angelic form (cf. Ezekiel 1: 10; Revelation 4: 7–8); the Psalms use the eagle as a symbol of spiritual regeneration. It is identified in spiritual iconography with Saint John (indeed, formerly, with Christ or the Word). The phoenix, 'ce bûcher qui soi-même s'engendre' (that funeral pyre who engenders himself), has since Origen been considered to be sacred, and this solitary bird symbolized the resurrection of Christ throughout the whole of the Middle Ages.

Note: The most likely source, although it has been unnoticed, of the passage we are dealing with is the *De ave Phoenice* of Lactantius, especially these lines:

Magnitiem terris Arabum quae gignitur ales
vix aequare potest, seu fera seu sit avis.

... levis ac velox, regali plena decore:
talis in aspectu se tenet usque hominum.

... Contrahit in coetum sese genus omne volantum
nec praedae memor est ulla nec ulla metus.
Alituum stipata choro volat illa per altum
turbaque prosequitur munere laeta pio.

... Ipsa quidem, sed non [eadem est] eademque nec ipsa est,
aeternam vitam mortis adepta bono.

(This bird that the Arabs' country engenders, no beast, no winged creature can equal its greatness ... it is light and fast, full of royal glory: this is how the phoenix is seen by men ... Winged creatures of every species come together in a group, forgetting all fear and all their prey. Surrounded by this choir of birds, the phoenix rises into the heavens and the happy flock follows it in pious homage ... In truth, he himself, but not [the same] and he is not the same, he attains eternal life through the happiness of death.)

This poem was imitated by Claudianus and paraphrased by Cynewulf (or someone from his group), but Lactantius remains the most likely source. Certainly we can, as René Pichon did, contest the claim that there is any Christian nature in the *De ave Phoenice* and instead argue that Lactantius wrote it before his conversion. It does not matter. It remains undeniably mystical.

Abelard, in the Laudes he wrote for the Saturday following Good Friday, takes up this myth and emphasizes its Easter meaning (see line 39 of our text): The marvellous bird, the unique Phoenix / which is re-animated by the third dawn, as it is brought back / ... rose up in its accustomed flight / when Christ rose into the heavens

/ ... Resembling Christ completely / it rose higher than all the animals, than all the birds' (Avis mirabilis phoenix et unica, / Quam et lux reparat, ut ferunt, tertia, / ... Similitudine Christi plenissima, Transcendit bestias et volatilia).

Apollinaire could thus have known the *De ave phoenice* by reading *Le latin mystique* (1892) of Rémy de Gourmont.

One more word about the Roc, which carries the ancestral skull. This giant bird from the Persian tradition is generally confused with the *sîmorgh* with which it shares certain features: it is also the king, gigantic and divine, of all the birds.[26]

To sum up, if we compare the actors of classes A and B at the poem's moment of the return of Christ (lines 52–70), class A is, by virtue of its features /modernity/, /European/,[27] /Christian/, in contrast with class B, whose actors include the features /archaic/ and/or /exotic/ and/or /mythical/ or /natural/. The actors do not all have the same degree of 'typicality': for example, the sirens are archaic and mythical, the hummingbird is only exotic and natural.

D. Extension of Class B

Many actors of this class carry the afferent feature /religious/. Several can symbolize Christ in the sense that they are archaic, exotic, or imperfect forms of him. Hence this hypothesis: The inferior Christs ('les Christ inférieurs' 153), lexicalize the features that are typical of class B. However, these Christs are also exotic (they come from Oceania and Guinea, 151).

This hypothesis is confirmed when we consider the human actors of class B in lines 42–52. During the ascension the priests (52) are not strictly speaking 'inferior Christs,' but they are at least servants of Christ. The angels, if they are not human, are also subordinate forms of divinity. This is especially evident in the enigmatic line 49: 'Icare Énoch Élie Apollonius de Thyane' (I know of no commentator who has tackled this line).

Some Church Fathers have seen in Icarus the image of a soul rising up on the wings of a false love, comparing him to Christ in order to establish the contrast. Enoch (see Genesis 4:1–7; lines 18–24) was, according to tradition, carried up into the heavens and never knew death. Elijah is the other person in the Bible who did not die: he travelled up in a chariot of fire. As the *return* of Elijah was announced, certain people mistook Jesus for Elijah (Mark 4:15). Philostratus, biographer of Apollonius, leads us to understand that he did not die. Hierocles compared him to Christ, bringing down upon himself the furious refutations of Lactantius and Eusebius (*Contra Hierocles*).[28]

In short, of these four humans, the first three were carried up or raised themselves up into heaven. The last three did not die. The first and the last two have been compared to Jesus. All four are archaic,[29] and/or mythical, as is the case for the birds of this same class B.

Note: As opposed to referential semantics, differential semantics treats proper nouns exactly as it does nouns. Here, it is the presumption of isotopy that allows us to select in each name the relevant features. That presumption is then reinforced by analysis of the context. Thus this enigmatic succession of proper nouns is part of what makes the cohesiveness of this text.

This first extension of class B allows us to confirm the stability of the type of semic molecule all of whose actors have at least one feature : 1 /religious/, 2 /ascensional/, 3 /inferior/, 4 /ancient/, 5 /foreign/, 6 /multiple/. Examples of occurrences:

'Adam's skull': 1, 2, 4
'Icarus': 2, 4
'Enoch': 1, 2, 4
'Roc': 1, 2, 4, 5
'these priests' (line 52): 1, 2 (cf. climb), 3 (in relation to airplane-Jesus[30]), 6.

Note: Certain of the constitutive semes of the molecule have affinities between them that are of the noemic order. /Religious/ and /ascensional/ support a rich symbolics that is not just of the Judaeo-Christian tradition (from Plato to the extactic wanderings of Taoists). /Foreign/ and /ancient/ sum up, along two different semantic axes, one and the same disposition relative to the *hic et nunc* of the represented enunciation. Finally, /inferior/ is often linked to the disjunctive terms of the *hic et nunc* and sometimes this is in a depreciative way (see in French, the accepted meanings of *peripheral* or *marginal*).

Let us now go on to lines 151–3: 'tes fétiches d'Océanie et de Guinée / ... Christ d'une autre forme et d'une autre croyance ... Christ inférieurs.' (Your fetishes from Oceania and Guinea / They are Christs of another shape and another creed / Inferior Christs). These lines lexicalize in a synthetic way the constitutive semic molecule of class B.

/religious/: 'Christ', 'fetishes'; /subordinate/: 'inferior'; /foreign/: 'from Oceania and Guinea'.[31]

We can now formulate a new hypothesis: since contiguity in fictive space is often coterminous with semantic equivalence, we should look to see whether the *ego* that is going to sleep among the inferior Christs might belong to the same class of actors:

- /religious/: 'la honte te retient / D'entrer dans une église et de t'y confesser ce matin' (shame restrains you from going into a church and confessing there this morning) 9–10; 'Vous [inclusive] n'aimez rien tant que les pompes de l'église' (You like nothing so much as the ceremonies of the church) 28; 'tu entrerais dans un monastère' (you would enter a monastery) 75.
- /inferior/: 'comme le feu de l'Enfer ton rire pétille' (your laugh crackles like hellfire) 77; 'je suis malade' (I am sick) 85; 'une maladie honteuse' (a shameful sickness) 86; 'j'humilie ... ma bouche' (I humble my mouth) 143.
- /foreign/: 'aux environs de Prague' (near Prague) 95; 'au Hradchin,' 103; 'à Coblence,' 107; 'à Rome assis sous un néflier du Japon' (in Rome, seated under a Japanese medlar tree) 108; 'à Amsterdam' ... Leyde ... Gouda,' 109–12. Cf. also pity for emigrants (121), the foreigner (140), knowledge of half-castes[32] (146–7).
- /ancient/: cf. 'l'âge' (116); 'j'ai perdu mon temps' (I wasted my time) 118; 'tu en as assez de vivre dans l'antiquité' (you've had enough of living in antiquity) 3.
- /multiple/: the ego of the represented narrator is in fact split into two actors, 'je' and 'tu'. The first is coterminous with the moment of the fictive enunciation (even in sentences in the past tense); for example: 'je m'en souviens' (I remember) 112; 'j'ai vécu' (I've lived) 118. The second belongs to the past (even in sentences in the present); for example: 'Te voici à Amsterdam' (Here you are in Amsterdam) 109. When the 'tu' coincides with the moment of fictive enunciation, it is devalorized; for example: 'la honte te retient ... ce matin' (9–10). That confirms that the disjunctive terms along the three axes of the represented enunciation undergo a dysphoric evaluation: the 'tu' (disjoined from the 'je'), ancient (disjoined from the present), foreign (disjoined from here). However, doubling is just a simpler form of multiplicity. The phenomenon of multiplicity is deployed within the ubiquitous nature of the 'tu' (lines 71–151), as underlined by the fact that temporal intervals are not ordered and the various loci are presented in parataxis (see the instances of 'te voici,' (here you are) lines 106–9).[33] If this feature is not lexicalized, it is however actualized in the occurrences of 'tu' by the inferences that are summarized above.

E. A Rereading

Now we can come back to the last lines. If 'sun', like Jesus, belongs to class A, I can defend the hypothesis according to which 'severed neck' belongs to class B.

(i) By default, 'neck' includes the feature /human/. Now, the only 'tu' in the immediate context includes that feature; and it belongs to class B.
(ii) 'severed neck', as we have seen, refers to 'the skull of Adam' (also belonging to class B).
(iii) Now, 'tu' is a sinner (see 9–10, 143, etc.); Adam also; and beheading was the form of capital punishment at the time.[34]

Thus 'tu', 'Adam', and 'severed neck' are three actors belonging to class B and all possessing the feature /culpability/.

Since the actors of the same class can be subsituted for one another (at least in the name of productive although reductive reading), we might, keeping in mind their metaphorical connections, also read in this line 'Jesus Adam.' This last line would then in its own way close off the cycle of prophecy,[35] or, in more Paulist terms, the story that goes from Adam and the Old Testament to the New Adam and New Testament.

However, this last line suspends, indeed *reverses* the direction of the narrative flow: the syntactic relation between 'sun' and 'severed neck' is certainly a parataxic equative, but the tactic succession of the two syntagms does not allow us to read any succession other than /euphoria/ (cf. 'sun' in the morning) followed by /dysphoria/ ('severed neck'):[36] that is, the elementary structure of pessimism.

We should not try to find an orthodox theology in this sin for which there is no redemption. Let us leave these mysteries for others. The only thing that interests us here is the semantic causes of the mystery effect. In order to clarify those causes we have to come back to the problem of referential impression. I noted above that 'soleil cou coupé' (sun severed neck) brought on no referential impression because this line did not refer to any constituted semantic domain. The example is not without validity but it is artificial, because it is given out of context. Subsequently the analysis allowed us to perceive the richness of the semantic relations between 'sun' and the other members of class A, between 'severed neck' and the rest of class B. Now, we have to formulate new propositions.

The problem of mediation between classes A and B should be posed here: why does this line exclude it? We must ask why John the Baptist is absent here, he being the mediating figure par excellence, since he was at the same time the last prophet and the first man to live in both the ancient and modern worlds, *sub lege* and *sub gratia*. This absence is quite relative because although he is not named, we find traces of him.

(i) Antithetical comparisons between the sun and the beheaded neck of the Baptist are many in *fin de siècle* art; for example in Gustave Moreau's *Salomé*. Flaubert admired that picture when he began *Herodias*, in which the faithful carry off the severed head 'at the instant when the sun was rising.' The symbolic antithesis is thus emphasized: 'The Essenian now understood these words [just pronounced by the Baptist]: "So that he might grow, I must be reduced."'

Mallarmé adds to this in his *Hérodiade*, especially in his *Cantique de saint Jean*, in which the severed head speaks: 'The sun which its supernatural pause exalts, quickly sinks again, Incandescent. I feel as in the vertebra, the darkness spreading.'

(ii) The Precursor can be included among the 'inferior Christs.'

(iii) Baptismal themes are present in this text (see 90–4).

None the less, we do not find in 'Zone' any mediation between the two ages of the world that correspond to classes A and B. Greek and Roman antiquity (3) are opposed directly by catholic modernity (5–8). The status of the Jews who live in 'this ancient world,' *sub lege*, is significant: 'Les aiguilles de l'horloge du quartier juif vont à rebours' (The hands of the public clock in the ghetto move withershins) 102. Now, the narrator shares this: 'Et tu recules aussi dans ta vie lentement' (And you too move slowly backward into your life) 103. Whereas traditionally Lazarus's resurrection is described as an allegory of Christ's resurrection, here 'Tu ressembles au Lazare affolé par le jour' (You ... looking like Lazarus unwitted by the daylight) 101. We find more Jews at the gare Saint-Lazare (125): their being fixed in a past time is reflected by their immobility (these paradoxical emigrants 'se déplacent rarement comme les pièces aux échecs' [move only now and then like pieces in a chess game]) 132. The last line therefore comes at an inconceivable moment in time that juxtaposes two ages with no mediation between them: the age of the first sin (76–7; 140–1), but when there was no redemption, and the age of promise, like the promise of a new morning, but in the midst of the anguish of a new era.

V. Directions the Research Can Take

The problem of referential impression is posed in very different ways according to which *threshold* or *level* of analysis you are talking about:

(i) At the level of the syntagm, and particularly of the word, one or more referential impressions can be called up; they correspond to *meanings* and *acceptions* that have been listed in the dictionaries,[37] and they also correspond to *uses* for them that have not been so recorded.

(ii) At the level of the utterance, the possible impressions are generally restricted by the establishment of a generic isotopy that accounts for the reciprocal selection, in context, of sememes. In exception to the rule, in the case of figures mentioned above, we can construct more than one isotopy (see line 2) or none at all (see line 155).

(iii) At the level of the text, and above all in the case of mythical texts (literary and/or religious especially), the production of referential impressions can become complex all over again, not this time because of the absence of linguistic determination (as is the case at the level of an isolated word), but rather because of a plurality of determinations. To the incidence we note in the immediate context, we see added several different incidences from faraway contexts.

To sum up, at the levels of the word, the utterance, and the text, referential impressions differ. At the first level they are potentially the most diverse because of the absence of determinations that have their source in the context. At the third level they are potentially the richest because of the overabundant supply of determinations coming from the context.

I can illustrate this by setting into perspective what I said above about the last line. If isolated, it does not produce any referential impression at the level of the utterance because of the lack of a codified semantic domain in language that can be common to the two syntagms and can bring about a mesogeneric isotopy. On the other hand, if we keep in mind the context, the two syntagms 'sun' and 'severed neck' take their place in the A and B classes of actors. This means that they can be indexed, through the afference of generic features, along different isotopies having to do with different domains; for example, see following table.

Domains	A	B
//geography//	/European/	/exotic/
//history//	/modern/ (e.g., 'airplane')	/ancient/ (e.g., 'Apollonius')
//religion//	/neo-testament/ (e.g., 'Jesus')	/vetero-testament/ (e.g., 'Adam')

Two types of interpretative strategies are then possible.

(i) The first, in the western hermeneutic tradition,[38] privileges a semantic domain and lexicalizes litigious contents there. For example, in the domain //religion//, 'sun' + /neo-testament/ might be rewritten 'Jesus'; and 'severed neck' + /vetero-testament/ might be rewritten 'Adam's skull'.

(ii) None the less the interpretative instructions that are explicit in the text are often deceiving and, in any case, they cannot take the place of solid methodology. For a linguistic analysis, the interpretative paths suggested by the text certainly remain privileged, but they are not exclusive. In addition, the 'message' of the text does not count any more than its 'structure': even if we were to suppose that the quest for textual meaning ends up with the creation of a stable configuration, that configuration is no more important than the path that led to it. It is also no more important than the other configurations, stable or unstable, that preceded it on the above path.

In concrete terms, in the case in point, I thus refuse any rewriting that might impose a univocal referential impression. I maintain then that 'sun' and 'severed neck' refer to the level of the syntagm and of the text, but not of the utterance. At the level of the text, which is what we are dealing with here, they refer to each of the other actors of their respective classes, without, for all that, being able to be substituted for them, and without its being the case that one or other of those actors can be substituted for them.

Note: In the acception of *refer*, is there not an abuse of terms? As we agreed at the beginning of this study, this is just a case here of intratextual reference, determined by the pairing[39] of several occurrences of just one semic molecule, and by the correlative superimposition of the mental images produced by the contents that include those occurrences.[40] 'Syntactic' anaphora is just a rudimentary case of this reference. More generally, relations that are often called *symbolic* (including what I have called *symbolic connection*) also have to do with this type of reference: we should be clear that they are intratextual and not intertextual.

In any case, substitutions within a class of actors do not occur *ceteris paribus*, since each actor can differ from the others not only in terms of its dialectic structure but also in terms of its thematic structure.[41] In short, the modulus for equivalence between actors can vary from one pair to the other.

Now, the interpretative strategy for rewriting that we set out above tends to sum up any given class of actors with reference to an actor type.[42] Hence it gives privileged status to a generic isotopy while at the same time ignoring specific differences between actors.

I should rather study the *degrees of typicality*[43] within classes of actors. These degrees are defined by the number and hierarchical position of the semes of the semic molecule that are manifested by the actor. The most typical actor might manifest them all. Now, the *referential force* (intratextual) of an actor develops in proportion to his degree of typicality:[44] the higher the degree, the greater the density of the semantic connections going from the actor toward the other actors of the same class (and indeed of other classes).

We can thus account for, without settling for an appeal to common sense, the differences in semantic importance (measured in terms of number of connections) between very typical actors (for example 'Jesus' in class A) and non-typical actors (for example 'hummingbird' in class B). The first can be connected to most of the others, the second ones can be connected to the most typical without, for all that, being connectable to each other. This can be visualized as follows:

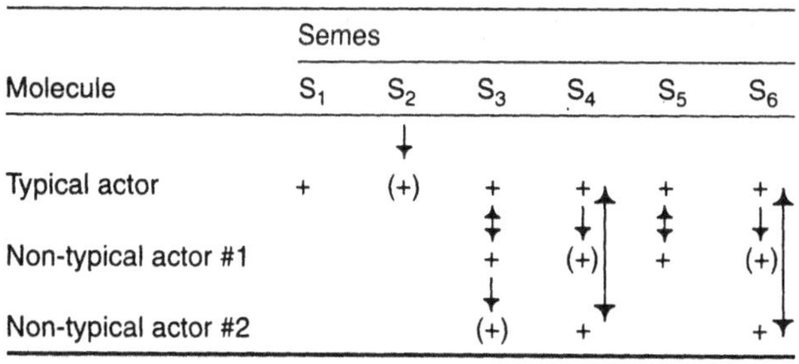

	Semes					
Molecule	S_1	S_2	S_3	S_4	S_5	S_6
		↓				
Typical actor	+	(+)	+	+ ↑	+	+ ↑
			↕	↓	↕	↓
Non-typical actor #1			+	(+)	+	(+)
			↓			
Non-typical actor #2			(+)	+ ↓		+ ↓

The arrows with heads at both ends symbolize semic connections; one-headed arrows symbolize possible relations of afference; features seen between parentheses are afferent features that are actualized in the case of a rewriting.

Does the (meso)generic isotopy in which a given highly typical actor is indexed have the privileged status of a dominant, indeed as a hierarchically superior actor?[45] Likely so. But the interpretative strategy I have adopted does not seek to rewrite litigious contents along a dominant or valorized isotopy; that would produce a flat reading.

More generally, I believe that a poly-isotopic text is not, strictly speaking, *plurivocal*. If we want to claim to have described its meaning, it is not enough to rhyme off one after the other its principal generic isotopies (even those that have been enriched by rewritings). More correctly speaking, such a text is *equivocal*. That, however, is a general property of mythical texts (especially literary and religious ones). That is why, even though their semantic structures are obviously finite, the readings thereof are infinite, including perhaps those that claim a descriptive validity.

The problem of reference was posed by logic in general terms, for all decidable propositions. In semantics I have posed the problem of a typology of referential impressions as a function of certain kinds of generic isotopy. But we cannot remain under the linguistic illusion that there are principles common to all texts; I have to emphasize that principles concerning the construction of referential impressions, even if they possess general psychophysiological substrats that are responsible for mental images, remain determined by cultural factors that have to do not only with language but with the type of discourse, genre, the social practice of which that genre is part. Here, in a poem, we have to keep semantic morphologies in mind. They set up relations between these semantic forms that we call semic molecules (in 'Zone' the two principal molecules, which constitute the invariables of classes A and B) and the perceptive resources flowing from generic isotopies.

Within our own tradition, we have to set up relations between semantic morphologies that are proper to genres and styles on the one hand and, on the other, aesthetic theories, explicit or not, to which they correspond and of which they are equally cause and effect. We should agree on the term *aesthesies* for these 'visions of the world' that are brought about and whose limits are set by various kinds of semantic morphologies.

When studying artistic realism, I identified (1992c, 1992d) the world visions of empirical realism and of transcendent realism. The link between them allows us to move from the empirical reality effect to the transcendent reality effect, via the metaphorical connection between two isotopies, on the condition that the comparing isotopy is positively evaluated. In the second line of 'Zone,' as we have noted, this traditional connection is derided. The other, more difficult, connecting path can be called antinomist: it destroys the empirical reality effect and creates a transcendental reality effect, not through isotopy, but rather through allotopy. It uses examples of this. Thus, the narrative and thematic transformation that is sought in the first line and that fails in the second in an ironic renewal or re-statement, succeeds in the last line in a strange apophasis, a divine unveiling and hiding of meaning; and all this occurs not through narrative mediation, but rather through a reversing of aesthetic techniques.

Notes

Introduction

1 For a discussion, see Coseriu, 1981. The *Fachtextlinguistik* that is currently being worked out appears much more promising, if only because it has abandoned universalist ambitions.
2 If one follows Morris and Carnap (and even Montague), pragmatics must be considered as a branch of semiotics.
3 For a discussion of this, see Rastier, 1988a.
4 This confusion is appropriate in this discipline. Note how Jackendoff (1983) assimilates semantics and cognition.
5 On universal grammars and their genealogy, see Rastier, 1988b.
6 The mediatic agitation twenty years ago around structuralism (then around post-structuralism) has undoubtedly contributed to obscure this: Linguistics was not a leading science (and it has paid dearly for this temporary illusion); but the comparative method, stemming from it, and the rational principles expressed by the alleged structuralism in question, has an impact that surpasses it and extends to all the social sciences.
7 To avoid repetition, the glossary at the end of this book clarifies the main concepts in this matter.
8 For example, I shall spare the reader my work on the automatic analysis of résumés on the observation of thyroid cancer.
9 In second place after religious texts, which, semantically speaking, have many traits in common with literary texts.
10 I reject the traditional opposition between form and meaning, once again in vogue and regrettably revived by formal grammars.
11 See, e.g., M. Imbert concerning Léviant's illusion (*Le Courrier du C.N.R.S.*, no. 66–8, 1987, appendix, 2).

12 See chap. 13, the analysis of 'Bergère ô tour Eiffel,' in Apollinaire's poem 'Zone,' and why we 'see' the shepherdess 'upright.' The elementary interpretative operations brought to the fore (cf. 1987a, chaps. 3 and 8) evidently depend upon these laws of perception.
13 The term itself indicates that it is exhausting, for the author as well as for the reader. The principle of exhaustiveness, as articulated by Hjelmslev and taken up again by the semiotic tradition that claims to draw from it, rests on an immanentism that I challenge later on.
14 Two disciplines, be they scientific or not, can very well share the same empirical object without sharing the same real object, or even the same objectives. The pretensions of certain linguists that they 'invalidate' the discourse of criticism have created the illusion of a competition where there was in fact complementarity.
15 I have taken the side of an empirical rationalism.

1: On the 'Objectivity' of Meaning

1 Moreover, in the same way as expression: letters, *a fortiori* phonemes, that can be identified only by means of very complex operations, are still poorly understood. Sound is no less a *cosa mentale* than the meaning.
2 See Greimas et Courtés, 1979 [1982] 'Hermeneutics' article.
3 See, for example, the collective work on Baudelaire's 'Les Chats,' where different critics claiming to use the same structural method widely contradict one another.
4 Ricoeur's study, *The Problem of Double-Meaning Considered as a Semantic Problem and as a Hermeneutic Problem*, can be reread from this point of view (1969, 64–79).
5 For example, according to Kristeva, (*Histoires d'amour*, 248–55), Don Juan only desires his mother (who is, for all that, absent in Molière) and finds satisfaction only in 'the icy embrace of the father' (the Commander, of course). Barthes warned us: 'Does not every story lead to Oedipus?' (1973, 75).
6 Why does Riffaterre see 'repressed sexual implications in Moses' *staff*' (1983, 23)?
7 It could be said that a 'fact' is a triplet composed of a setting, an observer, and an object.
8 A plausible reading proceeds from a principally intrinsic interpretation (see Rastier, 1987a, chap. 8).
9 That is why the study of linguistic 'content' is often devolved upon non-linguistic disciplines, such as logic and psychology.
10 We know that the phonatory muscles are slightly aroused when one 'thinks' (for example, while solving a mathematical problem) and the progressions of cerebral imagery allow one to see then the linguistic zones in action.
11 I have modified my terminology with regards to previous works: in thus defining

meaning and *signification* I link up with a long tradition (from Dumarsais to Ducrot), although several authors (such as Charaudeau and Martin) maintain the inverse use of the terms.

12 The mass of literature on linguistic ambiguity would become noticeably lighter if, instead of sentences isolated from a context, one studied at least paragraphs.

13 The theory of afferences is one of these means.

14 Its ancestors could be found among Pergamenian philologists rather than Alexandrian allegorists.

15 The very notion of *content* perpetuates the traditional image of the sign as the 'recipient' of a concept.

16 These are the very words of Daniel Kayser.

17 Admittedly, *several* descriptive readings can be produced by strategies that diversely connect licit interpretative operations: all then stem from what I have called intrinsic interpretation.

18 The rules of assimilation and dissimilation that I have brought to the fore are examples of these laws (see Rastier, 1987a, chap. 8, and 1991, chap. 7).

2: Difficulties of Avant-Garde Hermeneutics

1 See *Einführung in die literarische Hermeneutik*, Frankfurt, Suhrkamp, 1975.

2 See especially Ricoeur, *De l'interprétation. Essai sur Freud*, on psychoanalysis as hermeneutics.

3 Would it be appropriate to introduce here nuances between post-structuralism and post-modernism, deconstructionism and, why not, desirantism? Admittedly, it would, but one would have to consecrate an entire book to this, a book that the reader will gladly do without here.

4 See *De doctrina christiana*, I, 36, 40. If there are several interpretations that conform to the faith, they are equally justified.

5 This example is in no way exceptional. In the description of the 'blanquette de veau' in *L'Assommoir*, some eminent scholars suggested the reading of a libidinal isotopy, insisting bizarrely on the word *hole* (see chapter 9).

6 When Ricardou (1967) sees an allegory of *boustrophédon* in 'Le laboureur et ses enfants,' he does no more than reuse, for his own ends, the age-old topos that compares furrows to lines of writing, and of which we see the last occurrence in Rimbaud: 'A hand at the plough is the same as a hand with a pen.' For the history of this topos, see E.-R. Curtius, *Europäische Literatur und lateinisches Mittelalter*, Berne, Francke, 1948.

7 A. Ubersfeld, *Romantisme*, VI (1974), in a study of *Aux Feuillantines*, wherein she sees, in the collective reading of the Bible by the young Hugo and his brothers, 'the auto-erotic games of childhood and adolescence' (70).

8 Notably Aboulafia, Gikatilla, and Menahem Recanati.

9 See *La Estafeta de Urganda*, London, 1861; *El Mensaje de Merlín*, London, 1875; *La verdad sobre el Quijote*, Madrid, 1878. For example, in the name of the bachelor, *Perez de Alcobendas* (see I, 19), Benjumea read the words 'es lo Blanco de Paz,' which designates the Dominican who denounced Cervantes to the Dey of Algiers, and then to the Inquisition. One of his successors, José de Benito, proposes such anagrams as *Cide Hamete Benengeli = Io Miguel de Cerbantes i Saavedra horto igni* (see *Hacia la Luz del Quijote*, Madrid, Aguilar, 1960).

10 This inverse technique, for *gl* and *j*, the *notaricon* procedure used by the Jewish mystics that consisted in constructing a new word with the initials or the last letters of several words. In spite of all of Freud's authority, one comes to think that any old germano-phonic crossword puzzle enthusiast using the same method would have been able to propose other analyses that would be no less convincing.

11 Hermeneutic tradition, including psychoanalysis, has accustomed us to emphasize the hidden. It does not follow that posthumous manuscripts are necessarily inspired. Saussure strongly doubted the value of his research (see his letter to Meillet of 12 November 1906 [*L'Homme*, XI, 1971, 16]) and in the end his doubts dissuaded him from publishing them. The best technical refutation of his error (for all of its brilliance) remains F. Desbordes, 'A propos du Saturnien,' *Latomus*, 39, 1, 3–24.

12 *La dissémination*, Paris, Seuil, 1972.

13 *Revue française de psychanalyse*, Jan. 1970, 101–36; July 1971, 543–91.

14 'These semantic values can be immediate semantizations (of an onomatopoeic type) of the sex drive, without passing through identifiable morphemes' (Kristeva, 1974, 222).

15 'We were casting our eyes / (There were the two of us, I am sure of it) / Over the many charms of the countryside / O sister, comparing them to yours.'

16 Kristeva, 1974, 247.

17 Published when avant-garde hermeneutics was on the rise (cf. *Questions de poétique*).

18 Ibid., 434. The examples taken from the other 'Spleens' are less convincing; for example, one could compare 'Cependant qu'en un jeu PLein de sales parfums' (435) to 'Nous aurons des lits PLeins d'odeurs légères' ('La mort des amants').

19 It would also be within one's rights to search for the words 'Spleen et idéal' in the eighty-five poems of this section, the words 'Les fleurs du mal' in every poem, and find them disseminated everywhere. Every book contains thousands of anagrams of its title; just as of its author's name: does Jakobson not suggest reading the name Shakespeare in 'Th'expence of spirit in a waste of shame' and his first name in the words *well, yet*, and *men* (cf. op. cit., p. 374)?

20 'In a symmetric way, an abstract feminine-gender noun emerges in the third-to-last line of each stanza : 2 *pietà*, 6 *guistizia*, 9 *paura*, 12 *vertù*' (*Questions*, 307).

21 Let us overlook the fact that the demonstration lacks precision: the /r/ is not pertinent here, and it is surprising to see *pietà* itself cited among the words that surround and echo it.
22 Let us not even speak of *falsification*, as this concept is only of value in the 'hard' sciences.
23 The status of certain signs that make them up (the linked grammemes) is not clear. Will *pietà* and *pietoso* be counted as two occurrences of the same key-word, since the sign 'piet' – remains invariable?
24 For example, the verb *ramasser* (to gather) in Giono's *Noé*.
25 It is well known that the articulatory and acoustic properties of a phoneme vary greatly according to its position.
26 *Sémiotique de la poésie*, 144.
27 'This recently introduced term seems to be a new label for all sorts of well-recognized facts such as reminiscence, the use (explicit or camouflaged, ironic or allusive) of sources, quotation,' Segre, 1985b, 83. A more 'cognitive' but even more vague meaning is developed by Beaugrande and Dressler: 'an interdependence between the production and reception of a given text and the knowledge that the participants in communication have of other texts' (1984, 237).
28 'Pour une théorie des textes poly-isotopiques,' *Langages*, 31 (1973), 61.
29 In *Palimpsestes*, Genette manages by prudently limiting, his study of intertextuality to pastiches and parodies. Beyond these obviously convenient genres, would it not be necessary to study the theories and practices of *imitation*? For example, in the sixteenth century, Vida and Bembo advocated choosing an excellent author as parangon; while Ronsard recommended imitating as one pleases all the good authors, somewhat as a bee gathers nectar (an image he borrows from Horace!).
30 For example, it is the analysis of the narrative structure of *La bicyclette bleue* (R. Desforges) that allows one to find *Gone with the Wind* in it; that same sort of analysis of the film *La vie est un long fleuve tranquille*, which refers to *Aux champs* (Maupassant), etc.
31 See Rastier, 1987a, chap. 1.
32 As pointed out by A. Romizi (Milan, 1900), R. Ceserani (Turin, 1962). These connections are presented by Segre, 1985b, 84–6.
33 In fact, choosing an invariant from which connections can be worked out promotes it to the rank of organizing centre. From this stems the methodological illusion we have already seen concerning key word.
34 Later, the reader will find the theoretical foundation for this tripartition.
35 I use the sememes to designate the first four columns of the table, without neglecting the obvious differences between the contents such as 'virum' and 'cavallier,' for example.

36 For example, *if* 'lady,' *then* 'love.' Whence stems the oxymoron incarnated by the beautiful warrior (Clorinde, for example).
37 Note the chiasmas in Deschamps' line, which proceeds from the homologation 'ladies' : 'knights' :: 'loves' :: 'weapons.'
38 There appears a glaring inadequacy here of the connections made between the excerpts, which favour a contiguous relationship. The excerpt from Dante takes up the words attributed to Guido del Duca, and the narrator of *The Divine Comedy* intervenes in other places.
39 Admittedly, one would have to keep in mind diachronic factors, notably on the formation of the topic pair 'weapons' / 'loves,' which stems, according to some, from the conjunction of Carolingian material (the woman warrior) and Arthurian material (the love-struck woman); and is often taken up during the Renaissance; for example, the brilliant derision of Cervantes.
40 Particularly at the level of semantics, at least in its integralist (Lacanian) version, avant-garde hermeneutics bases its strategy on the avoidance of textual content. Meaning and significance are then denied in the name of the supremacy of the *signifier*, which is summarized in formulas that were formerly illustrious and rather witty: the line that separates the signifier from the signified must be understood as a 'barrier that resists signification,' so much so that 'the notion of the signifier has an active function in the determination of the effects wherein the signifiable appears to be subjected to its (the signifier's) mark, becoming, by this passion, the signified'; 'the signified slides under the signifier,' which is, for all that, defined as 'that which represents a subject by another signifier' (Lacan, *Ecrits*, Paris, Seuil, 1966, passim).

3: Situations of Interpretation and Typology of Texts

1 It does not relate the types of texts to specific languages. Up until now, most textual grammars have had a universal vocation. They are supposed to be worthwhile for every text, regardless of its language. But, why should a Finnish textual grammar not be different from a Guarani textual grammar?

This problem is of particular interest on the semantic level. Universal semantics are not rare, but semantics dealing with languages are. And yet textual structures stem for the most part from the semantic level.

2 They are not as rich, since, in general, they settle for making epilogues on a few figures like metaphor and metonymy. See Jakobson's famous but shaky study (1963).
3 This is precisely one of the tasks of textual linguistics.
4 Nevertheless, at one time the lofty mission of setting morals and, in this way, directing society was conferred upon it: notably in Isocrates, Posidonius, Cicero (*De oratore, De officiis*), right up to Martianus Capella, and even John of Salisbury (*Metalogicon*).

5 The relationship between rhetoric and poetics has never been clear. In any case, poetics is isolated from the trivium. However, in the thirteenth century, following Al-Farabi, poetics is often affixed, in teaching, to rhetoric and to the other disciplines of the trivium.

6 Hence the misadventures of the sonnet, which, for Dante, belongs to the 'illegitimes et irregulares modos' (*De vulgari eloquentia*, II, 3) and remains classified, right up to Rapin, among the 'espèces du Poème imparfait' (kinds of imperfect poems) (*Réflexions sur la poétique*, II, 1).

7 They also lack the meaning that is immanent to this situation. It is then easy to wax endlessly on ambiguities, confusing the object (utterance) with the artefact (the sentence). By stripping an utterance from its context and its surrounding to reduce it to a sentence, one essentially denies it its signification, and definitively, its meaning. It is again easy to call the residue the 'literal meaning' and to enumerate the 'possible derived meanings.'

8 Often the demands of theory prevail over that of language. Thus, Chomsky gives to his example *John is too clever to expect us to catch* this interpretation: 'John is too clever for us to expect to catch him' (1984, 14). On the other hand, for every American who is not a linguist, this sentence signifies something like: 'John is too clever to expect us to catch [the baseball],' since the absolute use of *catch* relates to this game.

9 Destutt de Tracy praised Dumarsais for having been the first to choose secular examples (citing Madame Deshoulières' 'L'idylle des moutons.' At least, he forgot the eternal *Socrates currit* transposed from Greek grammars. It remains true that the topics of examples has long since reflected apologetic preoccupations. However, is not every example taken from a master in some way apologetic?

10 When it establishes interpersonal communication as a parangon, conversational pragmatics perpetuates this idealization in its own way. After all, conversation is a set of totally codified genres, even when they give speakers an illusion of freedom.

11 For example, only in a society for which *time is money* does the expression *be brief* have much impact. It hardly suits the hurried businessmen of the comics. Even without evoking the meetings of the Académie française, everyone knows that social life, alas, prescribes loquacity on numerous occasions.

12 I depart from the use inspired by Anglo-Saxon linguistics, which assimilates discourse and text (see below).

13 Cf. Rastier, 1987a, chap. 2.

14 Without which the *Song of Songs* would be, as Voltaire says, only a 'Jewish eclogue.'

15 I do not deny, for all this, the even relative autonomy of the history of genres, and especially of literary genres, with regards to the other domains of history.

16 See, e.g., Genette et al., *Théorie des genres*, Paris, Seuil, 1986.

17 Here the word *discourse* is used in the sense of the text (cf. op. cit., 102 passim.).
18 According to Greimas and Courtés: 'The semio-narrative forms, postulated as being universal, [are] found in all linguistic and trans-linguistic communities' [1982] 83). Better yet, all texts (whatever they may be) would arise from a narrative syntax.
19 See especially Kristeva, *La revolution du langage poétique*. Since genres reflect the incidence of social factors, to 'subvert them' would revolutionize society.
20 However, parody, even in *Les chants de Maldoror* (Lautréamont) or *Ulysses* (Joyce), remains ambiguous, since, in its own way, it perpetuates the genres it ridicules. Since Sade is always cited as a parangon, let us remember that blasphemy has never been a guarantee of atheism.
21 When the word *philosophical* is used in this manner, it is not only philosophy but also thought that is renounced, which leaves only a few debased superstitions.
22 I have drawn up some of the reflections that follow on the advice of my colleagues at the Computer Science Laboratory for Mechanics and Engineering Sciences (Orsay). As we no longer teach eloquence to children, all that is left is to instil it into our machines.
23 This is a fitting reminder that semiotics exists not only around, indeed above, linguistics: it is also 'inside,' and it is too often forgotten, after Saussure, that there are several semiotic kinds of linguistic signs; moreover, as Bühler suggests, each linguistic sign can have several semiotic functions.
24 Cf. the title 'Die Axiomatik der Sprachwissenschaften' (*Kant Studien*, 38) under which this model was first presented.
25 The theory of metalanguage, created by Russellan logistic to describe paradoxes, remains interesting in the philosophy of language; but for all this it is not valid in linguistics. Natural languages function in the same way whether they refer to signs or to other 'objects.' The metalinguistic use of a language does not transform it into a metalanguage. Therefore, the notion of metalanguage stems only from the philosophy of reference and not, strictly speaking, from linguistics.
26 For a discussion of Bühler's and Jakobson's theories, see Coseriu, 1981, 50 passim.
27 If one then seeks to define a discourse, this tri-partition of functions cannot be used. For example, the authors no longer allude to it when they define scientific texts as 'having as their goal the extension and dissemination of knowledge of the "real world" ... by attempting to explore, enlarge or clarify the sum of knowledge that a society possesses on what has been determined to be an established fact ... by presenting or examining the evidence stemming from observation or documentation' (242).
28 Let us hazard an analogy with other types of exchanges (economic and matrimonial) that found human societies. The archetypal situation of communication is no more real than *the* family. As far as universals in these domains are concerned they are not

structures, but constraints placed on the formation of structures, such as the prohibition of incest, for example.

29 Admittedly, Jakobson takes the code into account, but simply in as much as it is regulated by the metalinguistic function (cf. *Essais*, 214–17).

30 The category of *subject* remains for us enigmatic and not useful in its ordinary usage. However, enunciation theories, since Benveniste's archetypal article ('De la subjectivité dans le langage') give the subject a prominent place, but without always accompanying this with a relational definition, as is the case with the first-person pronoun (see Benveniste, 1966, 260).

31 The word *enunciation* has often been used to designate interpretation as well. But, in fact, these last thirty years, researchers have almost exclusively given their attention to generation.

32 The Author, as a group of roles, does not have the civil status of a person, but may have a pseudonym.

33 I distinguish them by removing the initial capital. The Author is a semio-linguistic instance, a socially codified 'character'; the author is a person.

34 Cf. Kurt Schwitters's well-known phrase: 'Everything the artist spits out is art.'

35 Genres codify the type and number of roles of enunciation as such (clearly, just as they do of represented enunciation).

36 Or, in particular instances, several sociolects (e.g., Rabelais, Joyce).

37 According to Valéry, the writer has the right to violate grammar, but only on the condition that he causes it to bear offspring.

38 It was possible to describe this process in dialectology, for example, in the small linguistic communities that demarcate the valleys of the Alps.

39 Cf., e.g., Benveniste, on verbs derived from locutions (1966, chap. 23).

40 'Pure' linguistic communication is only a convenient abstraction for linguists who do not wish to be bothered with semiotics.

41 Certain texts, just like certain proverbs, include in their very genre a generalized instruction for symbolic rewriting, which allows one to transpose them indefinitely to new situations. In much the same way, relatively speaking, for sapiential texts. According to Confucius (*Interviews*, II, 11) 'The good master is he who, by reheating the old [texts], is capable of finding something new' (the character translated by *reheat* is used for cooking).

42 I do not claim to restore a single meaning: contrary to what the philologists of the last century presumed, textual content can be plurivocal.

4: Thematics

1 According to Richard, 1961, 24, a theme is 'a concrete organizing principle, a schema or fixed object, around which there would be the tendency for a world to

form and unfold.' In terms that are more linguistic and yet no less vague, Todorov defines the theme as 'a semantic category that can be present right throughout the text, or even in the whole of literature (example: the theme of death)' (T. Todorov and O. Ducrot, *Dictionnaire encyclopédique des sciences du langage*, Paris, Seuil, 1972, 283).

2 In France, in any given year, dozens of such studies are undertaken.

3 Even if one calls the theme *topic*, nothing is changed.

4 Cf. Rastier, 1987a, chap. 3.

5 We should note that no polysemy exists within a domain; as a general rule, to each domain there corresponds the single signification of a lexeme. Moreover, domains account for the generic oppositions that allow for the existence of metaphors: hence, 'Has Rocard converted his try?' is metaphorical because the domains of //sport// and //politics// are clearly distinguished from each other in our culture. As well, Jarry's text *The Passion of Our Lord As a Hill Climb* would be 'blasphemous' because the domains //sport// and //religion// are very distinctive; on the other hand, there could be cultures wherein sport is sacred, athletes deified, and where the transposition of such comparisons lose all their metaphoric character. Ancient Greece was not far from this.

6 Strangely, the contents of grammemes are never chosen as themes. Or, if so, they are transformed by translation into lexemes (e.g., the theme of *elsewhere* in Baudelaire). Otherwise, their study is passed on to linguists: *nothing* in the classical age would fall within their jurisdiction, and *nothingness* would revert to specialists in literature. Now, grammemes in no way deserve this ostracism and their sole particularity is that they remain indifferent to semantic domains, which allows them to be operational in every one.

7 By refusing the cryptic conceptions of textuality, we avoid postulating key contents.

8 This is notably the case for molecules that constitute narrative actors.

9 Cf. the theory of three styles long ago developed from Donatus's commentary on Virgil. The *stylus humilis* corresponds to the field of //breeding// (it evokes the shepherds, and the beech tree also suits it, cf. the *Bucolics*); the *stylus mediocris*, in the field of //agriculture// (it illustrates the peasants and the fruit trees, cf. the *Georgics*); the *stylus gravis*, in the field of //war// (to the warriors go the laurel and the cedar, cf. the *Aeneid*). As for the (topoi) I deal with them in part 4 of this chapter.

10 Here appears the theoretical limit that thematic criticism has not been able to surpass, due to its lack of a properly linguistic conceptualization. However, in practice, authors like J.-P. Richard have proposed unequalled descriptions.

11 I have looked at the construction of generic themes elsewhere (1987a), and notably at the identification of isotoping semes.

12 Interpretative processes are very complex and little studied. Research on learning in

automatic processing tiptoes around it, lacking a description of these 'common sense' processes, where analogic inferences, guided by the recognition of semantic forms, doubtless play the largest role.

13 'Ah! unworthy guest who abandons a woman whose honour you have stolen!'

14 'A cavalier wronged me by giving me his word and upon his honour a pledge of marriage, and has desecrated my bed and my virtue.'

15 'Ai hut, vile instrument of my dishonour and my infamy, wild den of thieves, that protects my offences.'

16 Philosophical problems raised by the equivalence of denominations and of definite descriptions are suppressed by the problematic of differential semantics; just as is the problem of *rigidity* of proper nouns (within the same text).

17 For a further explanation, see Rastier, 1987c. Where I diverge from Sowa has no place for discussion here.

18 I am careful to distinguish between primitives, which are methodological universals belonging to general linguistics, and features such as semes, which are the units belonging to a specific language.

19 These three levels correspond to three degrees of *integration*. I do not need to link them to three autonomous disciplines: lexicology, the 'deep' syntax of the sentence, textual analysis, or to separate the study of 'macrostructures' from that of 'microstructures.' In fact, the relations and the units of each level can be homologued or converted to other levels.

20 The cases cited are categories of general semantics, unrelated to any given language. On the other hand, the morphosyntactic cases (also called 'surface cases,' like the nominative, the agentive, and the sociative) are ruled out of this set. I challenge in fact the theory of cases used by Sowa, and reworked by Fillmore (the latest linguist to discover cases). I shall give details elsewhere of an inventory of the cases retained for a typology of processes: for example, the ergative of a transmission (with a dative) is obviously not 'the same' as that of a transformation (which does not have one).

21 Thematicized graphs have the status of types.

22 This reasoning, which Aristotle had already pointed out (*Rhetoric*, II, 26, 1403 a 17) is necessary for any textual analysis (see, for example, operations of *catalysis* in Hjelmslevian narratology).

23 See Riffaterre, 1983, 59 and 216–17.

24 Marivaux recreates the proverbial line 'The pitcher goes so often to water that, in the end, it breaks' (translator's note).

25 *Histoire de la littérature japonaise*, Paris, Fayard, 1985, I, 28.

26 Except by a postulate that would dogmatically position this quatern at the origin of every generative trajectory.

5: Dialectics

1 *Actant* is understood here in the sense Tesnière gave it (although I shall not distinguish between actants and circumstants). In order to avoid ambiguity, I prefer to keep *actant* for designating this mesosemantic unit, introducing the term *agonist* to designate the 'narrative' actant, which belongs to the macrosemantic level. The de facto homologation that narrative semiotics practices between these two types of units actually appears to be quite hazardous.

2 World of what is; world of expectations; possible worlds; counterfactual worlds (see Martin, 1983, 1987; and chapter 6 below, on dialogics).

3 Since Bédier, folkloristics is the domain of predilection for those undertaking research on narrative, and the area of the scientific revolution initiated by Propp.

4 Greimas postulates indeed the universality of narrative structures: 'the hypothesis that there exist universal forms of narrative organization has put Propp's research at the very heart of problems facing newborn semiotics' (Greimas and Courtés [1982] 204).

5 The canonical narrative structure of the Russian folk-tale is none other than that of tale number 300 (in Aarne and Thompson's classification). Propp correctly considers it to be typical, *within the limits of his corpus*. To make this captivating story of dragon-slaying the parangon of every semiotic manifestation would be betting on a sure loser.

6 For an overview of the debates, see especially Black and Wilensky, 1979; Rumelhart, 1980; Mandler and Johnson, 1980.

7 Although they were developed independently, Schank's and Greimas's theories present many analogies, as they share the same universalizing goal.

8 Researchers generally call signified *concepts* (for a discussion, see Rastier, 1987b).

9 The opposition between *form* and *substance*, inherited from Platonism by Aristotle, seems to me no more adequate in linguistics than in physics (where it was discredited at the turn of the century).

10 See Greimas, 1970, 119. Here it is a question of myth-narrative, but no other type of narrative will be clearly distinguished after this, since the narrative level corresponds to what one could call the utterance [as opposed to the enunciation] (see Greimas and Courtés [1982] 248). As this formulation is assimilated with that of the elementary structure of signification (see Greimas, 1970, 138), we can see how the notion of narrativity was then supposed to take into account every semiotic production.

11 In everything that follows, I rely on my analysis of Molière's *Dom Juan* (1971) in order to reformulate in a more systematic way concepts, in that analysis, that were of a more practical nature, so to speak. I borrow diversely, and equally, from Propp, Lévi-Strauss, and Greimas.

12 For example, 'Dom Juan,' 'unworthy guest,' 'brigand,' 'vile knight' constitute in the above cited example such an anaphoric chain. Admittedly, these contents are not identical, and not really equivalent. But that does not matter: it is a general property of languages to allow without a priori limits (except for conditions placed on particular uses) for anaphors without coreference. For example, in 'Do not give him this book. He already has it,' *it* has as a signified a meaning of book that is different from the first, without one being able for all that to stigmatize this sentence with an asterisk. In fact, coreference, like all questions of reference, essentially stems from logic rather than from linguistics. In 'I missed the bus but I shall catch it in five minutes,' *it* does not, strictly speaking, designate the same vehicle in the real world: but such latitude would only be intolerable in a logical language.

13 I use this term (illustrated by Kripke) in the framework of a differential semantics, and certainly without limiting the rigidity to the contents of proper nouns. Dom Juan, even as a hypocrite, remains Dom Juan; a knife without a handle and a blade, linguistically speaking, remains a knife: herein lies the principle of anaphors without coreference that I evoked earlier.

14 As her name indicates, this mean cousin is often compared to a beast. The animal isotopy in *La cousine Bette* is, in fact, quite dense and allows for the construction of a coherent *internal variation*.

15 For a discussion, see Rastier, 1974, 207–31. A 'character' can include several actors; or several 'characters' can make up the same actor.

16 In this, they pose the crucial problem of a semantics of action, even though in a way that is at times arbitrary (cf. the eleven primitive actions as described by Schank et al. 1975).

17 The position in time is independent of position in the text (even though, for Propp, the order of succession of functions is the obligatory, which is perfectly possible in a given genre).

18 They fit with the short fiction narratives I have analysed (see, e.g., chap. 11). For other types of texts and especially non-narrative texts, it is necessary to set up other functional categories, which opens the way for a comparative praxeology.

19 The status of these 'truths' and 'falsehoods' will be clarified in the next section.

20 Greimas (1966, 134) proposes a list of the actants in the sentence that is identical to that of the actants in mythical narrative (cf. ibid. 180); this assimilation is maintained in Greimas and Courtés, [1982] 3.

21 Admittedly, nothing prevents writing a monotonous text or finding a text monotonous where an agonist would subsume the actors whose every occurrence would occupy the same semantic case; but again nothing permits setting up this extreme case as a methodological principle.

22 This problem reappears all through Bremond's *Logique du récit*: how does one distinguish the deteriorations from the improvements?

23 Cf. Mallarmé's sonnet, 'Remémorations d'amis belges' (Rastier, 1972, 81).
24 For example, some texts are composed of a simple enumeration.
25 This is a matter of semantic syntagmatics, which are autonomous with regards to the linearity of the signifier: cf. chapter 7 below on tactics.

6: Dialogics

1 I willingly set aside the modalities proposed by various authors as *clear, legitimate, heretical, related by the Ancients, written in the Holy Scriptures*, etc. (cf. Seuren, *Operator and Nucleus*, Cambridge, Cambridge University Press, 1969). These so-called modalities depend exclusively on the semantic classes proper to the semantic universe described.
2 See Martin, 1983, 91 ff for a definition, and Sowa, 1984, 174 ff on the modalization of graphs.
3 Cf. the definitions proposed by Martin: 'we shall call *belief universe* or *universe* the indefinite set of propositions that, at the moment he expresses himself, the speaker holds to be true or wishes to accredit as such' (1983, 36) and: 'we shall call a given speaker's belief universe the application, at the moment of speech, of the set of decidable propositions in the set of truth values' (1987, 29).
4 The image of a graph is another graph obtained by changing its modalization, and situated in another world.
5 Replicates are graphs modalized in the same way as the graphs they 'copy' in another universe.
6 I use the term *propositions* instead of *graphs* to avoid terminological idiosyncrasy. But every semantic graph can be translated into one or several propositions.
7 The status of the represented enunciator will be defined later on. According to the way it is represented, the strategy by which the reader constructs the universe of reference will be constrained in various ways.
8 This *therefore* would call for a lengthy commentary, but for sake of brevity I limit myself to the evenemential level of the dialectic. However, a proposition that is true in two universes is not necessarily true in the universe of reference. We can reach the above conclusion because at the agonistic level Dom Juan and Sganarelle correspond to two opposite *agonists* at the agonistic level.
9 And this is undoubtedly Dom Juan's only crime, as the condemnation of hypocrisy is the only moral axiom that is part of the universe of reference. In antique theatre, the universe of reference was often attributed to a speaker or chorus; in contemporary theatre, one finds plays without a universe of reference (in Pirandello, for example) and where all the propositions remain undecidable.
10 In Turkish *Bakbac* means 'look, look!'
11 This could be represented simply by means of Beth's table.

12 The citation belongs totally to the text citing it. The fact that it is included makes it enter into new relations and modifies its semantics. This conforms to the principle that the global prevails over the local, and determines it.

13 This so-called death enables him to put off his own by giving him the subject matter for a story. In the same way, the tailor saves his own life by narrating the story of the barber.

14 See Kalinowski, *Sémiotique et philosophie*, Paris-Amsterdam, Hadès-Benjamins, 1985, chap. 6. Truth in the weak sense can be called analytical a posteriori. For me this weakness is constitutive: without it, semantics could never be distinguished from logic, which was preoccupied with the question of linguistic meaning before the former appeared on the scene.

15 See, for instance, during Gervaise's wedding meal, those 'lardons, toasted just right, smelling of a horse's hooves.' Or this sentence from M. Yourcenar: 'Coquettish villas did not as yet stain the dune' (*Souvenirs pieux*, Paris, Gallimard, 1976, 207).

16 These groups or *galaxies* generally bring together the universe of actors subsumed by a same agonist (for example in Molière's *Dom Juan*, Elvire, Dom Louis, the Statue, and the Ghost).

17 I take *narration* in the active sense, as the action of uttering a narrative. The adjective, *narrative*, alas remains ambiguous in current usage, where it refers sometimes to represented enunciation, sometimes to the uttered narrative. Modern aesthetics of the novel that continues to influence narratology, of course, does not favour coherent and univocal narrative structures, but rather a lacunary narration: if there remains a narrative, it is that of the narration.

18 See Benveniste's famous article 'On Subjectivity in Language' (republished in *Problèmes de linguistique générale*): 'The "subjectivity" we are dealing with here is the capacity of the speaker to set himself up as a subject' (259); 'Language is only possible because each speaker sets himself up as *subject*, by referring to himself as *I* in his discourse' (260).

19 Otherwise the contract is said to be deceptive.

20 By *focus* I mean the site of the origin of spatial, temporal, modal, evaluative, etc. marks.

21 The reader in *Jacques le fataliste* is a typical example.

22 I adapt this for our use by extending to the receiver the notion of *implied author* proposed by Wayne Booth.

23 I do not think that problems of subjectivity or objectivity fall within the scope of linguistics. Its only concern is with the linguistic devices that can create conventionally the impression of subjectivity or of objectivity.

24 Sainte-Beuve would be vindicated if Proust were confused with the narrator of *A La recherche*, or even with the actor called Marcel.

25 In the third book of his *Ars Grammatica*, which was invoked throughout the Middle Ages.
26 This is only a partial and approximative assimilation, all the more so as traditional classification is concerned only with the modes of enunciation and not the modes of interlocution. This 'generative' perspective (renewed today by theories of enunciation) has always fallen under the purview of rhetoric.
27 We have to distinguish between two kinds of inclusion: *embedding* (interlocution 'en abîme') and *interlacing* (non-signalled alternations of interlocutors, such as in 'indirect free style').
28 The represented receiver corresponds to an interpretive centre. Here are a few examples from Balzac's *Les paysans*: 'She leaned significantly on Émile Blondet's arm to make him share sentiments of indescribable subtlety that only women will suspect' (I, chap. 9); 'This summer evening made the magnificent landscape shimmer, which people of imagination will be able to appreciate' (II, chap. 2). From the readers named (*women, people of imagination*) can be distinguished designated readers ('a tench shows *you* its nose, a squirrel looks at *you*,' II, chap. 6) or simply implied (such as city dwellers in 'In the country they do not know the proper names of newspapers and they call them all *news*,' I, chap. 13).

7: Tactics

1 Although, according to him, only systems of symbols can have a biunivocal correspondence between the units of content and those of expression, which he calls *conformity*.
2 See Rastier, 1987a, chap. 3.
3 It has recently been discovered that the auditory system is an *active* transductor, whose functioning depends also on stimulations from the brain and translates its presumptions. This agrees with what we know about semantic perception itself.
4 We call *deterministic* an automatic parser that constructs syntactic and even semantic representations by scanning the text term by term with a window of constant width.
5 See the work of D. Dubois and L. Sprenger-Charolles (1988).
6 The word *linearity* reminds us that the written in linguistics has exorbitant prerogatives.
7 I have to leave aside here the level of the word, and the order of the morphemes that are part of this. Moreover, all the signs I mention in the paragraph (morpheme, word, syntagm, etc.) are considered only relative to their signifiers.
8 Cf. later on, in the extensive analysis of a sonnet by the same author, the links between a ternary thematic structure and a ternary tactic form.
9 I use the text of the Jerusalem Bible, without prejudging the Hebrew.
10 This expression is debatable, but *polysemy* is already taken.

11 In his studies on Slavic traditional poetry, he has described syntactic and morphological parallelisms but, for want of a semantic theory, he did not get very far.
12 Translators name this tree *eloeococca, pawlownia imperialis*, or *stercula platanifolia*, as they wish. One thing is certain, though; it occurs in the poetry of autumn.
13 This semantic counterpoint is, moreover, reduplicated phonetically in the original by a counterpoint opposing the tones of the monosyllables in the same position (in conformity with the rules of the genre).
14 The two arrows that are part of the operations of actualization are retrograde, which weakens the hypothesis of a deterministic interpretative path. The third arrow describes the inference *if* 'old man,' *then* 'philosopher.'
15 Translated from Sieffert, *Traités de poétique – Le Haïkaï selon Bashô*, Paris, P.O.F., 1983, 103. See also: 'On the back of the first page there is an old precept from the *renga: Spring on the fourth, tree on the eighth*, which means that in the fourth verse one avoids springtime, and in the eighth plants of great expanse. This is done so as not to impede the flowers. The haïkaï follows the same rule' (115). Prescriptions of the same kind are legion in this work, and extend also to the tactics of expression (from the position of the stanza on the page, for example, to the folding of the paper – that is part of another component of expression, the *mediatization* component).
16 Ibid., 102.
17 Without the dialectical rhythm proper accelerating: three dialectical intervals follow one another in this passage. Contemporary novelists (notably since Proust and Joyce) appreciate the contrast between a rapid rhythm and a slow tempo (cf. for example, the demonstrative exercise that Claude Mauriac's *L'Agrandissement* happens to be).
18 Are the deep structures nothing more than a reification of the linguist's need for rationality?

8: The Interaction of the Semantic Components

1 The limits of this work scarcely permit me to analyse the components of expression (notably morphological, tactic, media) or their interaction with the semantic components.
2 For example, Aragon's *Persienne*.
3 Let us avert attempts at 'squaring': although it happens to be quaternary, the elementary model presented here is not a 'semiotic square.'
4 Even though the choice of the expression is somewhat dubious, I mention here the concept of *parallelism* (as used in Artificial Intelligence).
5 Notably *The Modularity of Mind*, New York, Crowell, 1986, and *Psychosemantics*, Cambridge, Mass., MIT Press, 1987.

6 These presuppositions are part of the common sense of Artificial Intelligence and more generally of computer science. They are necessary in order to avoid the combinatory explosion and the elaboration of very complex algorithms that regulate parallel processes.

7 I am aware of Culioli's formula, according to which the object of linguistics is language apprehended through the diversity of natural languages. This compromise formula gives language more than its due. I prefer to say that the object of linguistics is languages, in their unity as well as in their diversity. Language unbound from languages is a privileged object only for philosophy, which created the concept.

8 For example, phraseology is found in the contact zone between the norms of the first type and those of the second. It is narrowly linked to a culture and to its history (including its political history) and is none the less indissociable from language. For example, it is impossible to understand a Chinese text without knowing the *cheng yu*, those quadrisyllabic expressions that number in the thousands and that are so many allusions to the classics, to ancient history, to myths, to fables.

9 Notwithstanding, in a given zone, none of the linguistic rules apply for good and unconditionally. No matter what has been said, they differ in principle from the rules of formal languages. The prejudice that a single grammar can account for a language contains in fact a normative aspect that can go unnoticed only in countries where language is regulated by teaching, standardized by the media, and especially stabilized by writing.

10 In brief, this is an elementary structure of what is called masochism (see the surprising *alas*).

11 It is only so for theories that restrictively affirm the preeminence – indeed the centrality – of syntax. As well as for ancient but very active logistic tradition that wants to assimilate the simple sentence to the logical proposition.

12 These two points of course must be specified and qualified in relation to the languages in question.

13 Nowhere does it become exclusive. A word can be idiolectal (e.g., compound adjectives in Hopkins).

14 These levels are the threshold of syntagmatic organization. They do not exhaust linguistic description. Short of the word (which is already a syntagm), there is the morpheme.

15 The levels of word and sentence are also codified by the norms of genre.

16 See *Le suicide et le chant*, Paris, Cahiers des brisants, 1988.

17 For example, in certain traditional African societies, proverbs are extensively used in legal jousts between litigants.

18 Including, in certain cases, that of proper nouns. For example, Paul Veyne has shown how *Lesbia* for Catullus designated a type and not an individual (to the consternation of impudent biographers).

9: Moon, Diana, Hecate

1 Des astres, des forests, et d'Acheron l'honneur,
Diane, au Monde hault, moyen et bas, preside,
Et ses chevaulx, ses chiens, ses Eumenides guide,
Pour esclairer, chasser, donner mort et horreur.

Tel est le lustre grand, la chasse, et la frayeur
Qu'on se sent sous ta beauté claire, prompte, homicide,
Que le haut Jupiter, Phebus et Pluton cuide,
Son foudre moins pouvoir, son arc, et sa terreur.

Ta beauté par ses rais, par son rets, par la craincte
Rend l'ame esprise, prise, et au martyre estreinte:
Luy moi, pren moy, tien moy, mais hélas ne me pers.

Des flambans forts et griefs, feux, filez, et encombres
Lune, Diane, Hecate, aux cieux, terre, et enfers
Ornant, questant, genant, nos Dieux, nous, et nos ombres.

Collected by Charles de la Mothe in *Les Amours d'Étienne Jodelle, parisien* [Nicolas Chesneau and Mamert Patisson, Paris, 1574, f. 1, v (II)]. I follow the text given in the very fine edition by Enea Balmas (*Œuvres complètes*, II, Paris, Gallimard, 1965, 393–4), in my eyes better than that of Albert Marie-Schmidt (*Poètes du seizième siècle*, Paris, Gallimard, Bibliothèque de la Pléiade, 1953, 711). References to the Marty-Laveaux edition (*Œuvres et Meslanges poétiques*, Paris, 'La Pléiade Françoise,' 1868, 2 vol.) are indicated by *M.-L.*; to the Balmas edition, by *E.B.* In the following pages, I have modernized spelling, which is of no import for the level of analysis chosen.

2 Texts are extremely complex formations, the exhaustive description of which remains very illusory. To orient the analysis, one needs to formulate hypotheses. Even if they happen to be founded on intuitions determined by cultural knowledge, that does not invalidate them: intuition is simply an implicit pre-analysis, which a rational description will help evaluate.

3 Quantitative data have a bad reputation in linguistics, and are not exploited in semantics. Nevertheless, nothing prevents us from exploiting them especially if they can be linked to qualitative data.

4 Of course, the features noted do not exhaust the content of each sememe.

5 This is microsemantic density.

6 The fact that the occurrences can be analysed in different ways does not put into question the stability of the classes.

7 This can be linked to the Renaissance paganism of this sonnet.

8 Three descriptions of the arrow of love that glistens, flies, and kills (this topos, illustrated by Petrarch, continues today: cf. the grotesque refrain by Julien Savage, 'She has the eyes of a revolver! She has a look that kills'). Moreover, Diana-Artemis is reputed to be responsible for sudden deaths: 'her arrows are always accurate, stunningly quick, and deadly' writes Joël Schmidt in his *Mythologie grecque et romaine* (Paris, Larousse, 1981, 49).

9 Q and T stand for *quatrain* and *tercet*. The commas indicate the limits between the semantic classes.

10 Line 7 is an exception: there is no god, on earth, who can be opposed to Diana. Her brother Phoebus is in the sky. A ternary structure is maintained, since two gods (and not a single one) are indexed in class A.

11 I adopted the useful course of action of designating the sememes under examination by the word in which they appear. But to be rigorous, albeit less readable, they should have been designated by their sole signifier. For example 'to hunt' (line 4) and 'the hunt' (line 5) do not designate two different sememes, but two occurrences of the same sememe, that appear in *hunt-* and that we could designate by 'hunt.'

12 On the phonetic level, we can neglect relations of contiguity, especially within the same prosodic group.

13 For an example of 'vertical' isophony, see Rastier, 1972, 104.

14 I shall not engage in the debate regarding the conformity and the non-isomorphism between the two planes of language.

15 However, in order for the conclusions of these experiments to be validly extrapolated for texts such as the one I have examined, the interaction between semantic rhythms and phonic rhythms would have to be taken into account; indeed, although sounds are forgotten, the memory of rhythm remains.

16 I do not modify the orientation of the arrows in use since Sowa (1984), without for all that forgetting that attribution is an endocentric relation (see Pottier, 1974).

17 Transformation in the syntactic sense of the term and not in the narrative sense. Cf. 'He opens the oysters with his knife <---> 'He uses his knife to open the oysters.' We are dealing with two different focalizations of the instrumental here.

18 Where we have:

$$\frac{\textit{/male/}}{\text{/female/}} \approx \frac{\textit{/superative/}}{\text{/inferative/}}$$

or also, 'Almighty power is on the side of the beard' (Molière).

19 It is impossible to take into account only case: this would amount to assimilating all the contents having the same case – so much so that dialectical analysis goes

necessarily hand in hand with thematic analysis. A 'formal' dialectics would give only trivial results.

20 And 'Diana' in the last tercet is associated only with the second world.

21 The universes are associated with actors. An agonist can thus subsume several universes, if it subsumes several actors.

22 This is the case for Artemis; but Roman legends of Diana are closely related to Greek myths. Moreover, in Latium, the sacrifice of men was practised for Diana of Nemi: each priest had to kill his predecessor in order to succeed him.

23 See also other poems of the same cycle:

Diane ses chiens mène, et aux parcs fait entrer
Ses cerfs: tu peux mener les grands héros en laisse
Ains les prendre en tes *rets* (396)

Libre et franc, je n'avais crainte d'être empêché
De playe, feu, prison, mais vivement touché
M'a l'arc, m'a le brasier, m'a la *rhetz* qui me fâche (397)

C'est un noeud gardien des *rethz* de vos beautés (401)

24 Jodelle did not hesitate to exploit this, in his 'Ode sur la devise de Noeud et de Feu' (398); or in this sonnet (394): 'Voilà le Feu, le Noeud, qui me brûle, et étreint ...' (where the capital letters are the interpretants). Just like the adopted name *Dictynne*, this motto is in perfect agreement with the love topos of the period. The poets of the period were very aware of this, as Pontus de Tyard, Amadis Jamyn, Philippe Desportes, Guillaume de Salluste du Bartas, Nicolas Rapin rivalled one another to celebrate this beautiful widow.

25 An interpretation produced by means of a descriptive process can rest on extratextual data without losing its intrinsic character (see Rastier, 1987a, chap. 7).

26 As though the time of enunciation simply paralleled the time of the utterance.

27 The imperfect aspect often prohibits the strict definition and the organization of the temporal intervals.

28 On the primary actant, see Pottier, 1987, chap. 10.

29 I owe this notion to Shank and Abelson, who introduced it in Artificial Intelligence.

30 Henri Morier, *Dictionnaire de poétique et de rhétorique*, 1961, Paris, P.U.F. defines *vers rapportés* (patched verse) 'as written in pairs, instead of the elements A, B, C, D, etc. of the first line being linked grammatically among themselves, they establish these links with the elements A', B', C', D', etc. of the second line. Such is the beginning of the epitaph that Jodelle dedicated to Marot: 'Quercy, the court,

Piemont, the universe / Made me, held me, buried me, knew me' (my translation; Quercy made me, the court held me, Piemont buried me, the universe knew me) 338.

31 See the fall of another of Jodelle's sonnets: 'If I fall into Hell, my only torment will be / To endlessly suffer the eye of a most beautiful Hecate.'

32 I shall expand on this parallel later on. Before justifying it, I should note that Judaeo-Christian tradition does not contradict this, because it esteems that humanity has already fallen into the world of sin.

33 Patched sonnets frequently introduce a chronological order between their semantic classes; for example, the allegory of Prudence that Giordano Bruno begins in this way (*Opere italiane*, ed. G. Gentile, Bari, 1908, II, 401): 'Un alan, un leon, un can appare / All; auror, al dì chiaro, al vespr'oscuro' (A wolf, a lion, a dog appear / At dawn, at noon, at obscure nightfall).

34 Practically, this is an upper limit for a French alexandrine (cf. *senaires* lines according to Morier).

35 In what follows I am much indebted to the works of G. Dumézil, J. Haudry, J. Varenne.

36 The same holds for the Germans where earth is called the 'median space' (got. *midjungars*). On the other hand, in Indo-European tradition, there exists a world that is intermediary between heaven and earth. For the Greeks, the sea can be looked on as an intermediary world; cf. the dividing up of the Universe among three brothers: Zeus, Poseidon and Hades.

According to the most ancient Indo-European cosmology, insofar as we have been able to reconstruct it (see Haudry, 1982), three heavens circumscribe the earth: a diurnal white sky, an auroral or twilight red sky, and a black nocturnal sky. For Graeco-Latin or Germanic conceptions, hell takes the place of the black sky, and earth, that of the red sky.

37 Moreover, 'triple Hecate' for the Greeks designates Selena, Artemis, and Hecate (see the triad Selena, Artemis, Persephone).

38 These three colours are also those of the three castes: white for the priestly caste; red for the noble warriors, black for the inferior caste (see Haudry, 1982).

39 The Greek *Khalkós*, which is normally translated by *bronze*, also signifies 'copper.'

40 These three ages correspond to the successive dominance of the three castes. On the two periods of the iron age, see Haudry, 1986, 7.

41 *Jupiter, 'dieu' (god)*, and *diurn* have moreover the same root.

42 For example, when the *Linga-Purana* (II, 39–42), a holy scripture of Hindu Puranic theism, describes the last period of human history, the horrible *kali-yuga* where we live, he affirms: 'Towards the end of the Yuga, the number of women increases, that of men decreases.'

43 No text has ever done so, even the *Rgveda*. This ideology is an explanatory model that has been worked out from linguistics and comparative mythology.

44 Why see in mythology only fastidious ornaments? When Jodelle sacrifices a goat to Dionysus to celebrate his first theatrical success, perhaps he goes beyond simple amusements for the literati. The power of Greek myths is not exhausted for our civilization: psychoanalysis owes a good deal of its effectiveness and in my opinion its greatest force to these myths.

45 Jodelle forged a reputation as a non-believer and a libertine. The three accounts of his death confirm this, in one way or another. His mediocre poems against the Protestants were written for alimentary reasons, and not as acts of faith. Under these conditions the *do not lose me* of line 11 appears to be a literal allusion to the *ne me perdas* of the *Dies irae* (verse 9, line 3), as the Maréchale or Diana is substituted for Jesus in this discreetly blasphemous invocation.

46 Translated from Haudry as the 'humide, the heroic, the immaculate' (1985, 22).

47 This elementary principle is valid beyond the line in indirect verse, successive lines, or successive verses. Hence, in one of the most continuous trivalent hymns of the *Rgveda* (X, 125), Vac, personified speech, is defined as she who supports the masculine gods of the three functions: 'I am the one who supports Mitra-Varuna, I support Indra-Agni, I also support the two Asvin.' Verses 4, 5, and 6 then respectively elaborate each of the three functions.

48 Cf. e.g. this epigram: 'Haec tria Castalii fontis remorantur alumnum: / Turpis, iners, coecus, crapula, somnus amor' (Daniel Meisner, *Thesaurus philopoliticus*, Frankfurt, 1624, I, tab. 30).

49 Unruffled, the latter goes to seven, even ten successive members (cf. Hildebertus Cenomaniensis, *Opera*, in Migne, *Patrologia latina*, 171, 1390 sq.).

50 In chapter 14 of *Les Recherches de la France augmentées par l'auteur*, Paris, 1611, maliciously entitled 'On some other poetic games we have borrowed from the Latin, and have paid in money of a better alloy than was loaned us.' 'I myself,' adds Pasquier, 'wanted to translate the Latin, verbatim, which is not a task without thorns: Shepherd, farmer, soldier, I feed, plough, defeat / Flocks, fields, enemies, with grass, plough, hands.' Tabourot, in chapter 13 of *Les Bigarrures du Seigneur des Accords* (1582), says of the same poem: 'Monsieur Tabourot, an official of Langres, has also miraculously translated this into two alexandrines: 'Shepherd, ploughman, Duke, I fed, dug, defeated with borders, / picks, hands, goats, fields, enemies.'

51 Until Weckherlin's explanation. For an overview, see D. Alonso, 1971.

52 Without being as clear as Monier Monier-Williams, *Sanskrit-English Dictionary* (Calcutta, 1946, 843): 'Figure of rhetoric that separates each verb from its subject and arranges verbs with verbs, subjects with subjects, so that they correspond respectively.'

53 In Vedic India, the third function is associated with earth, fecundity, the inferior (productive) classes, and pleasure. In ancient Greece, a divinity linked to fecundity, Persephone, illustrates the 'displacement' of the third function in the direction of the chthonian world: this daughter of Demeter becomes the spouse of Hades. She is sometimes assimilated with the last aspect of triple Hecate. Christian tradition has undoubtedly contributed to associating (as here with Jodelle) the chthonian world no longer with fecundity and pleasure, but with death and chastisement.

54 The first author he cites is Hildebert de Lavardin (1055–1133), who was a contemporary of Mammata's.

55 See B. Hauréau on the selected poetic works of Hildebert de Lavardin, *Notice et extraits des ms. de la Bibliothèque nationale*, 1878, 23, 2, 390: 'This laborious arrangement of words is the cachet of almost all the epigrams of the period.' J. Vianey, *Le pétrarquisme en France au XVIe siècle*, Montpellier, 1909, 112: 'These are sleight of hand tricks, where the poet juggles with three images at a time.' M. Raymond, *L'influence de Ronsard sur la poésie française*, Paris, 1927, I, 277, n. 2: 'Jodelle is fond of sonnets in "indirect verse," having a bumpy gait ... Union of linguistic pedantry and impotency, or too great facility.'

56 *Anthologia Palatina*, III, 241. This poem dedicated to wine can be translated as follows: 'You, audacity, youth, vigour, treasure, homeland / Of the timid, old, weak, poor, foreigner.' This is attributed by Krumbacher to Jean Kyriotes known as the Geometer (first half of the tenth century). The date of the lemma is unknown.

10: Goddamn! They Sure Made Short Work of the Blanquette of Veal!

The original French passage from *L'Assommoir*:

Ah! tonnerre! quel trou dans la blanquette! Si l'on ne parlait guère, on mastiquait ferme. Le saladier se creusait, une cuiller plantée dans la sauce épaisse, une bonne sauce jaune qui tremblait comme une gelée. Là-dedans, on pêchait les morceaux de veau; et il y en avait toujours, le saladier voyageait de main en main, les visages se penchaient et cherchaient des champignons. Les grands pains, posés contre le mur, derrière les convives, avaient l'air de fondre. Entre les bouchées, on entendait les culs de verres retomber sur la table. La sauce était un peu trop salée, il fallut quatre litres pour noyer cette bougresse de blanquette, qui s'avalait comme une crème et vous mettait un incendie dans le ventre. Et l'on n'eut pas le temps de souffler, l'épinée de cochon, montée sur un plat creux, flanquée de grosses pommes de terre rondes, arrivait au milieu d'un nuage.

1 I am thankful to N. Gelas, C. Kerbrat-Orrechioni, J.-C. Coquet, J. Fontanille, A.-J. Greimas, R. Martin, and B. Pottier for their remarks and suggestions.

2 P. Clarac has clarified, with an enthusiasm that convinced the Inspection Générale, what theoretically was expected of the explication de texte: 'It is a very difficult exercise, which should be applied only to texts having an exceptional richness and beauty, texts which students and teachers can approach only with respect, indeed trembling respect ... It should involve a very short text, barely a page, which will be studied in detail. Each of the words composing it, a master of our language chose it from among all others, in one of the more glorious moments of his genius. These are a sacred testimony' (translated from *L'enseignement du français*, Paris, P.U.F., 1963, 44). This is how he justified the linear procedure: 'the explication itself will naturally follow the meaning of the text ... We will thus follow the text in the order in which it is offered to us. Its order, or apparent disorder, is profoundly revealing of the intentions of the author' (ibid, 92–3).

3 They varied from : 'Sure, with white sauce or, alternatively, with rice,' to 'No, I have never eaten blanquette because of my religion.'

4 Of course, this does not preclude cultural hallucinations: a young West Indian concluded, for example, that blanquette causes thirst because it is too spicy.

5 Coseriu (1967, 77) makes the same observations, using a slightly different terminology. We should remember that all of the elements of a taxeme are interdefined; the same is obviously not true for all of the elements of a semantic domain.

6 For example, the morpheme *-s* corresponds to a sememe whose classeme is the generic seme /number/ and whose semanteme is the specific seme /plurality/.

7 This fact can be seen in relation to the kind of realism that generally is credited to Zola. For a discussion of this, see 120–30, and Hamon, 1984.

8 Our sample of schoolchildren represents no more than itself; I avoid presenting useless statistics. Indeed, syntagms such as 'the pieces of veal,' or 'the big loaves' function here as lexia.

9 The bottle/litre distinction is not perceived: a schoolgirl might write, for example: 'They opened a litre of champagne.'

10 For example, in the *Dictionnaire explicatif et combinatoire du français contemporain*, Mel'čuk, Iordanskaja, and Arbatchewsky-Jumarie use, as a 'lexical function,' an operator of intensity that they represent by *Magn* and that they define as follows: 'very,' 'intense,' 'to a high degree.' Examples: *Magn* (memory) = prodigious, excellent, surprising, of an elephant; *Magn* (noise) = infernal.

11 Certainly, a repetition does not have in and of itself an invariable content; at least those that have to do with the system of the language in question (and not, as is the case here, with usage) often express intensity: cf. Spanish *chiqu-it-it-o* (very small), Latin, *iam iam* (immediately); and Pottier, 1974, 304).

12 The context mentioned does not belong to the chosen extract. But the explication of a short extract precludes the construction of certain afferent semes and destroys part of the textuality. Of course, a superlative size is attributed to the salad bowl only a

few lines before this extract, but that might have been done anywhere in the text: the context is (at least) the whole text.

13 The actors violate the norms of good manners covering the relation between *speaking* and *eating*. First, they neither speak nor eat: 'they hardly spoke, they behaved correctly' (239); then they eat without speaking; finally, they speak while eating: 'they talked with mouths full' (ibid).

14 The opposition 'litre' versus 'bottle' is valid in the text: 'since the sealed bottles were empty, they turned to the litres' (250).

15 When in one and the same moment in time one sees contradictory evaluations or assessments, one can presume that a universe of assumptions corresponds to each evaluative norm.

16 Some have concluded that the narrator was one of the guests; and since in their way of thinking the narrator is not distinct from the author, Zola ate the blanquette. This conclusion is likely linked to the referential impression produced by the text, to such an extent that a student asked if the characters were all dead today, and another asked if Gervaise was indeed Zola's daughter.

17 Some schoolchildren solved the ambiguity of the semidirect style by affirming that Coupeau is first to exclaim; after that, Zola would take over ...

18 This obviously exclusive *ils* (they) confirms, by opposition, the inclusive nature of *on* (one) in our extract.

19 The scales are taxemes that are ordered according to relations of progressivity or linearity.

20 See the Lorilleux: 'They took enough for three days' (244). In my sample, valorization of quantity is typical of the boys; the girls more often than not show better manners. Is intensity a virile virtue? On the popular nature of an aesthetics of quantity, I agree, although I get there following entirely different paths, with certain analyses of P. Bourdieu, *La distinction*, Paris, Ed. de Minuit, 1979.

21 See R. Martin, 1983, on the concept of enunciative space.

22 One might suppose that this 'setting into place' of the real reader is linked to the *projective* nature of a naive reading (whence the well-known phenomena of identification, catharsis, etc.).

23 From here to page 130 if a word is underlined, it is my choice, in order to try the reader's 'sagacity.'

24 *Yellow* and *gold* do not exactly have the same content because *yellow* is dysphoric; thus, when Coupeau is drunk, 'the *fire* cauterized his *guts*' (cf. 'a *fire* in the *belly*'); 'everything appeared *yellow* to him' (379); or 'The sunset had that yellow colour of Paris sunsets, a colour that makes you want to *die* right away' (459). *Gold*, on the other hand, has a euphoric content, at least in Gervaise's universe: 'What are you drinking there? she asked the men sneakily, her eye *lit up* by the *gold* colour of their glasses' (391). The semic molecule under study is thus modified according to

narrative universe and moment: the feature /golden/ in the beginning of the novel and/or in Gervaise's universe finds its counterpart at the end and/or the narrator's universe in the feature /yellow/. These substitutions have to do with molecular dialectics.

25 Lantier's very body is *thick*: 'He had thickened, was fat and round' (266). And his name has the same effect on Gervaise as alcohol or gravy: 'She never would have believed that the name Lantier would give her such a *hot* spell in the *pit of her stomach*' (209, cf. also 269 and 39 on Lantier's greasy pomade).

26 Fat and alcohol have common semes: 'He had gone to drink a *drop* because he didn't feel well enough *oiled*' (188). The patron of L'Assommoir has a '*greasy* voice' (295); his 'full moon' is 'a real tub of *lard*.' Fat of this type results from drinking alcohol: for Coupeau, '*pichenet* and *vitriol fattened* him, absolutely ... But Lorilleux, angry at not having a *belly*, said that it was *yellow fat, bad fat*' (323). Hence the recurrence of round and yellow forms containing alcohol: the main room of L'Assommoir is 'decorated with great *casks painted a bright yellow*' (41); the still 'has a *copper pot-belly*' (50), and 'the damned vessel, round like a *belly* of a *fat* stove,' is compared to a witch who 'drop by drop spilled out the *fire* from her *entrails*' (391).

27 It is accepted that alcohol and fat are described in like terms; indeed, excretion is also linked to death: during the wake for Maman Coupeau 'a unique noise, a soft rustling, came out of the room. They all lifted their heads, looked at each other. It's nothing, said Lantier calmly, in a low voice. She is voiding herself. This explanation caused some to shake their heads, with a reassured air, and the company put their glasses on the table' (342–3). The juxtaposition of these two passages is not by chance. Maman Coupeau is described in the same way as the goose (cf. 240–1): 'One would never have believed that that old lady could be so fat and white' (333). The goose's end is consummated by 'a neighbour's *cat*' that 'finished off by burying the animal' (263); Maman Coupeau's is consummated by Nana, who ends up sleeping on her bed (352) after having watched her die: 'in front of this *white* mask, ... her young *cat's eye* pupils widened' (333). When the goose had appeared, Nana had the same reaction: 'Nana, her eyes opened unnaturally *wide*, raised herself to see' (241).

Indeed, a narrative analysis would show that the goose, Maman Coupeau, Gervaise are three actors having to do with the same agonist. With Maman Coupeau, Gervaise had 'buried a piece of her own life' (352); and the drunken pallbearer had been wrong: 'Gervaise had gone quite *white*. The pallbearer had brought a bier for her' (344).

Indeed, the goose is described with the same semantic features as Gervaise (/femininity/, /whiteness/, /blondness/, /fat/): 'Hell's bells! What a *woman*! What thighs and what a *belly*!' (241); 'the skin was thin and *white*, a *blond* skin hey! The men all laughed lewdly' (242). In a reciprocal way, Gervaise is described in terms of a fowl: 'Go ahead! touch the *beast*! ... And she was not supposed to *puck back*' (325). Coupeau says to her: 'stay on your back, big *turkey*' (117), or calls her 'Marie-good-beak' (389). She is compared to a 'little *white hen*' (156) and often wants to eat something good, 'the desire for which tickled her *crop*' (156).

28 'To drown' is frequently linked with Gervaise: 'a drowned look' (10); 'her face drowned with sweetness' (60); 'eyes drowned with tenderness' (253); and, during the meal, 'her drowned look was lost in the darkness' (253).

In the course of the meal, /death/ increasingly recurs: Coupeau 'was making a real cemetery in the dish' (242); 'the pile of dead negresses grew, a cemetery for bottles' (245). Gervaise says: 'a day comes when you are happy to depart this world' (246) and Nana says, 'look! die!' (248; see also 249, 257, and 258).

29 The feature /edible/ can be inferred in other contexts. At L'Assommoir, 'she *simmered* in a pleasant warmth' (392). After Maman Coupeau's burial: 'The *brie* disappeared, litres flowed like fountains. However, Gervaise *softened* under the blows' (351).

30 A few lines earlier, Coupeau had advised her in this to become a hooker: 'You're still okay when you *clean yourself up a bit*. You know, as they say, there's no *pot* so old that it can't find a lid ... Lady! if that was supposed to put *butter* in the spinach!' Gervaise is thus assimilated to stuff at the bottom of a cruddy pot: cf. connections with food, and particularly stew; as with /heat/ (*pot*), /yellow/ and /viscous/ (*butter*).

31 Analogical relations within associative networks allow one to constitute idiolectal taxemes; however, certain of these analogical relations proceed from phraseology and thus, to this extent, have to do with language. Thus, 'being dirty' and 'pig' are associated (cf. 'dirty as a pig'); just as is the case in French between 'calf' and 'tears' (cf. 'cry like a calf'): thus, Bijard calls Lalie, whom he whips, 'my calf' (377).

11: Daddy Hen

1 Maupassant published *Toine* in the 6 January 1885 issue of *Gil Blas*. Cf. *Contes et Nouvelles*, Paris, Bibl. de la Pléiade, II, 426–35. The text here is that established by F. Court-Pérez, ed. *Contes*, Paris, Hachette, 1981. The English translation is mine.

2 They, cumulatively, have the most narrative roles.

3 To make the reading easier, I adopt the following conventions: actors are designated by one of their designations, judged to be typical; these designations are not signalled by any particular written form.

4 Tactic effect: the consequence is announced before the cause.

5 However this exchange is not considered as such in the universe of the drinkers; at

least they are happily fulfilled when they hear Toine arguing with his wife: 'You'd willingly have paid to see it' (42).

6 Indeed with a sack of seeds (lines 55 and 62): now, chickens are fattened up with seed grains ...

7 The expression *give a child* marvellously sums up the underlying axiology. We expressly know that he has no daughter, and no boy is mentioned.

8 My italics. After this, too, unless otherwise stated, italics are my emphasis. The metaphorical connection between the ocean and woman is confirmed later on. As for the connection between love and drink, it is banal, from the *drunkenness* of Emma Bovary to the theory of the *glass of water* in Lenin.

9 The repeated *ça* (that) emphasizes the threat of dehumanization. See also line 70, *superhuman health*.

10 This threatening brandishing of the naked arm might lead to research on the semiotics of the 'bras d'honneur' (to give someone two fingers) in Normandy at the end of the nineteenth century.

11 It is marked by the perfective and singulative aspect of the simple past (preterite), which is opposed to the imperfective and iterative aspect of the imperfects seen in the first part.

12 I should add that she is compared to a 'screech owl' (lines 45 and 99); now, in our cultural tradition, the owl is linked to death: for example, Atropos takes it for his interpreter; cf. also La Fontaine, *Fables*, XI, 9.

13 Alas, we cannot in detail study the highly refined tactic structures of this text.

14 From the title on, the aphaeresis of his name, repeated several times, presages hemiplegia.

15 Cf. this sentence from Nerval: 'It always ended with a game of dominoes, a game that is especially quiet and meditative.'

16 'My belly isn't supple' (line 40) can be read as a humorous presaging of his paralysis.

17 We should remember that Toine calls her 'my board,' but does not knock her over.

18 Later I shall make it clear whether Prosper constitutes one actor of the agonist that the people from around there are part of, or whether he is of the order of another agonist.

19 The 'we'll see what will happen' (line 140) significantly takes up again the analogous formulae of lines 53 and 55.

20 The forced contract is a deceptive form of confrontation.

21 Cf. 'Toine suffered an attack' (line 75): This lexical interpretant confirms that the old lady and death are actors that can be substituted for each other.

22 Here we have a *contretemps* effect, a semantic rhythm that is common in literature. It is emphasized, as is the case at the end of the first episode, by an imperfective (lines 161–3) /perfective (line 164) alternance.

23 At this point in the text the covering of the eggs was still just a project (see 'this seed of future chickens [that would] hatch under his body heat'). In literary texts, lexia such as this 'sack of seeds' are often resemanticized: they are not only the object of a global interpretation, but also of an analytical interpretation.
24 This succession of the type *a b b a* in fictive time constitutes a dialectic rhythm.
25 This confirms that the covering of the eggs makes up for the excess charge he used to make for alcohol. This transformation affects the state of mind of the peasants: they used to come 'for laughs,' but are now *serious* (30).
26 In my provisional interpretation of the story, this claimed inconsistency emphasizes the preeminence of alliance over filiation; Toine demonstrates a perfect social integration, since he offers his 'child' to his 'son-in-law,' although he has manifested the desire to keep him himself.
27 His name, *Mâcheblé* (lit. *wheat chewer*), is thus justified, if one remembers that the chicks in the eggs were the 'seeds of future chickens.'
28 The old lady's territory, she whom Toine calls 'my board.'
29 It is constituted by interaction between *actors* within *functions*.
30 For a 'formal syntax,' the phrases *Pierre is cared for at the hospital* and *Pierre is cared for at home* should be represented in the same way. However, the first of these is passive and the second can be seen as active (has himself cared for ...): in order to establish this structural distinction we must resort to semantic considerations, indeed encyclopaedic.
31 Two great views of narrative dynamism compete for legitimacy today: the one we might call interactional emphasizes disequilibria in exchanges between actors. It is well represented in folklore studies (since Propp, cf. especially studies by Meletinski, Pop) in social anthropology (Lévi-Strauss), in comparative mythology (following Dumézil's work).

The second, not 'sociological' but rather psychological, links narrative dynamics to the actors' intentions (often confused with characters in the story): it can be seen in the always lively discourse of what we know as 'belles-lettres' (romantic psychology, which is of the humanist tradition); also in the discourse of psychoanalytical criticism (where impulses are the foundation of intentions and indeed contradict intentions); again in the discourse of cognitive psychology (see Abelson's theory of intentions, and his contribution to narrative analysis and in the area of Artificial Intelligence).
32 Some commentators have seen here, undoubtedly correctly, indirect instructions for a positive judgment. In a scholarly edition (*Contes: Scènes de la vie de province*, Paris, Bordas, 1976, 71), D. and P. Cogny propose this exercise: 'Show how Maupassant prepares sympathy and emotion on behalf of Toine, from the day he falls ill (with an illness that is, however, a deserved punishment).' The parentheses

show the difficulty authors have in reconciling the different internal versions of the story.

33 At least for the interpretative tradition that is in conformity with traditional genres such as the fabliau, an ancestor of the novel. One should note, for example, the comparison between Prosper and the fox.

34 Later I shall go in detail into the processes of animalization and feminization.

35 See also the six designations and descriptions of Toine (lines 1–2): they testify not only to his popularity among those from around there, but also demonstrate, being so numerous, the multiplicity of this collective actor.

36 As we can see, an enunciative position is a semantic point of reference that correlatively gives rise to spatial, temporal, aspectual, modal, and personal deictics as well as to judgments.

37 The psychological processes of identification that allow us to construct actors are of course oriented by linguistic indices.

38 If only in the case of everything that has to do with veridiction (see on page 56, how the violation of this contract by Scheherazade has an impact upon the interpretation of the *Story of the Little Hunchback*).

39 See lines 60 ff, and the pejorative judgments (and the abandoning of the subject *on*): 'his clients would bang on the tables and shake with laughter, stomp their feet and spit on the ground in their delirious fun.' One can think that these allotopies between judgmental features (afferent here) are the index of a change of enunciative position.

40 It belongs only to Toine's universe and that of those from around there, and not to the old lady's or the narrator's.

41 I use this word without referring to Riffaterre (1983). The versions studied above are narrative hypotexts. There are, of course, other kinds.

42 See, for example, parabolic texts and their instructions concerning research.

43 See also 'with his arms raised like wings.'

44 See also syntactic parallelisms and assonances such as 'dans le lit et dans le nid' (in the bed and in the nest), which underline semantic contiguities. All this doesn't prevent Toine's being called *cochon* (pig) in the old lady's universe, and *gros lupin* (big bunny) in Célestin Maloisel's universe: the animal isotopy is still very much there, in both universes.

45 Of course, it's just a matter of metaphorical comparisons. But if the author can mobilize all the resources of language, the reader should not be left to the last. I reject the procedure that reduces such comparisons to a meaning that is deemed dominant. As a general rule, they connect generic isotopies (see Rastier, 1987a, chap. 8).

46 See Buffon: 'le renard est célèbre par ses ruses et mérite en partie sa réputation' (the fox is famous for its tricks and in part deserves its reputation).

47 And his first name, Prosper, fits his role as beneficiary.

48 Technically, to the feature /animal/ that is inherent to 'hen', there is in addition, in this context and through afference, the feature /human/ that is inherent to 'lodger'. The dissimilation of isotopies suspends incompatibility.

49 The Robert dictionary, satisfying the taste of today, extends this to young girls.

50 The analogy between eating (consuming) food and consummating sex is most trivial.

51 Two internal variations of a story that can each be derived from the other with no axiological change might however be called *internal variants*.

52 Neither the ferret nor screech owl show, in this phrasing, any privileged relation with hens. The main thing is to remember the semantic features that are common in all descriptions of an actor: thus, the rooster, the screech owl, and the owl are associated here with descriptive features such as /round eye/, /screeching/.

53 This fecund production, as violent as it is, is no less chaste, and the biblical formula 'the time was approaching' (for the holy birth) would (for a productive reading) make the hatching into a nativity, and make Toine the virgin mother, the gathering of the peasants would be made into the adoration of the shepherds, and the chicken fricassee would become the Sacrifice.

54 Both belong to textual truth because they both have lexicalized units in all universes. Thus, the /animal/ isotopy is represented in the universes of the narrator, the old lady, Toine, Prosper and those from around there.

55 The words making up the insults and the phrasing of them bear witness to this.

56 These two terms have to do with the same semantic dimension.

57 According to common sense, a tired version of classical idealist ontology, appearance is by nature deceiving, and does not proceed from essence.

58 The western hermeneutic tradition, a product principally of patristic allegorism, naturally influences techniques of generation and interpretation of fictional texts: those techniques are such as to confirm the valorization of *hidden meaning*, which here is read derisively, along the animal isotopy.

59 From the initial confrontation on (see pigsty, wing [lines 54, 57]).

60 Also note that they are 'surrounded ... by trees.'

61 We should add that Tournevent is a locality: the site 'was the source of ... [the hamlet's] name' (line 7). See 'single-handed paternity' and 'Goddamn, what a baptism' (lines 209, 211).

62 The people from around there are little when compared to Toine (cf. 'this colossus').

63 These metaphorical connections are established by the *identity* of specific semes (inherent or afferent); they bring on a relation of *equivalence* between sememes that are indexed along different generic isotopies.

64 Global interpretative paths are highly non-linear, and constraints imposed by locality play only a secondary role here. Indeed, the thematic and dialectical analysis I am

carrying out here remains autonomous in terms of the tactic component that defines linear disposition. Certain comparisons can seem far-fetched. Even if they are barely plausible, their cumulative force does none the less constitute a whole package of presumptions that is hard to refute.

65 Cf. this sentence from Sartre: 'this woman ... is a hurricane.' American feminists have worked mightily to have cyclones named after men as well as women.

66 A word such as *undrinkable* certainly does not belong in this text and seems to be of the order of an extrinsic interpretation. I allow myself this little phraseological detour in order to emphasize that rapprochements such as this are already inscribed in the text (see also 'he can't swallow it').

67 The women get the sweets, the men get the pork. In Greece they say that a woman attracted to men 'likes the salty.'

68 As he does, undoubtedly, those of death, 'he could have made a tombstone laugh' (lines 30–1).

69 On the other hand, the old lady deprives him of liquid nourishment (soup) and then of movement. She finally deprives Toine of the last chick.

70 For example, in 'climb up to the crenel' (literally, to climb to the crenel; figuratively, to counter aggressively), the generic feature /military architecture/ is usually neutralized.

71 I have naturally taken 'to the letter' the expressions *that gives me to mourn*, *make a tombstone laugh*, and *make the devil laugh*.

72 Is he a man without God, according to P. Cogny? Or with God, according to Greimas, who proposed a biblical reading of *Deux amis*?

73 For example, for memory: the relation of type a: 'Toine' → 'cochon' in the old lady's universe; type b: 'Prosper' → 'fox'; type e: 'houses → 'birds'; type d: 'death' → 'old lady'; type f: 'death' → 'ocean wind'; type c: 'those from around there' → 'houses.'

74 I am keeping in mind here type relations and not the number of their occurrences. The remarks that follow therefore have to do with qualitative criteria.

75 As a function of other criteria I have shown above that it was not plausible.

76 They allow us to oppose, for example, the topographical isotopy (localized and dense) and the animal isotopy (unlocalized).

77 To simplify, I called, above, *isotopies* isotopic bundles: as a general rule reiteration of a generic feature is accompanied by the reiteration of other features linked to it; for example, the /human/ isotopy is generally part of a double unit, the other half being the isotope /animated/.

78 They show degrees of typicality.

79 In many (if not all) human societies and among many higher mammals, (simians, canines) to stare a fellow creature in the eye is interpreted as a sign of hostility.

80 It seems to be anthropologically well founded because laughter is appreciated everywhere for its vasodilating effects: as is the case here with Toine Brûlot's 'Fine.'
81 See also Plato, *The Republic*, X, 614 c: 'In the centre there were also judges who, after giving their sentence, ordered the just to take the road on the right, leading to the sky, after having hung a sign around them concerning their judgment. The convicted they ordered to take the descending way left, wearing also, but on their backs, a sign recounting all of their actions.' This kind of homologation is frequent in occult philosophies.
82 Cf. notably the *Hi ts'eu*, a small treatise added on to the *Yi King*.
83 The homologation *masculine:feminine::visible:hidden::cold:hot* is linked, for example, as shown by Granet, to the division of labour in ancient China: men, farmers or drovers, worked outdoors, especially in the summer; women, weavers, and seamstresses remained indoors. Beyond that, certain homologations can exhibit a transcultural validity, proceeding from perceptive and cognitive constraints. Texts belonging to so-called universal literature undoubtedly owe much of their universality to the anthropological nature of the archthematics they set into play.

12: The White Care of Our [Sail-]Cloth

1 Mallarmé, *Oeuvres complètes*, Paris, Gallimard, 1945, 27. Unless otherwise stated, all references are from this edition.
2 Especially Arrivé, Lerat, Klinkenberg, Tụtescu, Verrier, Vaina, Adriaens, Culler, Gelas, Kerbrat, the Groupe Mu, Greimas, and Courtés. R. Pommier begins with this question to us: 'What crazy phallus, what delirious uterus produced such a ridiculous pedant?' (1978, 17), and proves at least that French university polemics have not yet lost their verve.
3 Cf. 72: 'Without the helm's moving'; and 413 in connection with a teacher: 'once upon a time he took the helm.' Later on I shall evaluate the legitimacy of comparing such texts.
4 Cf. 477: 'lines / it should be / the Septentrion also North ... a constellation.'
5 In a case where the morpheme that we read can hold only one sememe, any equivocal meaning is impossible.
6 Setting aside the question of anaphorics, contents of grammemes are indifferent *vis-à-vis* semantic domains; thus I cannot index them along this type of isotopy. The actualization and neutralization of semes takes place while taking into account syntactic criteria (see Rastier, 1987a, III, 2). Given its deliberate ambiguities, Mallarméan syntax still authorizes, indeed prescribes, the interpretation of polysemies that have nothing arbitrary about them.
7 Cf. the Groupe Mu (1977, 101): 'From all evidence, what is manifested unequivocally in Mallarmé's poem is a story of sailors.'

8 This note is part of the immediate context of the poem because it figures, as the author wished, in the collection he published.
9 The first version of this poem had the title *Toast*. *Salut* likely was eventually the preferred choice because its polysemy allowed, as we have seen, for an indexing of its contents along several isotopies. Isotopic analysis can profitably be used by genetic criticism because the development of a text also consists of establishing its isotopies, which are primordial factors for its cohesion. See also the second line of *Toast funèbre*: 'Salut de la démence et libation blême' (54); and the various toasts to writers, 862–5.
10 Phrasing can accomplish the function of interpretant. Lerat here speaks of the autonymic anaphora of the title (1984, 109).
11 I first wrote 'purpose of the banquet'; it was neither clever nor false. Lerat thinks that it 'becomes syntactically impossible to gloss *souci* in terms of "purpose of the banquet" if you take into consideration the group of words *le blanc souci de notre toile*' (108). If you accept the glose 'sheet' for *toile* (white), then all is possible. The allotopy between 'white' and 'souci' is a strong enough indication of those hypallages so frequent in Mallarmé (cf. 'Neiger de blancs bouquets d'étoiles parfumées,' [30]).
12 We can make the comparison between the rites of *situational scripts* (cf. Schank and Abelson, 1977).
13 At least in French. For a discussion of quantitative criteria, cf. Arrivé, 1973, 58 and Rastier, 1987a, chap. 5.
14 On the theoretical status of connections, cf. Rastier, 1987a, chap. 8.
15 The Groupe Mu notes, where I use just the word *metaphor*: 'it is in fact a double metaphor, pointing us to the champagne of line 2 of the poem by way of "coupe" and pointing us to the ocean of line 3, by way of "se noie." And if indeed I can speak of metaphor, it is between "champagne" and "waves" whose foam is just one possible intersection, a manifested intersection' (1977, 69).
16 Cf. chap. 13, on 'Bergère ô tour Eiffel,' line 2 of 'Zone.'
17 One can in turn connect these rewritings: 'timonier' (helmsman) and 'president' have the feature /direction/ in common (cf. the Great Helmsman, President Mao).
18 We can agree here that for Mallarmé as for the other writers to whom he is speaking, the mythical isotopy /sailing/ (cf. sirens), is the object of a better evaluation than the practical isotopy /banquet/.
19 One can see what difficulties might arise here if one were to use the distinction between denoted and connoted isotopies: the connoted isotopy would be apparent, the denoted one latent.
20 //literature// is a domain that is recognized as such in lexicographical practice: the indicator *lit.* is of the same kind as *mar.* (marine), for example.
21 Cf. Robert dictionary: (i) nothing; (ii) that has never been touched, dirtied, soiled,

tarnished, or even used; (iii) where one is alone (not with other like people). This negativity is linked to the problematics of absence; in fact, the word waves off what is real by evoking the Idea, cf. the famous: 'Je dis: une fleur! et, hors de l'oubli où ma voix relègue aucun contour, en tant que quelque chose d'autre que les calices sus, musicalement se lève, idée même suave, l'absente de tous les bouquets' (368). I say: a flower! and, outside the forgetfulness where my voice relegates no contour, as something other that the calyxes known, musically arises, the even suave idea, the absent one (flower) from all bouquets.

22 See J.-P. Richard, 1961.

23 The idiolect in question is not coextensive with the whole work of Mallarmé, but it is with his non-remunerated writings, from 1866 to 1898.

24 H.-J. Frey proposes for *la coupe* another reading, that of 'cutting' (the poetic line) and remarks that then 'one and only one sounded signifier designates two things that have nothing to do with each other' (*Der Vers als Zeichen*, NZZ, #460, 4/10/1970, 49). This reading is possible. Frey however writes: 'The case of the word *la coupe* is a particularly neat example of the reign of chance (*Zufalls*) in language' (ibid.), whereas for Mallarmé the line refutes 'd'un trait souverain, le hasard demeuré aux termes' (with a sovereign stroke, chance left to the terms) 368.

25 We also know that Mallarmé used only black ink (the page – black on white – denying the constellated sky – white on black): 'Tu remarquas, on n'écrit pas, lumineusement, sur champ obscur, l'alphabet des astres, seul, ainsi s'indique, ébauché ou interrompu; l'homme poursuit noir sur blanc' (370); You noticed, one does not write, luminously on an obscure background, the alphabet of the stars, alone, is indicated, sketched or interrupted, man pursues black on white.

26 Cf. Dante: *Ormai la navicella del mio ingegno* (*Purg.*, I, 2).

27 The pen becomes 'la lucide aigrette de vertige' (cf. 'rocking') that 'bobs up and down' (/iterativity/), 470–1.

28 In relation to *Un coup de dés jamais n'abolira le hasard*, I see here an inversion: man can drown there ('naufrage cela direct de l'homme' (462)), and a siren is standing erect (cf. 471: 'en sa torsion de sirène debout'); whereas in *Salut* a man is standing erect and the sirens are drowning. That would seem to confirm, via a narrative analysis, that 'man' and 'siren' are opposed actors.

29 Cf. 'Toute pensée émet un Coup de Dés': a throw of dice, black dots on white, is like a constellation, white dots on black.

30 This is not the old extension of the acceptation of *lines* = *poetry*: 'Le vers est partout dans la langue où il y a rythme ... en vérité, il n'y a pas de prose: il y a l'alphabet et puis des vers plus ou moins serrés, plus ou moins diffus' (verse is everywhere in language where there is rhythm ... actually, there is no prose: there is an alphabet and then verse more or less tight, more or less diffuse) 867.

31 As, for example with *La porte du jour* (day's gate), which, in Somaize's dictionary, constitutes the molecule /passage/ + /luminosity/, lexicalized by *window*.

32 Making due allowances, Lévi-Strauss once claimed that the meaning of a myth is found in its relations of transformation with other myths. It remains true that those transformations themselves are regulated by a system that alone accounts for that meaning.

33 Cf. 'Nommer un objet, c'est supprimer les trois quarts de la jouissance du poème, qui est fait du bonheur de deviner peu à peu; le suggérer, voilà le rêve' (To name an object, is to suppress three quarters of the pleasure of the poem that comes from the happiness of slowly guessing; to suggest it, that is the ideal) 869. 'Evoquer, dans une ombre exprès, l'objet tu par les mots allusifs, jamais directs, se réduisant à du silence égal, comporte une tentative proche de créer' (To evoke in a shadow intentionally, the object unsaid by the allusive words, never direct, reduced to equal silence, is an attempt approaching creation) 113. More generally, Klinkenberg thinks, about i_3: 'such a reading fits well with what we know about the structures of modern poetry' (1973, 289).

34 Thus the parataxis between *foam* and *lines* is clarified. The words are of i_3 in connection with the relation of instrumental to the accusative, whereas they share along i_1 the same casual function.

35 However, connections between generic isotopies consist essentially of establishing elementary specific isotopies.

36 Such a representation seems preferable over the tabular representations to which the Groupe Mu would link my analysis; in effect, any sememe of a given isotopy can be connected to several others.

37 The indexations of anisotopic sememes along one or other isotopy are not considered to be connections.

38 Just as metaphorical dominance is a relation of the compared to the comparing.

39 The Groupe Mu has in turn correlated these isotopies – as is the case for those of all the poems – to three fundamental categories, arranged in a triadic model.

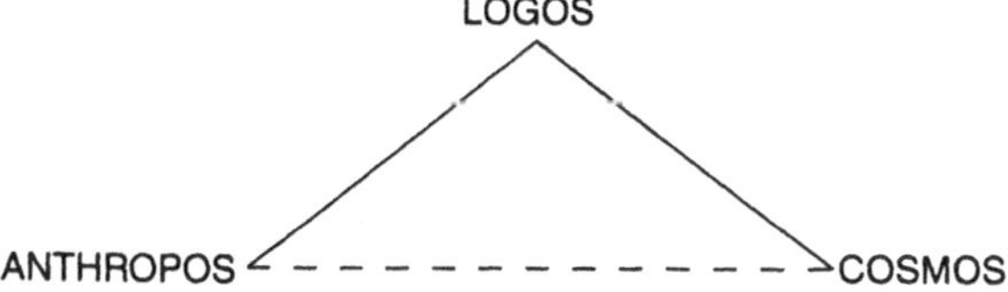

Referring to G. Durand, Jung, Eliade especially, the group thinks that the opposition *anthropos/cosmos* is primordial. Indeed it assimilates it to the opposition *interoceptivity/exteroceptivity* according to Greimas, which itself is a reprise of the opposition *noological/cosmological* in Ampère. Studying my first analysis of *Salut*, the group notes, 'One could easily *a priori* index in our three classes (anthropos-logos-cosmos) the sememes manifested in this text ... In particular that would give, in Logos, not only "lines," "designate" and the title "salut," but indeed "sirens," if we agree to extend the field under consideration so that it can take in signifiers whose referent is literary, mythical, semiotic, etc.' (1977, 84). It is difficult to see how one might follow through, because each of the isotopies I have identified includes sememes that can be placed indiscriminately within any one of the three '*a priori* classes.' Indeed, as far as generic isotopies of this kind are concerned, an a priori classification does not seem viable because the semantic domains that bring them on are linked to a determinate society and are susceptible of being modified – indeed created – idiolectally.

Although it is triadic, the Group Mu's model articulates a theory of poetry that has a twofold meaning: 'The strictly poetic effect according to us corresponds to two conditions: 1. Manifestation, direct or indirect, of a cosmos isotopy and of an anthropos isotopy. 2. Rhetorical mediation, explicit or implicit, between two isotopies' (ibid, 88). Logos then will become the mediator between anthropos and cosmos (cf. 99–103): here we again find the opposition between *thematic* (anthropos isotopy – interoceptive or noological) and *figurative* (cosmos isotopy – exteroceptive or cosmological). Semantics has given way to philosophy, since authors can assimilate this primordial opposition, primordial for them as for Greimas, to *spirituality* versus *materiality*.

40 The text can of course be studied on other levels, or relatively to other components. This opens up another avenue for research: to the three isotopies there correspond different dialectic structures. For example along i_1 and i_3 'sirens' corresponds to an opponent actor, not along i_2; along i_1 'lightnings' and 'winters' are two actors of the same agonist, and along i_3 they are two antagonists; 'star' corresponds to a helper along i_1, but corresponds to an object of value along i_3, etc. This poses important theoretical questions deserving their own treatment.

41 Cf. 'Une ordonnance du livre de vers poind innée ou partout, élimine le hasard; encore la faut-il, pour omettre l'auteur: or, un sujet, fatal, implique, parmi les morceaux ensemble, tel accord quant à la place, dans le volume, qui correspond' (An arrangement of the book of verse breaks out innate or everywhere, eliminates chance, again it must, to omit the author: now, a fatal subject, implies, among the parts together, an agreement as to the place, in the volume, that corresponds (366).

42 *Un coup de dés* appears in 1869 in the argument to *Igitur* (see 434).

43 A more systematic comparison would go beyond the bounds of this work.

44 *Salut* was even supposed to be distinguished from the other pieces of the collection by virtue of a different type face. This confirms its unique status (although no editor to date has acceded to the author's wish, as far as I know).

13: Referential Impression or the Sun and the Shepherdess

The original French poem 'Zone,' by G. Apollinaire :

À la fin tu es las de ce monde ancien

Bergère ô tour Eiffel le troupeau des ponts bêle ce matin

Tu en as assez de vivre dans l'antiquité grecque et romaine

Ici même les automobiles ont l'air d'être anciennes / La religion seule est restée toute neuve la religion / Est restée simple comme les hangars de Port-Aviation

Seul en Europe tu n'es pas antique ô Christianisme / L'Européen le plus moderne c'est vous Pape Pie X / Et toi que les fenêtres observent la honte te retient / D'entrer dans une église et de t'y confesser ce matin / Tu lis les prospectus les catalogues les affiches qui chantent tout haut / Voilà la poésie ce matin et pour la prose il y a les journaux / Il y a les livraisons à 25 centimes pleines d'aventures policières / Portraits des grands hommes et mille titres divers / J'ai vu ce matin une jolie rue dont j'ai oublié le nom / Neuve et propre du soleil elle était le clairon / Les directeurs les ouvriers et les belles sténo-dactylographes / Du lundi matin au samedi soir quatre fois par jour y passent / Le matin par trois fois la sirène y gémit / Une cloche rageuse y aboie vers midi / Les inscriptions des enseignes et des murailles / Les plaques les avis à la façon des perroquets criaillent / J'aime la grâce de cette rue industrielle / Située à Paris entre la rue Aumont-Thiéville et l'avenue des Ternes

Voilà la jeune rue et tu n'es encore qu'un petit enfant / Ta mère ne t'habille que de bleu et de blanc / Tu es très pieux et avec le plus ancien de tes camarades René Dalize / Vous n'aimez rien tant que les pompes de l'église / Il est neuf heures le gaz est baissé tout bleu vous sortez du dortoir en cachette / Vous priez toute la nuit dans la chapelle du collège / Tandis qu'éternelle et adorable profondeur améthyste / Tourne à jamais la flamboyante gloire du Christ / C'est le beau lys que tous nous cultivons / C'est la torche aux cheveux roux que n'éteint pas le vent / C'est le fils pâle et vermeil de la douloureuse mère / C'est l'arbre toujours touffu de toutes les prières / C'est la double potence de l'honneur et de l'éternité / C'est l'étoile à six branches / C'est Dieu qui meurt le vendredi et ressuscite le dimanche / C'est le Christ qui monte au ciel mieux que les aviateurs / Il détient le record du monde pour la hauteur

Pupille Christ de l'oeil / Vingtième pupille des siècles il sait y faire / Et changé en oiseau ce siècle comme Jésus monte dans l'air / Les diables dans les abîmes lèvent la tête pour le regarder / Ils disent qu'il imite Simon Mage en Judée / Ils crient s'il sait voler qu'on l'appelle voleur / Les anges voltigent autour du joli voltigeur / Icare Énoch Élie Apollonius de Thyane / Flottent autour du premier aéroplane / Ils s'ecartent parfois pour laisser passer ceux que transporte la Sainte-Eucharistie / Ces prêtres qui montent éternellement élevant l'hostie / L'avion se pose enfin sans refermer les ailes / Le ciel s'emplit alors de millions d'hirondelles / À tire d'aile viennent les corbeaux les faucons les hiboux / D'afrique arrivent les ibis les flamants les marabouts / L'oiseau Roc célébré par les conteurs et les poètes / Plane tenant dans les serres le crâne d'Adam la première tête / L'aigle fond de l'horizon en poussant un grand cri / Et d'Amérique vient le petit colibri / De Chine sont venus les pihis longs et souples / Qui n'ont qu'une seule aile et qui volent par couples / Puis voici la colombe esprit immaculé / Qu'escortent l'oiseau-lyre et le paon ocellé; / Le phénix ce bûcher qui soi-même s'engendre / Un instant voile tout de son ardente cendre / Les sirènes laissant les périlleux détroits / Arrivent en chantant bellement toutes trois / Et tous aigle phénix et pihis de la Chine / Fraternisent avec la volante machine

Maintenant tu marches dans Paris tout seul parmi la foule / Des troupeaux d'autobus mugissants près de toi roulent / L'angoisse de l'amour te serre le gosier / Comme si tu ne devais jamais plus être aimé / Si tu vivais dans l'ancien temps tu entrerais dans un monastère / Vous avez honte quand vous vous surprenez à dire une prière / Tu te moques de toi et comme le feu de l'Enfer ton rire pétille / Les étincelles de ton rire dorent le fond de ta vie / C'est un tableau pendu dans un sombre musée / Et quelquefois tu vas le regarder de près

Aujourd'hui tu marches dans Paris les femmes sont ensanglantées / C'était et je voudrais ne pas m'en souvenir c'était au déclin de la beauté

Entourée de flammes ferventes Notre-Dame m'a regardé à Chartres / Le sang de votre Sacré-Coeur m'a inondé à Montmartre / Je suis malade d'ouïr les paroles bienheureuses / L'amour dont je souffre est une maladie honteuse / Et l'image qui te possède te fait survivre dans l'insomnie et dans l'angoisse / C'est toujours près de toi cette image qui passe

Maintenant tu es au bord de la Méditerranée / Sous les citronniers qui sont en fleur toute l'année / Avec tes amis tu te promènes en barque / L'un est Nissard il y a un Mentonasque et deux Turbiasques / Nous regardons avec effroi les poulpes des profondeurs / Et parmi les algues nagent les poissons images du Sauveur

Tu es dans le jardin d'une auberge aux environs de Prague / Tu te sens tout heureux une rose est sur la table / Et tu observes au lieu d'écrire ton conte en prose / la cétoine qui dort dans le coeur de la rose

Épouvanté tu vois dessiné dans les agates de Saint-Vit / Tu étais triste à mourir le jour où tu t'y vis / Tu ressembles au Lazare affolé par le jour / Les aiguilles de l'horloge du quartier juif vont à rebours / Et tu recules aussi dans ta vie lentement / En montant au Hradchin et le soir en écoutant / Dans les tavernes chanter des chansons tchèques

Te voici à Marseille au milieu des pastèques

Te voici à Coblence à l'hôtel du Géant

Te voici à Rome assis sous un néflier du Japon

Te voici à Amsterdam avec une jeune fille que tu trouves belle et qui est laide / Elle doit se marier avec un étudiant de Leyde / On y loue des chambres en latin Cubicula locanda / Je m'en souviens j'y ai passé trois jours et autant à Gouda

Tu es à Paris chez le juge d'instruction / Comme un criminel on te met en état d'arrestation

Tu es fait de douloureux et de joyeux voyages / Avant de t'apercevoir du mensonge et de l'âge / Tu as souffert de l'amour à vingt et à trente ans / J'ai vécu comme un fou et j'ai perdu mon temps / Tu n'oses plus regarder tes mains et à tous moments je voudrais sangloter / Sur toi sur celle que j'aime sur tout ce qui t'a épouvanté

Tu regardes les yeux pleins de larmes ces pauvres émigrants / Ils croient en Dieu ils prient les femmes allaitent des enfants / Ils emplissent de leur odeur le hall de la gare Saint-Lazare / Ils ont foi dans leur étoile comme les rois-mages / Ils espèrent gagner de l'argent dans l'Argentine / Et revenir dans leur pays après avoir fait fortune / Une famille transporte un édredon rouge comme vous transportez votre coeur / Cet édredon et nos rêves sont aussi irréels / Quelques-uns de ces émigrants restent ici et se logent / Rue des Rosiers ou rue des Écouffes dans des bouges / Je les ai vus souvent le soir ils prennent l'air dans la rue / Et se déplacent rarement comme les pièces aux échecs / Il y a surtout des Juifs leurs femmes portent perruque / Elles restent assises exsangues au fond des boutiques

Tu es debout devant le zinc d'un bar crapuleux / Tu prends un café à deux sous parmi les malheureux

Tu es la nuit dans un grand restaurant

Ces femmes ne sont pas méchantes elles ont des soucis cependant / Toutes même la plus laide a fait souffrir son amant

Elle est la fille d'un sergent de ville de Jersey

Ses mains que je n'avais pas vues sont dures et gercées

J'ai une pitié immense pour les coutures de son ventre

J'humilie maintenant à une pauvre fille au rire horrible ma bouche

Tu es seul le matin va venir / Les laitiers font tinter leurs bidons dans les rues / La nuit s'éloigne ainsi qu'une belle Métive / C'est Ferdine la fausse ou Léa l'attentive

Et tu bois cet alcool brûlant comme ta vie / Ta vie que tu bois comme une eau-de-vie

Tu marches vers Auteuil tu veux aller chez toi à pied / Dormir parmi tes fétiches d'Océanie et de Guinée / Ils sont des Christ d'une autre forme et d'une autre croyance / Ce sont les Christ inférieurs des obscures espérances

Adieu Adieu

Soleil cou coupé

1 Adam speaks to the poet.
2 I prefer the term referential *impression* over *illusion*, a term popularized by Barthes and Riffaterre, but which is gratuitously pejorative.
3 A liminary poem in *Alcools* (1913), in *Oeuvres poétiques*, Paris, Gallimard, Bibl. de la Pléiade, 1965, 39–44.
4 Here I am dealing with truth in the strongest sense, and not truth in the weak sense that I used in chapter 6, on dialogics.
5 To the extent that the linguistic system does not fix a reference for morphemes, depending, aside from context (within the word especially), on the norms of general usage as well as communicational conditions of any given particular instance. Here, as in what follows, I refer in brief only to propositions I have defended elsewhere.
6 However, the arrow that goes from the signified to the referent should sometimes be reversed: often the presence, in a communicational situation, of a possible referent for a given sign allows one to identify the signified of that sign.
7 See the thesis by Denis (1987).
8 As for fiction texts, which is what I am studying here, the *R2* relation is of no immediate relevance (whatever the claim of such texts to 'realism').
9 For example, if in an amphitheatre filled with sixty people the speaker standing in front of the blackboard says, 'I'm picking up my blackboard eraser' (the French word for this is 'éponge,' meaning, in the first instance of course, 'sponge'), at least

one or two people – maybe people aching to go on holiday – will mentally visualize a marine zoophyte.

10 An isolated linguistic sign has no meaning, or at least its signified is indeterminate.

11 An inherent seme can be actualized by default; an afferent seme must be actualized by contextual indication.

12 I have based my argument on this observation when confirming that the theory of reference cannot be the foundation for a linguistic semantics.

13 The opposition /city/ versus /country/, or more precisely /intra-urban/ versus /extra-urban/ is lexicalized in French in such oppositions as *street* versus *road*, *bus* versus *highway bus* (in French *autobus* versus *autocar*). Indeed, if you keep in mind the succession in the utterance under study of sememes having to do with these two domains, you'll see this remarkable semantic rhythm: *c v c v cv* (in which *c* is short for //country// (in French //*campagne*//) and *v* is short for //city// (in French //*ville*//).

14 At the beginning of the poem, the represented enunciator is split into two actors: the 'je' is linked to positive assumptions and the 'tu' to negative assumptions (see above, 208).

15 *Tour Eiffel* is considered to be a lexia.

16 Of course, the sun is not strictly speaking circular; but we know that linguistic phrasing and scientific knowledge propose representations of reality that are often quite different. In French, the sun continues to rise and set as if Copernicus had never existed. With respect to other texts in *Alcools*, one might indeed question the relevance of the opposition /circularity/ versus /sphericity/: cf. 'Il vit décapité sa tête est le soleil / Et la lune son cou tranché' ('Les fiançailles'); ('He lives decapitated his head is the sun / And the moon his severed neck').

17 This seme is made explicit in an earlier poem: 'le soleil qui radiait / Dut paraître à leurs yeux extasiés / Le cou tranché'; ('the radiating sun / Must have appeared to their ecstatic eyes / The severed neck') ('Les Doukhobors,' 715). Cf. also: 'Sur nous tous les jours le guillotiné d'en haut / Laissera le sang pleuvoir'; ('On us every day the guillotined one on high / Will let the blood rain') ('Les poètes,' 720).

18 Here we see again the relation between signifieds and mental images. The signifieds constrain the mental images, but we have to formulate the hypothesis according to which a retroaction of conceptual representations happens to the semantic treatment, strictly speaking.

19 To this thematic study we should add a dialectical and dialogical analysis in order to account for substitutions of semes according to temporal or modal moments.

20 In fact this passage is divided into two parts (as will be confirmed later): ascension (lines 40–52) and Christ's return (lines 53–70).

21 Whose status was clarified elsewhere (1987a, chap. 9).

22 This detour via the inanimate allows us to avoid the principle of 'sexuisemblance,'

which, according to Genette, prevents us from comparing contents of the same gender.

23 Cf. the *Laetabundus*: 'Sol de stella / Sol occasum nesciens ...' or the Laudes hymn: 'O Sol salutis intimis / Jesu refulge mentibus ....'

24 These ornothological clarifications are not necessarily a waste of time. For example, the famous 'colombe poignardée' of the *Calligrammes* is also a known species.

25 On the express wishes of Adam himself, as is confirmed by Iacopo da Varazze. The iconography here is very rich.

26 Apollinaire, a curious reader if ever there was one, might have known, through a fine translation by Garcin de Tassy, another version of the Oriental myth of the king of birds (phoenix, Roc, or sîmorgh): *The Language of the Birds* of Farîd-ud-dîn'Attar. In that masterpiece of Islamic mysticism, all of the bird species take flight, from all corners of the world, to join their king, a giant bird named Sîmorgh. Thirty arrive and recognize themselves in him (*sî morgh* signifies in Persian 'thirty birds'). 'Attar's work especially develops the *Story of the Bird* of Avicenna, which Apollinaire might have known by less direct means.

If one rejects this rapprochement, and if one clings to the Roc of the *Thousand and One Nights*, a transformation is still very apparent: the king of the birds is replaced by the airplane, a superlative bird that does not fold its wings (cf. line 53), whereas the Roc is among those birds that come to fraternize with it.

In short, pagan beliefs (Roc, phoenix, sirens) are subordinate to Christian belief; cf. 'Tu me protégeras à l'ombre de tes ailes' (You will protect me in the shadow of your wings) Psalm 16:8; 'Tu mettras ton espoir dans ses ailes' (You will put your hope in his wings) Psalm 35:8.

27 Cf. 'Seul en Europe tu n'es pas antique ô Christianisme,' line 7.

28 Apollinaire was naturally interested in Apollonius. He uses him in a story of *L'hérésiarque et Cie* (The Heresiarch and Company). He no doubt knew that his solar theology brought him close to monotheism. At the end of the hagiographic novel that he devotes to him, Philostratus begins to doubt that he had died. He wonders if he had simply disappeared into the temple of Athena at Lindos, or the temple of Dyctinna in Crete: 'he entered and, behind him, the door closed, as though it had been locked and one heard the voices of young girls singing. And this is what they sang: "Leave the earth behind, come towards heaven, come." That is to say: "Elevate yourselves above the earth."'; cf. P. Grimal, *Romans grecs et latins*, Paris, Gallimard, 1958, 1337)

29 This is underlined by the very rare rhyme *Thyane / aéroplane*. Note also, in connection with the tactic structure of the line, that the order of the names corresponds to a chronological succession (mythical past for Icarus, Enoch, then Elias in the biblical story, beginning of the Christian era for Apollonius, who lived in the first century) and an evaluative hierarchy (pagan, then Jewish, then para-Christian).

Finally one should note that all four, in a sign of subordination, *move aside* in order to let pass 'these priests who mount continually, elevating the Host' (line 52).

30 The /multiple/ feature is in fact afferent to each of the actors of class B, not only when multiplicity is lexicalized, but, also in the case of proper nouns such as Adam, Roc or Icarus, because of the fact that they are included in an enumeration.

31 The repetition of *autre* (another), line 152, confirms the disjunctive nature of the feature /exotic/.

32 *Métive* in the French original conjoins exoticism archaism, being an ancient form of *métisse* / half-caste).

33 A confirmation of our hypothesis: the 'images' of the ego are multiple, cf. 'Fearfully we watch octopus in the depths / And among the seaweed swim fish, metaphors of the Saviour' (lines 93–4). Now, in the bestiary of Apollinaire, the octopus, infamous and inky, is the image of the writer-ego: 'Jetant son encre vers les cieux, / Suçant le sang de ce qu'il aime / Et le trouvant délicieux, / Ce monstre inhumain, c'est moi-même' (Spewing its ink towards the sky, / Sucking the blood of those it loves / And finding it delicious, / This inhuman monster, is myself) (*Bestiaire*, xx).

34 'Adieu, Adieu' (line 157): these words – which cannot fail to evoke God (Dieu), in this context – can also pass for the last words of a condemned man.

35 Adam is to a greater or lesser extent considered to be a prophet in all Abrahamic religions. For the Ebionites, as we know them through the pseudo-clementine texts, he is even the True Prophet (cf. *Hom.*, VIII, 420); the oneness of Adam and Jesus is one of the Gnostics' favourite themes. For Shiite theologians, Adam is the first prophet. Even Manicheists recognize him as such.

36 The first version supports this evidence: 'Le soleil est là c'est un cou tranché ... Le soleil me fait peur il répand son sang sur Paris.' (The sun is there its neck severed ... The sun frightens me it spreads its blood over Paris).

37 Here is an important psychological correlate: 'mental images have their greatest effects when the context is minimal'; cf. Denis, 1987. The 'evocative' force of short genres, such as the haiku, undoubtedly owes a lot to this property of semantic perception.

38 Be it lay or religious, it matters little.

39 Appariement means here *pattern-matching*.

40 I thus would rather use the terms *referentiation* for pairing of the perception of an object and a signified, and *imagization* for pairing of a signified and a mental image.

41 The dialectic structure of an actor is defined in terms of the totality of the agonist roles that subsume that actor; its thematic structure is defined in terms of the totality of the semes belonging to the molecule that gives it its type.

42 As is the case in narrative analysis, we tend to name (something open to debate) the agonist using the name of the most typical actor.

43 On typicality in cognitive psychology, see Dubois, 1986.

44 Beyond intratextual reference, typicality has close links with referentiation. To explain, for example, the meaning of the word *fruit* one can show an apple; for *tool*, one can point to a hammer or a monkey wrench (rather than to a diamond or an awl), etc. It is the same thing for imagization, which is undoubtedly nothing more than sophisticated referentiation: experiments carried out in cognitive psychology confirm, for example, that the mental image brought on by the word *fruit* (not in the context of enticement) will be that of a typical fruit (such as the apple of northern France or the orange of the south).

45 On the hierarchy and dominance of generic isotopies, see Rastier, 1987a, chap. 8.

Glossary

acceptation	sememe whose meaning includes afferent semes that obey social norms.
actant	unit of the utterance having a semantic case.
actor	unit of the evenemential level of the dialectic, composed of a semic molecule with which a group of roles is associated.
actualization	interpretative operation that allows us to identify a seme in context.
afference	an inference that allows us to actualize an afferent seme.
afferent seme	extreme of an antisymmetrical relation between two sememes that belong to different taxemes. E.g. /weakness/ for 'child'. An afferent seme is actualized by contextual information.
agonist	a type that is constitutive of a class of actors; a unit having to do with the agonistic level of dialectics.
agonistic level	level of dialectics constituted by agonists and of sequences. Only stories include this level, a level that is hierarchically superior to the evenemential level.
allotopy	contextual relation of exclusive disjunction between two sememes (or two groups of sememes) that include incompatible semes.
anisotopic	adjective describing, in relation to a given isotopy, a sememe that has no 'isotopizing' seme and of all semes that are incompatible with it.
archdialectics	that part of dialectics has to do with the series of operations that cause valuated contents to succeed each other in textual time.
archthematics	that part of thematics accounts for the division of semantic universes into valuated spaces.
assimilation	actualization of a seme by presumption of isotopy.
associative network	totality of relations that allow one to identify the recurrence of a semic molecule.

bundle	totality of isotopies brought about by the recurrence of elements of the same semic molecule.
classeme	group of generic semes belonging to a sememe.
coherence	unity of a linguistic succession or chain, defined in terms of its relations with its surroundings.
cohesion	unity of a linguistic succession or chain, defined in terms of its internal semantic relations.
component	systematic instance that, being in interaction with other instances of the same order, regulates the production and interpretation of linguistic chains.
connection	relation between two sememes that belong to two different generic isotopies.
dialect	functional language (as opposed to historical language).
dialectics	semantic component that articulates the succession of intervals in textual time, such as states that are created in texts and the processes that unfold in texts.
dialectic function	interaction between actors. It is dependent upon which types are involved.
dialectic sequence	dialectic unit of the agonistic level, constituted by homologation of isomorphic functional syntagmas.
dialogics	semantic component that articulates modal relations between universes and between worlds.
dimension	class of very general sememes, independent of domains. Dimensions are grouped into smaller closed categories (for example, //animate// versus //inanimate//).
discourse	the totality of codified linguistic usages attached to a given type of social practice (for example, juridical discourse, medical discourse, religious discourse).
dissimilation	actualization of opposing afferent semes in two occurrences of the same sememe or in two 'parasynonymous' sememes.
domain	group of taxemes, linked to the social context, such that in a given domain there is no polysemy.
elementary interpretative operation	see 'actualization,' 'assimilation,' 'dissimilation,' 'virtualization.'
evenemential level	level of dialectics constituted by actors and functions.
extrinsic interpretation	interpretation that produces unactualized semes in a linguistic chain.

generic seme	element of a classeme. It marks the fact that a sememe belongs to a semantic class.
genre	program of positive or negative prescriptions (and licences) that regulate the production and interpretation of texts. All texts have to do with a genre and all genres have to do with a discourse. Genres do not belong to the language system, strictly speaking, but rather to other social norms.
grammeme	morpheme that belongs to a closed class, in a given synchronic state.
hierarchy	relative evaluation or assessment, in a given semantic universe, of the various classes that define generic isotopies.
hypotext	a partial representation of a text, endowed with its own cohesion.
idiolect	use of a language and of other social norms that are proper to a given enunciator.
imagization	pairing of a signified with a mental image.
inherent seme	seme whose occurrence is dependent on a type, by default (for example, /black/ for 'crow').
interlaced	this is said of lexicalized isotopies whose sememes alternate in successions or chains that are at a lower level than the dimension of the utterance.
internal version	hypotext of a story; if along one and the same generic isotopy (that is, within one and the same variation) several narrative structures can be constructed, and they can define an equal number of internal versions.
interpretant	linguistic or semiotic element that allows one to establish a semic relation.
interpretation	the assigning of meaning to a linguistic chain.
interpretative path	succession of cognitive operations that allow one to assign meaning to a linguistic sequence.
intrinsic interpretation	interpretation that brings out semes (inherent and afferent) that have been actualized in a linguistic chain.
isosemy	an isotopy that is prescribed by the functional system of language (for example, agreement of adjectives etc., grammatical rection).
isotopizing	said of a seme whose recurrence creates an isotopy.
lexeme	morpheme that belongs to one or more open classes, in a given synchronic state (for example, *run-* in *running*).
lexia	a stable grouping of morphemes, constituting a functional unit.
macrogeneric	relative to a semantic dimension.
meaning	content of a linguistic unit, defined in terms that are relative to its context and communicational situation.
mesogeneric	relative to a semantic domain.

metaphorical connection	connection between lexicalized sememes: such connection that there is a relation of incompatibility between at least one of their generic features, and a relation of identity between at least one of their specific features.
microgeneric	relative to a taxeme.
morpheme	the minimal sign, undecomposable in a given synchronic state.
poly-isotopy	in the limited sense, the property of a linguistic chain that includes several generic isotopies whose isotopizing semes are in a relation of incompatibility; in the larger sense, the property of a chain that includes more than one isotopy.
reading	a text produced by the transformation of a source-text that it is supposed to describe, scientifically or not.
role	elementary dialectic valence of an actor. Each function confers a role on each of the actors participating in that function.
semanteme	totality of semes that are specific to a given sememe.
semantic case	a primitive semantic relation between actants. Cases mark the arcs of thematized graphs. Being universals of method, they are not to be confused with the morphosyntactic functions of particular languages.
semantic isotopy	effect of a syntagmatic recurrence of one and the same seme. Relations of identity between occurrences of the isotopizing seme bring about relations of equivalence between sememes that include them.
semantic rhythm	a regulated correspondence between a tactic form and a thematic structure, be it dialectic or dialogic.
seme	semantic feature, element of a sememe, defined as the extreme of a binary relational function between sememes.
sememe	content of a morpheme.
semic molecule	stable grouping of semes, not necessarily lexicalized, or whose lexicalization can vary (a 'theme,' when it can be defined semantically, is nothing more than a semic molecule).
sentence	syntactic structure of an utterance or of a succession of embedded or coordinated utterances.
signification	content of a linguistic unit defined by abstracting context and communicational situation. Any given signification is an artefact.
sociolect	usage of a functional language proper to a specific social group.
specific seme	element of the semanteme that sets the sememe in opposition to one or more sememes of the taxeme to which it belongs. E.g., /feminine sex/ for 'woman.'
successives	said of lexicalized isotopies that alternate in sequences that are on the same level or on a hierarchically superior level to the utterance.

superimposed	said of a totality of generic isotopies of which one is lexicalized and of which at least one is not lexicalized. The construction of non-lexicalized isotopies is accomplished by establishing symbolic connections.
surroundings or context	the totality of the semiotic phenomena associated with a linguistic chain; or more generally, a non-linguistic context, sometimes called pragmatic.
symbolic connection	connection between two sememes (or groups of sememes) such that starting with one lexicalized sememe (or group), one can lexicalize another sememe (or group of sememes).
tactics	the tactics of the content is a component that regulates the linear disposition of semantic units.
taxeme	minimal class of sememes in language, within which the semantemes of those sememes are defined as well as their common microgeneric seme.
text	autonomous linguistic chain (oral or written) that constitutes an empirical unit and that is produced by one or more enunciators in a given communicational situation. Texts are the empirical object of linguistics.
textuality	totality of the properties giving cohesion and coherence and that render a text irreducible to just a succession of utterances.
thematics	study of invested contents and of their paradigmatic structures.
thematized graph	a semantic graph whose nodes are instanciated by variables.
topic	sociolectal part of thematics.
topos	the normative axiom that underlies a socialized afference.
universe	totality of the semantic graphs that are associated with a given actor at a specific moment of textual time.
use	a sememe whose meaning includes afferent semes that obey a set of localized or idiolectal norms.
utterance	a predication that is considered in its linguistic context and relative to its situational context.
variation	hypotext relative to a generic isotopy.
virtualization	neutralization of a seme, in context.
word	integrated grouping of morphemes.
world	totality of semantic graphs associated with an actor and modalized in the same way in the same interval of textual time.

Bibliography

Adam, J.-M. 1987. Textualité et séquentialité: L'exemple de la description, *Langue française*, 74, 51–72.

Alonso, D. 1971. *Pluralità et correlazione in poesia*, Bari, Adriatica Editrice.

Bal, M. 1977. *Narratologie*, Paris, Klincksieck.

Balmas, E. 1962. *Un poeta del rinascimento francese: Etienne Jodelle*, Florence, Olschki.

Barthes, R. 1973. *Le plaisir du texte*, Paris, Seuil.

Beaugrande R. de. 1980. *Text, Discourse and Process*, Londres, Longman.

Beaugrande, R. de, and W. Dressler. 1984. *Introduzione alla linguistica testuale*, Bologna, Il Mulino.

Benveniste, E. 1966–74. *Problèmes de linguistique générale*, 2 vol. Paris, Gallimard.

Berger, B. 1930. *Vers rapportés: Beitrag zur Stilgeschichte des französischen Renaissancedichtung*, thèse de Fribourg-en-Brisgau, Karlsruhe, Malsch & Vogel.

Black, J., and R. Wilensky. 1979. An Evaluation of Story Grammars, *Cognitive Science*, 3, 213–30.

Bolte, J. 1904. Die indische Redefigur Yatha-samkhya in europäischer Dichtung, *Archiv für das Studium der neueren Sprachen und Literatur*, 112, 265–76.

Bremond, C. 1973. *Logique du récit*, Paris, Seuil.

Bronckart, J.-P., éd. 1985. *Le fonctionnement des discours*, Neuchâtel, Delachaux et Niestlé.

Brown, G., and G. Yule. 1983. *Discourse Analysis*, Cambridge, Cambridge University Press.

Bûhler, K. 1965. [1934] *Sprachtheorie*, Stuttgart, Fischer.

Chatman, S. 1978. *Story and Discourse*, Ithaca, Cornell University Press.

Chomsky, N. 1984. La connaissance du langage, *Communications*, 51, 7–24. [Originally in English, *Philosophical Transactions of the Royal Society of London*, 1981.]

Cohn, D. 1981. *La transparence intérieure*, Paris, Seuil [1978. *Transparent Minds*:

Narrative Modes for Presenting Consciousness in Fiction. Princeton NJ, Princeton University Press].
Coseriu, E. 1976. L'étude fonctionnelle du vocabulaire, *Cahiers de lexicologie*, 27, 30–51.
– 1977. *Tradición y novedad en la ciencia del lenguaje*, Madrid, Gredos.
– 1981. *Textlinguistik: Eine Einführung*, Tübingen, Narr.
Couffignal, R. 1966. *L'inspiration biblique dans l'œuvre de Guillaume Apollinaire*, Paris, Minard.
Denis, M. 1987. *Formes imagées de la représentation cognitive*, Université de Paris VIII, thèse de doctorat d'État.
Doležel, L. 1979. Extensional and Intensional Narrative Worlds, *Poetics*, 8, 193–211.
Dubois, D. 1986. *La compréhension de phrases: Représentations sémantiques et processus*, Université de Paris VIII, thèse de doctorat d'État.
Dubois, D., and L. Sprenger-Charolles. 1988. Perception/interprétation du langage écrit: Contexte et identification des mots au cours de la lecture, *Intellectica*, 5, 113–46.
Dumézil, G. 1945. *Tarpeia*, Paris, Gallimard.
– 1947. *Naissance d'archanges*, Paris, Gallimard.
– 1977. *Les dieux souverains des Indo-européens*, Paris, Gallimard.
– 1981. [1968] *Mythe et épopée*, I. Paris, Gallimard.
Dyer, M. 1983. *In-Depth Understanding: A Computer Model of Integrated Processing for Narrative Comprehension*, Cambridge, Mass., MIT Press.
Fayol, M. 1985. *Le récit et sa construction*, Neuchâtel, Delachaux et Niestlé.
Genette, G. 1982. *Palimpsestes*, Paris, Seuil.
– 1983. *Nouveau discours du récit*, Paris, Seuil.
Greimas, A.-J. 1966. *Sémantique structurale*, Paris, Larousse.
– 1970. *Du Sens*, Paris, Seuil.
– 1983. *Du Sens II*, Paris, Seuil.
Greimas, A.-J., et J. Courtés. 1979. *Sémiotique: Dictionnaire raisonné de la théorie du langage*, Paris, Larousse. [1982. *Semiotics and Language: An Analytical Dictionary*, trans. D. Patte and L. Crist, Bloomington, Indiana University Press].
Guiraud, P. 1967. *Structures étymologiques du lexique français*, Paris, Larousse.
Groupe MU. 1977. *Rhétorique de la poésie*, Bruxelles, Complexe.
Grunig, R. 1982. La sémantique des mondes possibles et ses limites, *DRLAV*, 26, 63–89.
Hamon, P. 1984. *Texte et idéologie*, Paris, P.U.F.
Haudry, J. 1982. Les trois cieux, *Études indo-européennes*, I, 1, 23–48.
– 1985. *Les Indo-européens*, Paris, P.U.F.
– 1986. La tradition indo-européenne au regard de la linguistique, *L'information grammaticale*, 29, 3–11.
Jackendoff, R. 1983. *Semantics and Cognition*, Cambridge, Mass., MIT Press.

Jakobson, R. 1963. *Essais de linguistique générale*, Paris, Minuit.
- 1973. *Questions de poétique*, Paris, Seuil.
Kalinowski, G. 1982. Vérité analytique et vérité logique, *Actes sémiotiques*, Documents, IV, 40.
Kittredge, R., and J. Lehrberger. 1982. *Sublanguage*, Berlin – New York, De Gruyter.
Klinkenberg, J.-M. 1973. Le concept d'isotopie en sémantique et en sémiotique littéraire, *Le français moderne*, 41, 3, 285–290.
Kristeva, J. 1974. *La révolution du langage poétique*, Paris, Seuil.
- 1985. *Histoires d'amour*, Paris, Denoel.
Le Ny, J.-F. 1989. *Science cognitive et compréhension du langage*, Paris, P.U.F.
Le Ny, J.-F., M. Carfantan, and J.-C. Verstiggel. 1982. Accessibilité en mémoire de travail et rôle d'un retraitement lors de la compréhension de phrases, *Bulletin de psychologie*, 35, no. 356, 327–34.
Lerat. P. 1984. *Sémantique descriptive*, Paris, Hachette.
Lévi-Strauss, C. 1964. *Le cru et le cuit*, Paris, Plon.
Linsky, L. 1974. *Le problème de la référence*, Paris, Seuil.
Lintvelt, J. 1981. *Essai de typologie narrative: Le problème du point de vue*, Paris, Corti.
Mandler, J.-M., and N. Johnson. 1980. On Throwing out the Baby with the Bathwater: a Reply to Black and Wilensky's Evaluation of Story Grammars, *Cognitive Science*, 4, 305–12.
Martin, R. 1983. *Pour une logique du sens*, Paris, P.U.F.
- 1987. *Langage et croyance*, Bruxelles, Mardaga.
Molinié, G. 1987. *Essais de stylistique française*, Paris, P.U.F.
Nef, F. 1983. *La description de la deixis temporelle du français moderne*, Université de Paris IV, thèse de doctorat d'État.
Pisani, V. 1939. Corresponsioni tri- et polimembri, *Annali della scuole norm. sup. di Pisa*, II, 8.
Pommier, R. 1978. *Assez décodé!* Paris, Roblot.
Pottier, B. 1974. *Linguistique générale*, Paris, Klincksieck.
- 1987. *Théorie et description en linguistique*, Paris, Hachette.
Prince, G. 1980. Aspects of the Grammar of Narratives, *Poetics Today*, I, 3, 49–64.
Propp, V. 1970. *Morphologie du conte*, Paris, Seuil. [*Morphology of the Folktale*, Austin, University of Texas Press, 1968.]
Rastier, F. 1971. Les niveaux d'ambiguïté des structures narratives, *Semiotica*, III, 4, 289–342.
- 1972. Systématique des isotopies, in A.-J. Greimas, éd. *Essais de sémiotique poétique*, Paris, Larousse.
- 1974. *Essais de sémiotique discursive*, Paris, Mame.
- 1985. Sémiotique de la poésie, *Le français moderne*, 53, 1–2, 143–6 (review of Riffaterre, M., 1983).

– 1986. Microsémantique et textualité, in Charolles et al., *Research in Text Connexity and Text Coherence*, Hambourg, Buske.
– 1987a. *Sémantique interprétative*, Paris, P.U.F.
– 1987b. Présentation, in 'Sémantique et I.A.,' *Langages*, 87, 5–19.
– 1988a Problématiques sémantiques, in *Hommage à Bernard Pottier*, Paris, Klincksieck, vol. 2, 671–86.
– 1988b. Paradigmes cognitifs et linguistique universelle, *Intellectica*, 6.
– 1992a. Réalisme sémantique et réalisme esthétique, *TLE*, 10, 81–119. [Translation: Semantic Realism and Aesthetic Realism, *Substance*, 71–2 (1993) 74–97.]
– 1992b. La généalogie d'Aphrodite: Réalisme et représentation artistique, *Littérature*, 87, 105–23.
Ricardou, J. 1967. *Les chemins actuels de la critique*, Paris, Plon.
Richard, J.-P. 1961. *L'univers imaginaire de Mallarmé*, Paris, Seuil.
Ricoeur, P. 1965. *De l'interprétation: Essai sur Freud*, Paris, Seuil.
– 1969. *Le conflit des interprétations*, Paris, Seuil.
– 1976. *Interpretation Theory*, Notre Dame, Texas Christian University Press.
– 1981. La grammaire narrative de Greimas, *Documents du G.R.S.L.*, 15.
– 1984. *Temps et récit, II: La configuration du temps dans le récit de fiction*, Paris, Seuil.
Riffaterre, M. 1971. *Essais de stylistique structurale*, Paris, Flammarion.
– 1981. L'illusion référentielle, in *Littérature et réalité*, Paris, Seuil, 91–108.
– 1983. *Sémiotique de la poésie*, Paris, Seuil.
Rumelhart, D.E. 1980. On Evaluating Story Grammars, *Cognitive Science*, 4, 313–16.
Ryan, M.-M. 1985. The Modal Structure of Narrative Universes, *Poetics Today*, 6, 4, 717–55.
Sabah, G. 1978. *Contribution à la compréhension effective d'un récit*, Université de Paris VI, thèse de doctorat d'État ès sciences mathématiques.
Schank, R., et al. 1975. *Conceptual Information Processing*, Amsterdam – New York, North Holland – American Elsevier.
Schank, R., and R. Abelson. 1977. *Scripts, Plans, Goals and Understanding*, New York, Lawrence Erlbaum Associates.
Scheglov, Y., and A. Zholkovsky. 1987. *Poetics of Expressiveness*, Amsterdam – Philadelphie, Benjamins.
Scherer, J. 1977. Le '*Livre*' de Mallarmé, Paris, Gallimard.
Schmidt, A.-M. 1953. *Poètes du seizième siècle*, Paris, Gallimard, Bibliothèque de la Pléiade.
Scholes, R. 1982. *Semiotics and Interpretation*, New Haven, Yale University Press.
Scholes, R., and R. Kellogg. 1966. *The Nature of Narrative*, Oxford, Oxford University Press.
Searle, J. 1985. *L'intentionalité*, Paris, Minuit.

Segre, C. 1985a. Les isotopies de Laure, in H. Parret and H.-G. Ruprecht, éd. *Exigences et perspectives de la sémiotique*, Amsterdam – Philadelphie, Benjamins, vol. 2, 811–25.

– 1985b. Testo letterario, interpretatione, storia: Linee concettuali e categorie critiche, in A. Asor Rosa, ed. *Litteratura Italiana*, 4, Turin, Einaudi, 21–140.

Sowa, J. 1984. *Conceptual Structures*, Reading, Mass., Addison-Wesley.

Vaina, L. 1974. Pour une hiérarchie des isotopies du contenu d'un texte poétique, *Cahiers de linguistique théorique et appliquée*, XI, 2, 317–26.

– 1977. Les mondes possibles du texte, *Versus*, 17, 3–13.

Van Dijk, T. 1979. *Macro-structures*, Hillsdale, N.J., Erlbaum.

– ed. 1985. *Handbook of Discourse Analysis*, 4 vol. London, Academic Press.

Zumthor, P. 1972. *Essai de poétique médiévale*, Paris, Seuil.

Name Index

Subject Index

www.ingramcontent.com/pod-product-compliance
Lightning Source LLC
LaVergne TN
LVHW020437080826
844660LV00033B/1307

* 9 7 8 0 8 0 2 0 8 0 2 9 5 *